# Refugees and the violence of welfare bureaucracies in Northern Europe

Manchester University Press

# Refugees and the violence of welfare bureaucracies in Northern Europe

*Edited by*
Dalia Abdelhady, Nina Gren and Martin Joormann

Manchester University Press

Copyright © Manchester University Press 2020

While copyright in the volume as a whole is vested in Manchester University Press, copyright in individual chapters belongs to their respective authors.

An electronic version of this book is also available under a Creative Commons (CC-BY-NC-ND) licence, thanks to the support of Lund University Library, which permits non-commercial use, distribution and reproduction provided the editor(s), chapter author(s) and Manchester University Press are fully cited and no modifications or adaptations are made. Details of the licence can be viewed at https://creativecommons.org/licenses/by-nc-nd/4.0/.

Published by Manchester University Press
Altrincham Street, Manchester M1 7JA

www.manchesteruniversitypress.co.uk

British Library Cataloguing-in-Publication Data
A catalogue record for this book is available from the British Library

ISBN   978 1 5261 4683 0   hardback

First published 2020

The publisher has no responsibility for the persistence or accuracy of URLs for any external or third-party internet websites referred to in this book, and does not guarantee that any content on such websites is, or will remain, accurate or appropriate.

Typeset
by New Best-set Typesetters Ltd

# Contents

| | |
|---|---|
| List of figures | *page* vii |
| List of tables | viii |
| List of contributors | ix |

| | |
|---|---|
| 1 Introduction – Dalia Abdelhady, Nina Gren and Martin Joormann | 1 |

**Part I    Governing refugees**

| | |
|---|---|
| 2 Social class, economic capital and the Swedish, German and Danish asylum systems – Martin Joormann | 31 |
| 3 Lesson for the future or threat to sovereignty? Contesting the meaning of the 2015 refugee crisis in Sweden – Admir Skodo | 50 |
| 4 Representations of the refugee crisis in Denmark: deterrence policies and refugee strategies – Martin Bak Jørgensen | 67 |
| 5 Minimum rights policies targeting people seeking protection in Denmark and Sweden – Annika Lindberg | 85 |

**Part II    Disciplining refugees**

| | |
|---|---|
| 6 Images of crisis and the crisis of images: a visual analysis of four frames of representation of 'refugeeness' in Swedish newspapers – Jelena Jovičić | 105 |
| 7 Media constructions of the refugee crisis in Sweden: institutions and the challenges of refugee governance – Dalia Abdelhady | 122 |
| 8 (De-)legitimation of migration: a critical study of social media discourses – Marie Sundström and Hedvig Obenius | 144 |

**Part III    The meaning of refugeeness**

| | |
|---|---|
| 9 Living bureaucratisation: young Palestinian men encountering a Swedish introductory programme for refugees – Nina Gren | 161 |

10 Aspiration, appreciation and frustration: Syrian asylum
seekers and bureaucracy in Germany – Wendy Pearlman 180
11 The trauma of waiting: understanding the violence of the
benevolent welfare state in Norway – Nerina Weiss 195
12 Bureaucratised banality: asylum and immobility in Britain,
Denmark and Sweden – Victoria Canning 210

*Index* 227

# List of figures

1 Election campaign poster for the Social Democratic Party
   (Sweden) (source: *TT-nyhetsbyrån*/Svenska Dagbladet)　　　*page* 7
2 Swedish migration bureaucracy (source: www.domstol.se/
   upload/Arende/Migration/fran_ansokan_till_avgorand_eng_
   stor.gif)　　　36
3 Accommodation at *Udrejsecenter Sjælsmark* (source: author)　　　220
4 Image of walkway at *Udrejsecenter Sjælsmark* (source: author)　　　220

# List of tables

1 Overview of the distribution of images across four visual frames *page* 110
2 Frame distribution of news articles in Swedish newspapers in 2015   126

# List of contributors

**Dalia Abdelhady** is Associate Professor at the Department of Sociology at Lund University in Sweden. She is the author of *The Lebanese Diaspora: The Arab Immigrant Experience in Montreal, New York and Paris* (New York University Press, 2011) and the co-editor (with Ramy Aly) of the *Routledge Handbook of Middle East Diasporas* (2020). She has also written about the children of immigrants' transition from school to work, and media representation of Syrians refugees, both from within a comparative perspective.

**Martin Bak Jørgensen** is Associate Professor at the Department of Culture and Learning at Aalborg University in Denmark. He has published articles in journals such as *International Migration Review, Journal of Migration and Integration, Critical Social Policy, Ethnologia Europaea – Journal of European Ethnology* and *Political Geography*. He is an editorial member of *Comparative Migration Studies*.

**Victoria Canning** is Senior Lecturer in Criminology at the University of Bristol in the UK. She has spent more than a decade working on the rights of migrants, in particular, women survivors of violence. She is a trustee at Statewatch, associate director at Border Criminologies at Oxford University and co-coordinator at the European Group for the Study of Deviance and Social Control. She is the author of *Gendered Harm and Structural Violence in the British Asylum System* (Routledge, 2017)

**Nina Gren** is Senior Lecturer of Social Anthropology at Lund University in Sweden. She is a social anthropologist whose research interests are found within the anthropology of migration. Her book *Occupied Lives: Maintaining Integrity in a Palestinian Refugee Camp in the West Bank* (American University in Cairo Press, 2015) analyses the many ways Palestinian refugees maintain continuity, morality and a normal order despite repeated emergencies during the second intifada. She has also researched Palestinian diasporic practices in Denmark and Sweden.

**Martin Joormann** is Lecturer in Sociology of Law at Lund University in Sweden, where he received his PhD in 2019. He is the author of articles such as 'Asylstaffetten: A longitudinal Ethnographic Study of Protest Walks against the Detention of Asylum Seekers in Sweden' (2018), *Justice, Power and Resistance*. He also serves as editor for several international journals.

**Jelena Jovičić** is a PhD candidate in Sociology at Stockholm University in Sweden. Her work focuses on the increased criminalisation of asylum seeking through law, policy and political debates, and how these processes are co-opted in the visual media uses and reproductions of such discourses. In doing so, she highlights the gendered and racialising practices in visual media(s), their intersections and violent outcomes. She also explores the possibilities and boundaries laying at the intersections of academia, art and activism.

**Annika Lindberg** received her PhD in Sociology at the University of Bern in Switzerland. She is co-author of the collaborative ethnography *Migrants Before the Law: Contested Migration Control in Europe* (Palgrave Macmillan, 2018) and part of the Freedom of Movements Research Collective, which recently published *Stop Killing Us Slowly: A Research Report on the Motivation Enhancement Measures and the Criminalization of Rejected Asylum Seekers in Denmark* (Roskilde University, 2018).

**Hedvig Obenius** is a PhD candidate in Welfare Law at Linköping University in Sweden. Her work focuses on the study of migration through the lens of critical legal cartography. She is currently working on several publications, among them one project (together with Anna Lundberg) that will counter-map the legal landscape on human smuggling.

**Wendy Pearlman** is Associate Professor, and Martin and Patricia Koldyke Outstanding Teaching Professor, in Political Science at Northwestern University in the US. She is the author of four books: *Occupied Voices: Stories of Everyday Life from the Second Intifada* (Nation Books, 2003); *Violence, Nonviolence, and the Palestinian National Movement* (Cambridge University Press, 2011); *We Crossed a Bridge and it Trembled: Voices from Syria* (Custom House, 2017); and *Triadic Coercion: Israel's Targeting of States That Host Nonstate Actors* (co-authored with Boaz Atzili, Columbia University Press, 2018). Pearlman is also the author of several articles on a range of topics, including political fear, protest cascades, transnational diffusion and rebel fragmentation.

**Admir Skodo** is a Researcher at the Swedish South Asian Studies Network (SASNET) at Lund University in Sweden. His research focuses on historical and contemporary links between forced migration, geopolitics, state-building, diaspora politics and migration policy. His work has been published by *Journal of Refugee Studies*, The Migration Policy Institute, the

*Times Literary Supplement* and the *Independent*, among others. During 2017–2018 he was a Commissioned Instructor for the Swedish Migration Agency.

**Marie Sundström** holds a Master of Science in Sociology of Law from Lund University in Sweden. Her main research interests are critical studies of migration, the dynamics of discrimination and inequality, social justice studies, media studies (including social media) and critical discourse analysis. She is currently working as a Research Assistant in political science at Linnaeus University.

**Nerina Weiss** is a Senior Researcher at Fafo Research Foundation in Norway. She has a PhD in Social Anthropology from the University of Oslo and worked as a Marie Curie Fellow at Dignity: The Danish Institute Against Torture from 2011–2013. Her research interests include political violence, mobilization, migration, gender as well as torture and trauma. She is the co-editor of *Violence Expressed: An Anthropological Perspective* (Routledge, 2012).

# Acknowledgements

This book would not have been possible without the kind support of a number of individuals and institutions. We are grateful to the Centre of Middle Eastern Studies, Lund University, which hosted and financed an initial workshop on studying refugees in Northern Europe, from which the idea of this book came about. Lund University Libraries have also been kind enough to pay for the costs of making the volume Open Access. The authors of the various book chapters have been patient in responding to our comments and editing. Our colleagues at Lund University's Department of Sociology, Centre of Middle Eastern Studies and Department of the Sociology of Law have provided us with encouraging and fruitful discussions in relation to our research interests. Our publishers at Manchester University Press, especially our editor Thomas Dark, should also be acknowledged as vital to this project. Last, but not least, we want to extend our thanks to the refugees, street-level bureaucrats, NGO workers and volunteers who have discussed their thoughts and experiences of migration as well as of welfare state bureaucracies within the various research projects that this volume builds upon.

1 Dalia Abdelhady, Nina Gren, and Martin Joormann

# Introduction

Summer 2015. While the beaches of Greek islands received boat after boat of refugees, a large part of the space of the central station in Copenhagen was occupied by young Danish volunteers who distributed sandwiches, drinks, blankets, and second-hand clothes to crowds of people on the move, most fleeing wars in Syria and Afghanistan. Locals bought train and bus tickets so the travellers could continue their journey onwards to Sweden and beyond. Across the strait forming the Swedish–Danish border, the Sound (hereafter Öresund), in Malmö, Swedish volunteers were doing the same as their Danish counterparts. Only a few weeks later did Malmö municipality and the local branch of the Swedish Migration Agency send some of their employees to meet those who were on the move. The asylum seekers were slowly registered and accommodated by different authorities. After their encounters with police and border patrol agents, they met caseworkers from the Migration Agency, healthcare professionals for medical check-ups, employees and managers from refugee camps, schoolteachers for their children, and many more representatives of the welfare state. Those encounters were to shape and form their experiences from that point onwards.

From the news reports, it became evident that the situation was more or less the same at train stations and border crossings all over Europe. Within a few weeks, however, a refugee crisis had been declared by media outlets and politicians in many countries of Europe. The crowd at the Scandinavian stations was replaced by police officers after the Swedish government implemented border controls. The Danes followed suit. From that point onwards, the trains between Copenhagen and Malmö were stopped twice on their 40-minute journey; first, at the train station next to Copenhagen international airport, and second, at the next train station across the Öresund in Sweden, Malmö Hyllie. Guards met all travellers, asking for passports and ID cards, severely delaying the trains. Fewer and fewer people in line waiting to have their papers checked were asylum seekers. The crowd soon consisted of local commuters and European travellers. Talk of the refugee crisis almost vanished from public discourse a few months later. What remains, however, are debates about what institutional arrangements are best suited to 'integrate' the refugees and maximise their utility for the welfare state they encounter.

Despite the spotlight, whether during the 'long summer of migration' in 2015 (Hess et al., 2016; Odugbesan and Schwiertz, 2018), which led to the constructed notion of a refugee crisis, or in the many welfare state interventions that target refugees across Europe, little is known about the experiences of refugees in their countries of settlement. Even less is known about those daily experiences in the established bureaucracies of the Northern European countries where increasing numbers have settled.[1] Through interrogating the phenomenon of the 2015 'refugee crisis', and its foreplay and aftermath in the context of Northern Europe, this edited volume analyses the tensions that emerge when strong welfare states are faced with large migration flows. With an eye to the daily strategies and experiences of newly settled populations, this book tackles the role played by different actors such as state agencies, street-level bureaucrats, media discourses, and welfare policies in shaping those experiences. As we argue later in this introduction, the receiving states encountered those groups of people on the move as largely embodying high levels of risk that had to be mitigated through various mechanisms. The assumption of risk triggered the desire to control the flows of people and control the individuals who embodied the perceived risks. When control and discipline were being challenged, the sense of crisis took over public discourses and policy environments, triggering exaggerated responses that were camouflaged under the term refugee crisis. Writing prior to 2015, Peter Gatrell (2013, p. 17) reminds us that 'there is a tendency to regard refugee crises as temporary and unique rather than as "recurring phenomena"'. Gatrell's statement draws attention to crises as recurring phenomena, ones that strengthen governance through risk. As recurring phenomena, governing crises also involves the enactment of violence, which is the argument we put forth in this volume.

Given the significant similarities and differences between the welfare states of Northern Europe and their reactions to the perceived refugee crisis of 2015, the book focuses primarily on the three main cases of Denmark, Sweden, and Germany. Placed in a wider Northern European context – and illustrated by those chapters that discuss refugee experiences also in Norway and the UK – the Danish, Swedish, and German cases are the largest case studies of this edited volume. To focus on these three national contexts is meaningful because they include 1) Denmark, a country with one of the most restrictive asylum policies in Europe; 2) Sweden, having one of the – formerly – most generous asylum systems in the Global North;[2] and 3) Germany, which, since 2015 and of all EU member states, has received the largest number of asylum applications (UNHCR, 2017).

## The aim of the book: studying refugees and welfare state bureaucracies

It is difficult to approach the state methodologically and conceptually, to define its boundaries, and to disentangle the power structures within the context of state–society relations. Empirical research can, however, analyse some of the effects that the state's institutions and its employees have on people's everyday lives – and vice versa. With regards to the mechanisms that the state applies to govern its population, the analytical significance of studying bureaucratic practices has been highlighted: 'The ongoing nature of governance requires maintenance and administration. This suggests that scholars interested in the workings and the effects of the state should look, at the very least, to the bureaucracies that keep it running' (Bernstein and Mertz, 2011, p. 6). One example of such research is the study of refugee asylum and reception, which has been conducted in and across different national contexts (e.g. McKinnon, 2008; Canning, 2017; Maroufi, 2017; Sager and Öberg, 2017; Gateri, 2018).

This is also the subject of the book, which contributes to debates on the governance of non-citizens and the meaning of displacement, mobility, and seeking asylum by providing interdisciplinary analyses of a largely overlooked region of the world, with two specific aims. First, we scrutinise the construction of the 2015 crisis as a response to the large influx of refugees, paying particular attention to the disciplinary discourses and bureaucratic structures that are associated with it. Second, we investigate refugees' encounters with these bureaucratic structures and how these encounters shape hopes and possibilities for building a new life after displacement. This allows us to show that the mobility of specific segments of the world's population continues to be seen as a threat and a risk that has to be governed and controlled. Focusing on the Northern European context, the volume interrogates emerging policies and discourses, as well as the lived experiences of bureaucratisation from the perspective of individuals who find themselves the very objects of bureaucracies.

In his classical conception, Max Weber (2009, p. 245) defined a bureaucracy as a 'permanent structure with a system of rational rules ... fashioned to meet calculable and recurrent needs by means of normal routine'. This definition, while offering an ideal type and not an empirical reality, is taken to reify a vision of a bureaucracy that is impersonal and merit-based, and founded on rational-legal administrative structures, which promises a variety of practical freedoms. While Weber saw the risk of bureaucracies as resulting in an 'iron cage' (*stahlhartes Gehäuse* in the German original, see Weber, 2009) governed by mundane, stagnant administrative structures, more contemporary studies highlight the ways these structures reproduce axes of discrimination and inequality. Bureaucracies involve power dynamics that affect the everyday lives of citizens (Herzfeld, 1992; Bernstein and

Mertz, 2011), sometimes with violent outcomes (Graeber, 2015). We address such violent outcomes associated with bureaucracy later in this introductory chapter but, before we do that, we highlight the relevance of focusing on bureaucracies in understanding experiences with forced displacement and important features of the Northern European context.

In his formative book, *The Making of the Modern Refugee*, Peter Gatrell (2013) draws attention to an international refugee regime that constructs refugee migration as a problem which is amenable to a solution, and argues that humanitarianism 'fashion[s] the modern refugee as a passive and traumatised object of intervention' (Gatrell, 2013, p. 13). As a legal category, the label refugee 'seek[s] to "discipline" life and knowledge to realise dominant interests in society' (Chimni, 2009, p. 12). As Liisa Malkki (1992) convincingly argued, nation state projects include a naturalisation of the links between people and place as well as a sedentary bias. This implies that populations on the move (be they nomads or forced-displaced), both across national borders and within a state's territory, are seen not only as abnormal but also as a politico-moral problem (Malkki, 1992). 'Historically, refugees' loss of bodily connection to their [national] homelands came to be treated as a loss of moral bearings. Rootless, they were no longer trustworthy as "honest citizens"' (Malkki, 1992, p. 32). Regarding forced-displaced people,[3] the bureaucratic labelling of refugees creates stereotypes and generalisations in the process of registering and providing support to those who have sought international protection (Harrell-Bond, 1986; Zetter, 1991). This process partly averts attempts by refugees to express individual or collective will, although at times it has also been resourcefully used as a basis for political mobilisation (Malkki, 1995; Gren, 2015; Joormann, 2018; Odugbesan and Schwiertz, 2018).

Roger Zetter (1991) highlights explicitly 'the extreme vulnerability of refugees to imposed labels' as well as 'the non-participatory nature and powerlessness of refugees in these processes' (p. 39; see also chapter 9 below). Yet, Zetter (1991) argues, labelling is not simply imposed but is a dynamic process, negotiated between the forced-displaced and those institutions that attempt to support them. As Lacroix (2004) has shown, the intersection between bureaucratisation and 'refugeeness' is not as simple as extending the denial of refugees' agency, collective will, and, thus, democratic or political participation. There remain possibilities, although limited, for forced-displaced people to act collectively and engage in the politics of the receiving country and/or their countries of origin. Specifically, with regards to the effects of bureaucratisation on refugees' agency, it is important to note that bureaucratisation is not unique to refugees but marks the lives of most people around the world, not least citizens in Northern Europe. Few people who seek asylum, however, are prepared to handle those bureaucratic interventions which asylum processes and integration programmes demand

(Jackson, 2008; Whyte, 2011). People are subjected to multiple layers of bureaucracies around the world, but those who are labelled refugees or seek such a status are especially so. It is our contention that Northern European welfare state bureaucracies maintain a level of discipline and control over the daily lives of their welfare clients that reproduces axes of exclusion and inclusion through mundane everyday interactions. Such tension between welfare and discipline calls for specific investigations of the encounters between refugees and the welfare states of Northern Europe.

Northern European welfare states are known for their efficiency and the support that their national as well as local institutions of government enjoy among citizens (Fitzgerald and Wolak, 2014).[4] A strong claim to bureaucratic efficiency, either imagined or real, is an important characteristic that sets apart Northern European countries from Europe's South. Asylum systems such as the Greek or the Italian – largely due to their geographical location, and their politically and economically subordinated position within the Dublin system[5] – are struggling to register, process, and accommodate people who seek asylum (Georgoulas, 2017; Mallardo, 2017; see also Herzfeld 1992; Pardo and Prato, 2011; Navaro-Yashin, 2012). At the same time, the bureaucracies of Northern Europe can trap applicants in the bureaucratic iron cage discussed above, which makes steel-hard claims to the rule of law, primarily understood as legal correctness, certainty, and efficiency (Johannesson, 2017; Joormann, 2019). This being noted, it is important to highlight that there are significant differences between the welfare states of Northern Europe. Some provide only a minimum safety net for their citizens; the German system's minimal financial aid to the long-term unemployed (Hartz IV) is a case in point. Others, for instance the Swedish welfare state, are meant to serve all members of society – including, arguably, full citizens and legally residing non-citizens more or less alike.[6]

More importantly, Northern European welfare states have undergone processes of privatisation and marketisation that influence the overall workings of welfare state institutions. Graeber (2015, p. 17) describes the current state of the world as 'the age of total bureaucratisation', in which the private and public sectors seem to have fused. In his view, paradoxically, the privatisation of contemporary welfare states and their services, aiming to reduce government interference in the economy and society, have instead produced 'more regulations, more bureaucrats and more police' (Graeber, 2015, p. 9). This holds true to Northern European welfare states, in which citizens' individual responsibility and activity are increasingly emphasised over the state's responsibility to support citizens (see Pedersen, 2011; Bruun et al., 2015; Rytter, 2018). We believe that this is part and parcel of the neoliberal turn influencing welfare states in Northern Europe and, therefore, of special relevance to the analyses offered in this volume.

## The context of the book: re-bordering Northern Europe

Differences in social welfare policies withstanding, the reactions to the long summer of migration in 2015 depict the convergence in Northern European states' approaches to the provision of asylum. We understand this as a process of re-bordering, which entails reverting back to pre-Schengen national border controls within the EU.[7] Sweden's government, at first, prided itself in receiving the highest rate of asylum seekers per capita in the EU (Barker, 2018). In a matter of months, however, this welcoming policy was replaced by the re-emergence of a strict border between the two Nordic countries and EU member states Denmark and Sweden through extensive passport controls targeting asylum seekers. As an immediate response, in order to avoid becoming a bottleneck for unwanted migrants on their way north, Denmark established general passport controls on its border with Germany. Having said this, it should be emphasised that travellers on their way south, i.e. from Sweden through Denmark to Germany, could generally continue to cross these borders without being checked at all.[8] While stricter border controls were implemented and accompanied by a more stringent asylum law (Meier-Braun, 2017), Germany has not started to control its borders in the face of asylum seekers in the same meticulous way as Sweden and Denmark did (see Dietz, 2017; Meier-Braun, 2017; Hoesch, 2018).[9]

We see this process of re-bordering as strongly intertwined with the workings of the welfare state system. For example, as part of the campaign for 2018's national elections (see Figure 1 below), Sweden's Social Democrats linked immigration control to the welfare state (Lindberg, 2017). Below the photograph of two border patrol officers checking passports on one of the trains that cross the Öresund, the claim that 'We protect Sweden's security' is followed by the announcement that 'the Swedish [Welfare] Model will be developed, not dismantled'. Presenting (unwanted) border crossers as a threat to Swedish national and social security, one can identify within this advertisement a discourse that constructs migration control as a policy tool to 'develop' rather than 'diminish' the welfare state. As chapter 7 in this volume shows, the legal restrictions on asylum seeking introduced in Sweden at the end of 2015 were strongly couched in a discourse that was based on the importance of the welfare state and its institutions and less so on engaging in an argument about the moral responsibility of providing asylum to those seeking refuge.

When considering welfare states such as Sweden, immigration policy brings together two fields: immigration control and welfare policy (Myrberg, 2014). Immigration control regulates who is allowed to enter the country and deals with controls that are mostly external to the nation state. Welfare policy regulates the provision of social rights to the inhabitants of the country and, thus, focuses on distributive measures that are internal to the

1 Election campaign poster for the Social Democratic Party (Sweden)

nation state (see chapter 5 below). Following the argument that 'the idea of distributive justice presupposes a bounded world within which distribution takes place' (Walzer, 1983, p. 31), Swedish political scientist Karin Borevi (2012, p. 32; see also Öberg, 1994) argues that two general options can be discerned regarding the question of who is allowed to enjoy national welfare: 1) a system where everyone with legal residence in the country has equal access to the welfare policy but with limitations concerning who is allowed to immigrate; or 2) a system of relatively free immigration policy but with a differentiated right to welfare for different categories of inhabitants (for example, limited benefits for certain groups of non-citizens). The latter system resembles the guest-worker model, where migrants are expected to return after some time. Varieties of this second model have been applied in, for instance, Germany and Austria, as well as in the Scandinavian countries in the early decades of labour migration after the Second World War.

Since the 1970s, however, the first model, focusing on equal access and limited immigration, has become the preferred choice for Northern Europe's welfare states, although in different forms.

Over time, our three main cases (Sweden, Denmark, and Germany) have moved away from the first option outlined by Borevi. One example that clearly illustrates this approach is the temporary law in Sweden, which has been in force since July 2016 and will remain (at least) until July 2021. According to this package of temporarily more restrictive regulations, only applicants who receive (full) refugee status via UNHCR's resettlement programme (quota refugees) are granted permanent residence permits (hereafter PRPs). For other protection-seeking people whose applications have been accepted, temporary residence permits (hereafter TRPs) are issued.[10] Refugees who live in Sweden on a TRP, despite the fact that they are legally recognised as 'in need of protection', are granted only limited rights to family reunification. They indeed face increased 'maintenance requirements' for family reunification under the temporary law. This means that people who live in Sweden on a TRP must be able to financially provide for the family members who plan to move to Sweden. Furthermore, the Swedish welfare state has significantly reduced the benefits available for the most vulnerable group of people who seek asylum: rejected applicants (who might often be in the process of appealing their case, see chapter 2 below). This regulation limits assistance for maintaining livelihood and housing from local social services. Those aspects which led to Sweden being a relatively refugee-welcoming destination until recently have been reduced to a 'minimum level' (as the Swedish government used the term in 2015–2016). Indeed, the current situation in Sweden illustrates that the reality of governing welfare and immigration in today's Northern European countries has moved away from both of Borevi's models – 1) full access to welfare but limited immigration, or 2) relatively free immigration policy but with a differentiated right to welfare – as outlined above (for the Danish case, see chapter 5 below). Instead, a third alternative consisting of limited immigration and limited access to welfare has emerged.

Yet it should not be assumed that such restrictive policies are necessarily successful in meeting their goal of deterring people from seeking asylum or establishing permanent residence in their host societies. As empirical research has shown time and again (see Banakar, 2015), the socially practised 'law in action' is strongly dependent on the interpretation that the responsible actors perform when they apply regulations. In other words, those changed norms and rules of refugee reception have to be not only implemented but also discursively interpreted and socially practised at different levels. In the EU context, this administration operates at the national but also at the supra-national and local levels (see e.g. chapters 9 and 12, this volume).

In most countries of Northern Europe, the reception of refugees is handled at the local level, and the pressure on municipalities across Europe to find pragmatic solutions has risen (Ireland, 2004, pp. 7–8; Caponio and Borkert, 2010, pp. 9–13). Municipalities and other local political and bureaucratic institutions have increased in importance for the settling and integration of refugees. Simultaneously, bordering mechanisms are being exercised within the borders of the nation state, adding another dimension to the process of re-bordering. In chapter 5 of this volume, Lindberg investigates this internal bordering by focusing on those Danish and Swedish welfare regulations and practices that are currently used to exhaust unwanted migrants in order to make them leave. In chapter 12, Canning takes on the notion of internalised bordering and highlights the micro-level, everyday forms of social control which deliberately encroach on the autonomy of people seeking asylum in the Danish, Swedish, and British contexts. Such encroachment replicates the experiences of borders in daily experiences and practices.

Given examples such as the Danish and Swedish minimum (welfare) rights policies that are currently enforced, the localisation of refugee management makes the encounter between forced-displaced people and state bureaucracies a daily affair, which would be escaped more easily were the state an omnipresent yet abstract actor. In those day-to-day encounters between the state and refugees, street-level bureaucrats (Lipsky, 1980) such as police officers, caseworkers at the Migration Agency, language teachers, and social workers are crucial and often constitute the only direct contact with the state and its policies. In this volume, chapters 4, 5, 9, 10, 11, and 12 highlight the clashes between refugees' assumptions about the relatively welcoming societies of Northern Europe and the local realities of restrictive policies, asylum processing, integration programmes, and unwelcoming or even hostile discourses about forced-displaced people. Chapters 2, 3, 6, 7, and 8 probe the ways in which re-bordering is a process that is legitimised, justified, and also manipulated at the political, legal, and cultural levels. At the centre of these processes of re-bordering and their consequences, we argue, is a perception of risk and a desire to manage refugees through mitigating risks. This process of mitigating risks is characterised by bureaucratic violence, which we discuss in the following sections.

### Deconstructing the refugee crisis: governing through risk

A critical approach to Northern Europe's most recent refugee crisis can benefit from applying Ulrich Beck's analysis of Risk Society. There is an abundant literature on ways that people's mobility is seen as dangerous and threatening (e.g. Turner, 2007; Isotalo, 2009), and various strands of research document the risks associated with migration and displacement, such as health risks (e.g. Kentikelenis et al., 2015), behavioural risks (e.g. Hosper et al., 2007), and security risks (e.g. Faist, 2002). The very decision to migrate is believed to entail a number of risks (see e.g. Heindlmaier and Blauberger, 2017). Security risks associated with migration have legitimised extraordinary policies related to asylum and migrant rights (Hampshire, 2011; see also Bourbeau, 2015). Securitisation withstanding, we believe that the approach to migrants and asylum seekers is part of a larger neoliberal governmentality strategy that is constitutive of Beck's risk society. Moreover, the sedentary bias in viewing migration and displacement (see Malkki, 1995; Bakewell, 2002) constructs and amplifies the problems associated with the mobility of people. When sedentarism is naturalised, mobility, movement, and migration pose a problem and an anomaly, and the mechanisms of control have to ensure that certain cross-border mobility is curtailed (Malkki, 1995) and contained. There is the risk that 'bogus' claims to asylum are presented; government practices and employees have to ensure the credibility of claims. Once granted asylum, there is a risk that people will cluster in ethnic neighbourhoods and establish urban 'ghettos', which is controlled for by ensuring distribution of accepted refugees among the different municipalities to 'share the burden'. Once settled, there continues to be a risk that refugees will roam around the nation state and disappear from the municipalities' purview. Registering refugees and enrolling them in introductory programmes forces their regular interaction with state officials and their continuous surveillance. Introductory programmes perform the added function of mitigating the risks of refugees becoming endlessly unemployed and, thus, long-term recipients of welfare assistance (see e.g. Valenta and Bunar, 2010; Brochmann and Hagelund, 2012; Schmidt, 2013; Myrberg, 2017). The shift to TRPs, as discussed above, is a clear reflection of the risk that refugees may become permanent inhabitants depending on social welfare in a context where many citizens experience their welfare state as threatened due to constant budget cuts, privatisation, and lowered taxes.

Settlement, introductory programmes, and temporary status are different examples of the logic of governmentality and its reliance on disciplinary power. According to Foucault (1979), disciplinary power is that which is exercised through administrative systems and social services, such as prisons, schools, and mental health services. As disciplinary institutions, they rely on mechanisms such as surveillance, assessment, the organisation of space, timetables, and daily routines, which ensure that people behave in certain ways or are being disciplined without having to resort to the use of corporal violence. Disciplinary mechanisms ensure the control of populations and promote norms of human conduct in modern society. In face of migration risks, they become increasingly important and relevant to disciplining the roaming populations and mitigating the risks they pose.

# Introduction

Beyond disciplinary power, the heightened assumption of risk and the exaggerated responses they trigger create certain forms of violence. Adam et al. (2000, p. 215) argue that established risk definitions are a magic wand with which a 'society can terrify itself and thereby activate its political centres and become politicised from within'. In Sweden, the Social Democrats' 2018 election campaign poster (Figure 1) demonstrates such an attempt to mobilise around policing the border. Once risks are established, activated, and politicised, it is then expected that resources will be allocated by governments to regulate and manage such risks. This is also reflected in the construction of the need to strengthen the welfare state in face of the refugee influx. As evident in the Social Democrats' election poster, political discourse aimed at strengthening the welfare state can resort to scapegoating migrants and constructing them as the cause of various problems facing the nation state (see e.g. Wodak, 2019). As historical narratives attest to, scapegoating is often synonymous with violence (Arendt, 1973).

The conceptualisation of risk as mechanisms with which 'society can terrify itself' fits particularly well with Danish asylum policy. While Denmark had a severely restrictive refugee policy already prior to 2015, the risk of becoming a bottleneck for people on their way north to (or through) Sweden was used to further securitise Danish policies (Gammeltoft-Hansen, 2017; see also chapter 4 below). In a risk society, laws like the Danish 'Jewellery Law'[11] (see chapter 2) have become widely uncontested among the domestic public, given the accepted state of emergency brought about in response to an increased number of asylum applications. More akin to a panic attack than a refugee crisis, the book's three countries of focus suddenly perceived themselves as being threatened by a large inflow of unwanted bodies that they were not prepared to receive and manage (see chapter 7 on the absence of a Swedish plan and the anxieties associated with such absence). Re-bordering and the more repressive policies it involved were immediate first reactions to the panic. The measures were considered to be temporary; for example, in Sweden they were presented as bringing about a much needed 'breathing space'. As many of the contributions in this volume point to, however, they are part of a long process of control and exclusion that preceded the declaration of crisis in 2015.[12]

A risk society relies on large bureaucratic structures to deal with and safeguard against perceived risks. Analysing the establishment of risk bureaucracies that emerged following the War on Terror, Heng and McDonagh (2011, p. 1) state that 'the emergence of such risk regulatory regimes however is neither assumed nor predicted. The subjective and constructed nature of risk perceptions suggests that any emergent regulatory framework based on increased risk consciousness can never be considered a foregone conclusion.' In other words, the ambivalent nature of risk dictates the continual construction and negotiation of the meaning of risk. In the context of the refugee crisis, Abdelhady (2019) demonstrates that media discourses communicated ambivalent and incoherent representations, ultimately leading to a crisis of meaning. Such an ambivalent understanding of risk (see also chapter 6) constructs risk as a process that can, depending on the perspective, have not only negative but also positive consequences. This conceptualisation of risk is close to how the word is used in the (neoliberal) language of corporate business and the global financial market: a certain action includes risks, but it can lead to considerable gains. Risk management industries, which seek to reduce those risks that public discourse identifies as the most threatening, have increasingly permeated the approach of governments to immigrants in general and refugees specifically (see e.g. Heng and McDonagh, 2011).

Given this understanding of risk, one can argue that public discourses in Northern Europe approach refugee migration as a risk – if in different ways. Refugees were imagined as real or potential terrorists, sexual assailants, unemployed welfare recipients, religious maniacs, and cultural others – basically as risks to the norms and cohesion of the receiving societies (Abdelhady and Malmberg, 2018). As a result, throughout Europe's North, the political will to control the immigration of people who seek asylum contributed to the expansion of bureaucracies that administer refugees through risk management techniques. Such risk management, arguably, is interested in regulating the future. Just as the War on Terror that followed 11 September 2001 benefitted from the lack of an ability to declare the end of the need for war, risk management lacks an ability to declare itself successful in mitigating risks. As a result, both the War on Terror and risk management become infinite strategies that continue to justify the control of certain bodies and the outright exclusion of others.

As noted above, however, risk is subjective and constructed, and therefore cannot be taken as a foregone conclusion. Chapters 6 and 7 illustrate the ambivalent understanding of the refugee risk in the case of Sweden. Ambivalence emerges as a result of views stressing that refugees are a much-needed economic resource that can contribute to the welfare state once integrated and turned into, among other things, docile and productive labour (e.g. De Genova, 2009; Holgersson, 2011). Such ambivalence, in this and other contexts, results in the negotiation of its meaning in daily interactions. The chapters in this book provide evidence of the ways risks introduced by the inflow of asylum seekers are defined and negotiated at the point of encounter between the refugees and the risk management industries of Northern Europe's welfare states. The diverse effects that these different yet interconnected bureaucratic interventions, and the ambivalent attitudes towards refugees, have on the lives of people who seek asylum – and vice versa – is a subject matter that is empirically investigated in this volume. These diverse effects, however, share their foundation in risk management and enactment of bureaucratic violence as we explain in the next section.

**Refugees and bureaucratic violence**

We suggest that Weber's iron cage, one that is brought about by bureaucratic institutions in Northern Europe in the experience of refugees, can be better understood in conjunction with the concept of bureaucratic violence. Hannah Arendt (1969) explained the relationship between bureaucracy and violence as follows:

> the greater the bureaucratisation of public life, the greater will be the attraction of violence. In a fully developed bureaucracy there is nobody left with whom one could argue, to whom one could present grievances, on whom the pressures of power could be exerted. Bureaucracy is the form of government in which everybody is deprived of political freedom, of the power to act; for the rule by Nobody is not no-rule, and where all are equally powerless we have a tyranny without a tyrant.

While Arendt's essay was written in the context of the 1960s' students' movements and the violence they triggered in the US and France, her remarks draw attention to the universality of the resort to violence whenever revolutionary change is attempted. In Arendt's analysis, violence is not physical but mostly manifests itself in the denial of rights and freedoms, especially the right to appeal and resist the injustices of power. A growing literature on the intersections between bureaucracy and violence points to the 'spaces where state and bureaucratic organizations exert force and social control and engender struggle across multiple scales' (Eldridge and Reinke, 2018, p. 95). David Graeber (2015, pp. 32–33) describes the process of total bureaucratisation and the violence it is ready to perform as follows:

> Security cameras, police scooters, issuers of temporary ID cards, and men and women in a variety of uniforms acting in either public or private capacities, trained in tactics of menacing, intimidating, and ultimately deploying physical violence, appear just about everywhere – even in places such as playgrounds, primary schools, college campuses, hospitals, libraries, parks or beach resorts, where fifty years ago their presence would have been considered scandalous, or simply weird.

Graeber's description refers to the readiness to use physical violence in daily surroundings, which is only one aspect of the kind of violence we refer to. A different perspective on bureaucracy is offered by Akhil Gupta (2012), who demonstrates the structural violence (see also chapter 2) embedded in the practices of the postcolonial Indian state even when that very same state wishes to ameliorate suffering. Gupta describes the arbitrariness of decisions taken by bureaucrats, and the widespread corruption embedded in systems of care. Such contradictory processes, the author shows, systematically reproduce and normalise suffering.

An important element of bureaucratic violence takes the form of waiting. As Pierre Bourdieu explains, waiting demonstrates how the effect of power is experienced (see also Khosravi, 2014). 'Making people wait ... delaying without destroying hope is part of the domination' (Bourdieu, 2000, p. 228). Javier Auyero (2012) also takes on the experience of waiting (see chapter 11) that poor people have to go through as they interact with state bureaucracies in Argentina, and argues for the construction of subordinate political subjectivation as an outcome of bureaucracies. In Auyero's book, poor people wait for identification documents, at the welfare office, or for relocation in a toxic industrial hinterland. This analysis allows us to understand the ways state interventions and bureaucracies regulate the lives of poor people. In the process of waiting, subordination is normalised, and poor people's citizenship is curtailed. In the end, waiting emerges as one of the punitive methods of state violence. Or, as Shahram Khosravi (2014) writes, 'waiting generates feelings of "powerlessness and vulnerability"'.

In this volume, we expand the analysis of spaces where the state exerts bureaucratic control engendering struggle, harm, and violence. The outcomes are analysed not only as products of abstract structures, but ones that are administered through processes of decision-making (see chapters 2 and 3), paperwork (see chapters 9 and 10), mass/social media discourses (see chapters 6, 7, and 8), inaction (see chapter 11), and exclusion (see chapters 4, 5, and 12). Thus, the authors in this collection illustrate the ways in which bureaucracies interact with refugees face-to-face, structure their lives outside of these personal interactions, and reproduce different forms of violence that diminish their access to citizenship and human rights.

The concept of bureaucratic violence has its roots in postcolonial studies, which drew our attention to ways bureaucratic violence has historically been used to discipline or even wipe out colonised populations (e.g. Fanon, 2008, 2014, see also Lewis and Mills, 2003; Dwyer and Nettelbeck, 2018). Apart from the most infamous violence of the German Nazi-government of the Second World War, both Sweden and Denmark have ruled and administered indigenous populations like the Sami people and the Greenlanders with colonial methods. Other minority groups, such as the Roma, have also been harshly governed (Arbetsmarknadsdepartementet, 2014). The abduction of children to foster care or compulsory schooling, and forced sterilisations directed against marginalised social groups and indigenous populations are cases in point (see also Broberg and Tydén, 2005; Farver, 2010; Sydow Mölleby et al., 2011; Sköld, 2013). When states govern vulnerable minorities, violent interventions of the state are frequently considered necessary 'for their own good'. Duran (2006) has defined 'colonial bureaucratic violence' as the various mechanisms through which institutions alienate, isolate, and oppress Native people. In the process, institutions also ignore and deny the importance of indigenous cultures (see also the notion of epistemic violence in Spivak, 1990; Evans, 1997). While Duran writes about Native Americans who endured cultural genocide, the definition provided is useful for our purposes. While we do not wish to equate colonial violence with neoliberal bureaucratic violence, we wish to show that bureaucracy in contemporary Northern Europe, in its interest in being impersonal, efficient, rule-based, and formal, ends up alienating and oppressing newly arrived refugees whose cultures and hopes and dreams are often ignored in multiple interactions and different ways (see especially chapters 9, 10, and 11). These mechanisms are equally believed to be necessary for the clients' own good and should not necessarily be considered any less coercive than those carried out by colonial powers. As Fassin (2015, p. 2) concludes about the French state and its street-level bureaucrats, they 'represent a dual dimension of order and benevolence, of coercion and integration.' The chapters in this volume, in different ways, show that impersonal rules dehumanise and exclude newcomers in ways that end up replicating some of the features of colonial violence.

Based on the analyses we offer in this volume, it is no coincidence that the disciplining bureaucratic practices that intervene in the lives of refugees bring to mind colonial practices. Colonialism and bureaucracy (on which colonialism depended) aim to control every aspect of human life, as is evident in the bureaucratisation of schools, hospitals, municipalities, and social services that were all part of the colonial project. For example, Mitchell (1991) illustrates that the colonisation of Egypt relied on large bureaucracies that institutionalised order, made the colonised legible to colonial power, and maintained discipline over colonised bodies. In European discourses, racialised refugees and other non-European migrants are often conflated with the colonial Other of historical times. It is, indeed, one effect of postcolonialism that many colonised and racialised subjects migrate to the (former) colonial metropoles of Europe. Racial imaginations also influence who is considered to belong to the nation and, indirectly, who is considered worthy of assistance from the welfare state (see e.g. Fox, 2012).[13]

Writing already in the 1980s, Nobel (1988, pp. 29–30) referred to an 'arms race against humanitarianism' coupled with an 'escalation of unilateral measure against refugees'. Nobel's analysis of the phenomenon of forced displacement is as true today as at the time he was writing:

> The overwhelming majority of the refugees originate in the Third World. The direct causes of their flight are conflicts kept alive mostly by super-power politics and by weapons forged and manufactured at bargain prices in the rich countries, who export death and destruction, and import the natural and partly processed products of the poor countries. At the same time they refuse to a great extent to receive the refugees who try to escape the suffering and the sorrow generated by super-power politics. (p. 29)

The refusal to receive those escaping suffering is at the core of the analysis provided in this book. When reception is coerced, either through legal resettlement or, as in most cases, by irregular entry, the problem facing the rich countries of Northern Europe (three of which provide the geographic focus of this book) becomes that of bureaucratic management. This serves as the basis for controlling most aspects of refugees' lives, while simultaneously alienating, isolating, and oppressing them. We propose the study of this process of discipline and coercion of refugees in an attempt to mitigate their imminent risk through conceptual tools offered by the framework of regimes of mobility.

## Regimes of mobility

The different contributions in this book are theoretically and methodologically influenced by the 'mobility turn' within analyses of migration and mass movements of people. In discussing the contours of the mobility turn, Glick Schiller and Salazar (2013) draw our attention to the need to analyse 'regimes of mobility'. According to the authors, 'the regimes of mobility framework brings attention to the relationships between mobility and immobility, localisation and transnational connection, experiences and imaginaries of migration, and rootedness and cosmopolitan openness' (Glick Schiller and Salazar, 2013, p. 183). From our perspective, refugees' encounters with the welfare state are sites where these relationships can be interrogated and analysed beyond an insistence on those binaries that the regimes of mobility framework refutes. For example, it is within the encounters with bureaucracies that we can examine states' interests in controlling mobile populations, managing their social mobility, and motivating their further mobility (to another country and/or back home). Similarly, it is within these encounters that we can understand the contradictions between cosmopolitan openness in state policies towards the protection of refugees and exclusionary practices of re-bordering (see Benhabib, 2004, 2014). The ongoing encounter between established bureaucracies and mobile subjects is one that is characterised by unequal distributions of power. Such inequality is hard to conceive when the analysis is focused on either the state and its policies/practices or the migrants' narratives of mobility. It is precisely at the encounter between the two that the regimes of mobility framework – and our volume as an extension of it – enables us to specify the inequality and interlinks between state and migrant.

As an integral part of our reading of this framework, the reference to regimes brings attention to ways individual states and international entities regulate and surveil the mobility of individuals, often through bureaucratic measures. At the same time, the attention paid to the notion of regimes reflects the importance of analysing forms of governmentality and hegemony that shape such mobility (Hall, 1997; Foucault and Ewald, 2003; Glick Schiller and Salazar, 2013, p. 189). In our understanding, practices of bureaucratisation in Northern Europe often aim at handling both governmental policies towards mobile people and street-level bureaucrats' work processes in different institutions. Regimes of mobility are thus affected by practices that have little to do with mobility and more with institutional requirements and bureaucratic logics, including 'audit culture' (see also Strathern, 2000). Audit culture is the process by which the rules and methods of accountancy and financial management are used for the governance of people and organisations, and the social and cultural effects of this process. A focus on accountability colours policy delivery with increased standardisation, documentation, and evaluation. Today, this influences both work units and individual street-level bureaucrats within Northern European welfare states (see also Bruun et al., 2015). In chapters 2, 3, and 5, Joormann, Skodo, and Lindberg analyse recent developments regarding refugee mobility and the ways they have re-configured the governmentality of refugees at the local, national, and regional levels.

Within migration research, the mobility paradigm distinguishes mobility from movement by highlighting its meaningfulness: 'to ignore the way movement is entangled in all sorts of social significance is to simplify and strip out the complexity of reality as well as the importance of those meanings' (Adey, 2009, p. 35). The meanings of mobility can come from an array of sources including the media, government, workplace policies, and legal interpretations, the latter two having ongoing direct material effects on the bodies of the subjects of these discourses and policies (Blomley, 1994). The focus on the specific constructions of and effects on refugee bodies is the approach taken by Abdelhady, Canning, and Jovičić: As chapters 6, 7, and 12 show, albeit in different ways, control over refugees' bodies is associated with institutional practices that legitimise and perform the desire to control.

Furthermore, focusing on meaningfulness underscores a subject-based approach and brings into question the power dynamics shaping these subjective experiences (Rogaly, 2015). A critical approach to mobility (Massey, 1993; Söderström et al., 2013) examines such power dynamics and demonstrates the ways mobility entails a complex relation to places (Waters, 2014), a mixture of freedom and coercion (Gill et al., 2011), and simultaneous experiences of success and stagnation (Abdelhady and Lutz, under review) that need to be understood within specific institutional arrangements. In chapters, 9, 10, and 11, Gren, Pearlman, and Weiss interrogate the power dynamics integral to bureaucratic interactions that shape individual experiences and the associated imaginaries that influence much of these experiences. The three chapters discuss how meaning-making, aspirations, and mobility strategies are linked to both institutional settings in the receiving country and migrants' cultural and social understandings of what a good life constitutes. This understanding is key within the regimes of mobility framework that this book extends.

**Chapters in the book**

In Part I, 'Governing refugees', four chapters portray the political and legal contexts within which the refugee crisis and the accompanying mechanisms to manage mobility risks can be understood. In chapter 2, Joormann provides an introduction to the constructions of refugees in and through political discourses and legal procedures in Sweden, Germany, and Denmark. His analysis underscores the relevance of class as a category of stratification, which plays an important (yet sometimes contradictory) role in the granting of asylum. In chapter 3, Skodo elaborates on the Swedish case by showing how the construction of refugees as a national risk ultimately impeded the ability to respond to the influx of large number of refugees in 2015. Relying on the analysis of a government report, the chapter unearths the official public theories expressed in this report and puts forth two key findings. First, it reveals a fundamental difference between the national and local government. The national government saw 2015 as a threat to sovereignty, while the municipalities saw it as a strain on the bureaucracy that was successfully managed, the lessons and resources of which were lost on the government and the state precisely at the moment when new practices were established that could effectively deal with another mass entry. Second, this difference does not imply an entirely autonomous sphere of action for the local government, since the national government curtailed the autonomy of the local government. Skodo shows that far from threatening Swedish state sovereignty, as the Swedish national government and mainstream media claimed, the 'refugee crisis' has justified, asserted, and extended sovereignty by recourse to national and international law, and an associative chain link between asylum seekers, illegal immigration, terrorism, and crisis. In chapter 4 Bak Jørgensen focuses on the framing of crisis in the Danish context, the deterrence policies that this framing created, and some of the reactions these policies triggered among certain segments of civil society. In his analysis, Bak Jørgensen unpacks three interrelated concepts: deterrence policies, institutional uncertainty, and deportable populations. Similar to Skodo's analysis, Bak Jørgensen shows that the specific framing of crisis legitimised restrictive policy shifts that receive widespread support in Danish public life. These policies also feed into a climate of uncertainty and expand the category of deportable populations, exemplifying a form of bureaucratic violence. In chapter 5, Lindberg illustrates the implementation of the minimum rights approaches adopted by the Swedish and Danish governments in view of making their respective countries less attractive for persons seeking protection. While the discussed policies form part of a wider

European trend whereby welfare regimes are instrumentalised for the purpose of border and migration control, Lindberg argues that restrictions to minimum welfare services assume particular significance in highly bureaucratised welfare states, and should be understood as a particular form of state violence.

Part II, 'Disciplining refugees', is illustrated in three chapters. Jovičić, in chapter 6, examines visual material and associated imageries of refugees and shows that the changing visual discourses can best be illustrated though four visual frames: victimisation – refugee bodies constructed as voiceless victims caught in suffering; securitisation – refugee bodies enmassed and posing threats to destabilise sovereignty of the 'nation state'; reception – images of refugees being welcomed and integrated in Sweden; and humanisation – private portraits of people fleeing depicted as complex individuals and active political subjects. In chapter 7, Abdelhady expands the cultural analysis and shows that the refugee crisis of 2015 was constructed as a crisis facing institutions, as they were unable to cope with the demands of bureaucratically managing and assisting those who came to Sweden seeking help. The author underscores the salience of the institutional crisis rather than moral panic that shaped the public framing of crisis in 2015. The chapter concludes that even though Sweden sees itself as a generous, righteous country, a restrictive turn can still be justified through invocation of notions of order, discipline, control and management, without challenging the nation's self-image. Chapter 8 continues the focus on Sweden and the meaning of asylum from the perspective of social media users who may not have experienced mobility. In the chapter, Sundström and Obenius analyse the debate surrounding a decision to deport an elderly woman, which was later overturned by one of Sweden's Migration Courts. The analysis highlights the dichotomy of inclusion/exclusion as a form of discursive violence that is exercised bottom-up, bringing new insight into an important aspect of the dehumanisation of asylum seekers and refugees.

In Part III, focusing on 'The meaning of refugeeness', the counterproductive consequences of the refugee regime are further illustrated. In chapter 9, Gren interrogates the Swedish introductory programme that is expected to aid in integrating refugees. Instead of focusing on integration, Gren illustrates experiences of frustration, loss, and dependence, which often thwart the hopes and dreams of mobile youth who arrive in Sweden. Despite policy-makers' attempts to individualise the programme and to offer extensive support, institutional requirements and the disciplining of refugees have immobilising effects, not least when it comes to social mobility and higher education. Following the same interest in uncovering the perception of bureaucratic interventions from the perspective of the refugees themselves, in chapter 10, Pearlman brings the focus to the context of Germany. Pearlman's findings echo Gren's as they illustrate the mismatch between mobility and hopes on the one hand, and frustrations and dependence on the other. The entrapment in different bureaucratic regulations and institutional procedures are experienced as hinderances to establishing oneself in the new society. In chapter 11, Weiss turns to Norway and tackles one specific form of frustration, that of waiting. In illustrating the ways in which the welfare state exerts violence on refugees, Weiss depicts the ways bureaucracies negatively impact lived experiences, despite attempts at empathy and care by individual street-level bureaucrats, of those waiting to be resettled in a municipality and to start a new life. Even though Weiss' interlocutors have received permanent residency, lack of willingness and coordination between different welfare state institutions prolong the waiting and create a situation of bureaucratic violence. In chapter 12, Canning turns attention to the ways the externalisation of controls through physical barriers – walls, wires, and border policing – is increasingly supplemented with more banal and bureaucratic internal constrictions which work to encourage immigrants to leave. Detention, degradation, and destitution have become the modus operandi for facilitating the removal of unwanted migrant bodies in the UK, Denmark, and Sweden. Canning provides a vivid look into the ways external and internal border controls are executed in Britain, Denmark, and Sweden. Although there are similarities, each country uses the strategies differently, particularly since the increase in immigration to Europe from 2015.

Collectively, the chapters in this volume investigate how refugees are constructed not only as a threat, and/or scapegoats for gaining votes and political power, but also as a specific category of people in need of welfare state interventions. It is the aim of this book to disentangle the different policy fields and to investigate their impacts on the daily experiences of newly arrived refugees. The importance of daily experiences also stems from the nature of the bureaucracies themselves. We go beyond the analysis of restrictive discourses, regulations, and practices and focus on the construction of different notions of 'crisis' and the different manifestations of violence that emerge when refugees encounter Northern European welfare states and their bureaucracies. Thus, we discuss asylum processes and integration programmes as phenomena that must be understood in the context of the bureaucratisation of everyday life. As such, the chapters offer insights that go beyond the most recent construction of crisis in 2015 to investigate long-term approaches to state–society relations, and political, social, and cultural membership in the welfare state.

### Notes

1  By 'Northern Europe', we refer to those countries in Europe's North-West that are not post-communist states and, in this sense, share a history of having developed into welfare states (currently neoliberalised) with a population that

is marked by recent immigration from Global Southern countries: e.g. people from the former colonies in the UK and the Netherlands, workers and their families who moved from Turkey to Germany, or people who came as refugees from various places to the Nordic countries. Thus, 'North' refers to the geographical location of the countries, while 'West' is understood historically (hence including, e.g., Finland but not the Baltic countries).

2 Abiri (2000) argues that the generosity of the Swedish system has in fact fluctuated considerably over the years. Others such as Brekke (2004), Noll (2005), Barker (2012), and Joormann (2019) provide evidence that problematise the notion of generosity showing the inhumanity and arbitrariness of the Swedish refugee regime.

3 Abram and associates use the term 'forced-displaced people' to refer to those people who are 'categorised and labelled as refugees, asylum seekers, internally displaced people, and stateless people' (Abram et al., 2017: 8). When we use the word 'refugees', we use it as an overarching term, while we use 'asylum seekers' in those contexts where it is important that the person(s) in question are waiting for a decision on their asylum claim.

4 According to statistics published by the EU, trust in national governments is highest in the Netherlands, followed by Sweden, Luxembourg, Finland, and Germany (European Commission, 2017).

5 Since 1 September 1997, the Dublin system (currently 'Dublin III' [EU Regulation 604/2013]) is central to the administration of asylum in Europe. With the Dublin system, the signatory states agree that they have the right to expel asylum seekers to another Dublin-signatory state. This opens up for expulsions to the country where the applicant is registered to have entered 'Europe' as defined by the area that encompasses the territory of the Dublin system's signatory states (see e.g. Brekke and Brochmann, 2015).

6 In the context of refugee asylum, it is important to stress that many financial benefits are not granted to asylum seekers whose applications are pending. Or, as the Swedish Social Insurance Agency, *Försäkringskassan*, clearly states on its webpages: 'When you are waiting for a residence permit you do not have the right to [receive] money from *Försäkringskassan*. But when you have received a residence permit you *may* have the right to money from *Försäkringskassan*' (Swedish Social Insurance Agency, 2018, our translation, emphases added; see also chapter 9).

7 The Schengen Agreement, signed in 1985, is a treaty that guarantees the freedom of movement for people and the abolishment of border checks within the specific geographic area of Europe (https://ec.europa.eu/home-affairs/what-we-do/policies/borders-and-visas/schengen_en).

8 One-and-a-half years later, in May 2017, these 'strengthened border controls' were again loosened (Joormann, 2017). By then, the numbers of asylum applications in Sweden had diminished significantly, while business interests and the regional authorities were pushing for a model of border controls with less impact on the travel of commuters, tourists, and other (wanted) border-crossers (Barker, 2018).

9 Even prior to 2015, scholars observed the intensification of border controls and criminalisation of immigration in Europe's North (Abiri, 2000; Aas, 2007; Bosworth and Guild, 2008; Barker, 2013). Importantly, such accounts explain

that refugee migration is discursively constructed and framed increasingly as a security problem (see Abdelhady and Malmberg, 2018). The increased number of refugees arriving to Europe in the aftermath of the popular uprisings in the Middle East have only intensified this discursive construction of threat and the consequential securitisation (Abdelhady and Malmberg, 2018).
10 During the first half of 2017, 12.1 per cent of accepted asylum seekers in Sweden were granted PRPs, while the remaining 87.9 per cent received TRPs based on refugee status or another protection status. See, in Swedish, www.migrationsverket.se/download/18.4100dc0b159d67dc6146d5/1506929524658/Beviljade+uppeh%C3%A5llstillst%C3%A5nd+2017.pdf (Accessed 19 October 2017).
11 The 'Jewellery Law' stated that refugees' valuables worth more than 10,000 DKK (approx. 1,200 GBP) should be confiscated by Danish authorities (see Crouch and Kingsley, 2016).
12 Similarly, literature on the exclusion of Arab Americans post 11 September 2001 points to the fact that the resulting policies followed established norms and procedures that preceded the terrorist attacks (see e.g. Cainkar, 2009).
13 Our three main cases, Denmark, Germany, and Sweden, all had their own colonial ambitions/projects (although not as successful as, for instance, Great Britain and France).

## References

Aas, K. F. (2007). *Globalization and Crime*. London: SAGE.
Abdelhady, D. and Malmberg, G. F. (2018). 'Media Representation of the Syrian Refugee Crisis: Islam, Securitization and Self-Reflection', in O'Donnell, E. (ed.) *Anti-Judaism, Islamophobia, and Interreligious Hermeneutics: How Conflicts in the Middle East and Beyond Shape the Way We See the Religious Other*. Leiden: Brill Publishers, pp. 107–136.
Abdelhady, D. (2019). 'Framing the Syrian Refugee: Divergent Discourses in Three National Contexts', in Menjivar, C., Ruiz, M., and Ness, E. (eds.) *The Oxford Handbook of Migration Crises*. Oxford: Oxford University Press, pp. 635–656.
Abdelhady, Dalia and Lutz, Amy (under review). *Perceptions of Success Among Working Class Children of Immigrants in Three Cities*.
Abiri, E. (2000). *The Securitisation of Migration: Towards an Understanding of Migration Policy Changes in the 1990s. The Case of Sweden*. Gothenburg: Gothenburg University.
Abram, S., Feldman Bianco, B., Khosravi, S., Salazar, N., and de Genova, N. (2017). 'The Free Movement of People Around the World Would be Utopian: IUAES World Congress 2013: Evolving Humanity, Emerging Worlds, 5–10 August 2013', *Identities*, 24(2), pp. 123–155.
Adam, B., Beck, U., and Van Loon, J. (2000). *The Risk Society and Beyond: Critical Issues for Social Theory*. London: SAGE.
Adey, P. (2009). *Mobility*. London: Routledge.
Arbetsmarknadsdepartementet (2014). 'Den mörka och okända historien. Vitbok om övergrepp och kränkningar av romer under 1900-talet' (The Dark and

Unknown History: A White Paper on Abuse and Violations of Roma People During the 1900s), Ds 2014: 8, Stockholm: Elanders Sverige AB.

Arendt, H. (1969). 'Reflections on Violence'. *The New York Times Review of Books*, 27 February. www.nybooks.com/articles/1969/02/27/a-special-supplement-reflections-on-violence/ (Accessed 30 August 2019).

Arendt, H. (1973). *The Origins of Totalitarianism*. New York: Harcourt.

Auyero, J. (2012). *Patients of the State: The Politics of Waiting in Argentina*. Durham: Duke University Press.

Bakewell, O. (2002). 'Document. Returning Refugees or Migrating Villagers? Voluntary Repatriation Programmes in Africa Reconsidered', *Refugee Survey Quarterly*, 21(1–2), pp. 42–73.

Banakar, R. (2015). *Normativity in Legal Sociology: Methodological Reflection on Law and Regulation in Late Modernity*. New York: Springer.

Barker, V. (2012). 'Global Mobility and Penal Order: Criminalizing Migration, A View from Europe', *Sociology Compass*, 6(2), pp. 113–121.

Barker, V. (2013). 'Nordic Exceptionalism Revisited: Explaining the Paradox of a Janus-Faced Penal Regime', *Theoretical Criminology*, 17(1), pp. 5–25.

Barker, V. (2018). *Nordic Nationalism and Penal Order: Walling the Welfare State*. London: Routledge.

Benhabib, Ş. (2004). *The Rights of Others: Aliens, Residents, and Citizens*. Cambridge: Cambridge University Press.

Benhabib, Ş. (2014). 'Defending a Cosmopolitanism Without Illusions. Reply to My Critics', *Critical Review of International Social and Political Philosophy*, 17(6), pp. 697–715.

Bernstein, A. and Mertz, E. (2011). 'Introduction – Bureaucracy: Ethnography of the State in Everyday life', *PoLAR: Political and Legal Anthropology Review*, 34(1), pp. 6–10.

Blomley, N. (1994). 'Mobility, Empowerment and the Rights Revolution', *Political Geography*, 13, pp. 407–422.

Borevi, K. (2012). 'Sweden: The Flagship of Multiculturalism', in *Immigration Policy and the Scandinavian Welfare State 1945–2010* (pp. 25–96). London: Palgrave Macmillan.

Bosworth, M. and Guild, M. (2008). 'Governing through Migration Control: Security and Citizenship in Britain', *British Journal of Criminology*, 48(6), pp. 703–719.

Bourbeau, P. (2015). 'Migration, Resilience and Security: Responses to New Inflows of Asylum Seekers and Migrants', *Journal of Ethnic and Migration Studies*, 41(12), pp. 1958–1977.

Bourdieu, P. (2000) *Pascalian Meditations*. Stanford: Stanford University Press.

Brekke, J.-P. (2004). *While we are Waiting: Uncertainty and Empowerment among Asylum-Seekers in Sweden*. Oslo: Institutt for Sam-funnsforskning.

Brekke, J. P., and Brochmann, G. (2015). 'Stuck in Transit: Secondary Migration of Asylum Seekers in Europe, National Differences, and the Dublin Regulation', *Journal of Refugee Studies*, 28(2), pp. 145–162.

Broberg, G. and Tydén, M. (2005) *Oönskade i folkhemmet. Rashygien och sterilisering i Sverige* (Unwanted in the People's Home: Racial Hygiene and Sterilization in Sweden), Stockhom: Dialogos.

Brochmann, G. and Hagelund, A. (2012). *Immigration Policy and the Scandinavian Welfare State 1945–2010.* London: Palgrave Macmillan.

Bruun, Maja Hojer, Krøjer, Stine, and Rytter, Mikkel (2015) 'Indledende perspektiver. Forandringsstaten og selvstændighedssamfundet' (Introductory Perspectives: The Changing State and the Society of Independence), Temanumer Velfærdsstaten (Thematic Issue the Welfare State), *Tidsskriftet Antropologi*, 72, pp. 11–37.

Cainkar, L. A. (2009). *Homeland Insecurity: The Arab American and Muslim American Experience after 9/11.* New York: Russell Sage Foundation.

Canning, V. (2017). *Gendered Harm and Structural Violence in the British Asylum System.* Oxon: Routledge.

Caponio, T. and Borkert, M. (eds.) (2010). *The Local Dimension of Migration Policymaking.* Amsterdam: Amsterdam University Press.

Chimni, B. S. (2009). 'The Birth of a "Discipline": From Refugee to Forced Migration Studies', *Journal of Refugee Studies*, 22(1), pp. 11–29.

Crouch, D. and Kingsley, P. (2016). 'Danish Parliament Approves Plan to Seize Assets from Refugees', *The Guardian*, 26 January. Available at: www.theguardian.com/world/2016/jan/26/danish-parliament-approves-plan-to-seize-assets-from-refugees (Accessed 21 May 2018).

De Genova, N. (2009). 'Conflicts of Mobility, and the Mobility of Conflict: Rightlessness, Presence, Subjectivity, Freedom', *Subjectivity*, 29, pp. 445–466.

Dietz, A. (2017). *Ausländer- und Asylrecht* (Foreigners and Asylum Rights). Baden-Baden, Germany: Nomos Verlagsgesellschaft.

Duran, E. (2006). *Healing the Soul Wound: Counseling with American Indians and Other Native People.* New York: Teachers College Press.

Dwyer, P. and Nettelbeck. A. (eds.) (2018). *Violence, Colonialism and Empire in the Modern World.* London: Palgrave Macmillan.

Eldridge, E. R. and Reinke, A. J. (2018). 'Introduction: Ethnographic Engagement with Bureaucratic Violence', *Conflict and Society*, 4, pp. 94–99.

Evans, I. (1997) *Bureaucracy and Race: Native Administration in South Africa*, Berkeley: University of California Press.

Faist, T. (2002). '"Extension du domaine de la lute": International Migration and Security before and after September 11, 2001', *International Migration Review* 36(1), pp. 7–14.

Fanon, F. (2008). *Black Skin, White Masks.* New York: Grove Press.

Fanon, F. (2014). *The Wretched of the Earth.* London: Penguin Classics.

Farver, M. (2010). 'I den bedste mening? Om et eksperiment med grønlandske børn og mulighederne for forsoning mellem Danmark og Grønland' (With the Best of Intentions? About an Experiment with Greenlandic Children and the Possibilities for Reconciliation Between Denmark and Greenland). Unpublished MA Thesis, Roskilde University.

Fassin, D. (2015). 'Introduction: Governing Precarity', in Fassin, D. et al. (eds.) *At the Heart of the State: The Moral World of Institutions*, London: Pluto Press, pp. 1–14.

Fitzgerald, J. and Wolak, J. (2014). 'The Roots of Trust in Local Government in Western Europe', *International Political Science Review*, 37(1), pp. 130–146.

Foucault, M. (1979). 'Govemmentality'. *Ideology and Consciousness*, 6(5–21), p. 1975.

Foucault, M. and Ewald, F. (2003). *Society Must Be Defended: Lectures at the Collège de France, 1975–1976* (Vol. 1). New York: Macmillan.

Fox, C. (2012) *Three Worlds of Relief: Race Immigration, and the American Welfare State from the Progressive Era to the New Deal*. New Jersey: Princeton University Press.

Gammeltoft-Hansen, T. (2017). 'Refugee Policy as "Negative Nation Branding": The Case of Denmark and the Nordics', in Fischer, K. and Mouritzen, H. (eds.) *Danish Foreign Policy Yearbook*. Copenhagen: Danish Institute of International Studies.

Gateri, H. (2018). *Exploring Barriers, Refugees and Refugee Claimants' Experience Accessing Reproductive Health Care Services in Toronto*. PhD, York University.

Gatrell, P. (2013). *The Making of the Modern Refugee*. Oxford: Oxford University Press.

Georgoulas, S. (2017). 'Border Crimes: The Case of Lesvos', *Oxford Border Criminologies Blog*. Available at: www.law.ox.ac.uk/research-subject-groups/centre-criminology/centreborder-criminologies/blog/2017/05/border-crimes (Accessed 4 May 2018).

Gill, N., Caletrio J., and Mason V. (2011). 'Introduction: Mobilities and Forced Migration', *Mobilities*, 6, pp. 301–316.

Glick Schiller, N. and Salazar, N. B. (2013). 'Regimes of Mobility Across the Globe', *Journal of Ethnic and Migration Studies*, 39(2), pp. 183–200.

Graeber, D. (2015). *The Utopia of Rules: On Technology, Stupidity, and the Secret Joys of Bureaucracy*. New York: Melville House.

Gren, N. (2015). *Occupied Lives: Maintaining Integrity in a Palestinian Refugee Camp in the West Bank*. Cairo: The American University in Cairo Press.

Gupta, A. (2012). *Red Tape: Bureaucracy, Structural Violence, and Poverty in India*. Durham: Duke University Press.

Hall, S. (ed.). (1997). *Representation: Cultural Representations and Signifying Practices*. London: SAGE.

Hampshire, J. (2011). 'Disembedding Liberalism? Immigration Politics and Security in Britain since 9/11', in Givens, T., Freeman, G. P., and Leal, D. L. (eds.) *Immigration Policy and Security U.S., European, and Commonwealth Perspectives*. London: Routledge, pp. 109–129.

Harrell-Bond, B. (1986). *Imposing Aid: Emergency Assistance to Refugees*. Oxford: Oxford University Press.

Heindlmaier, A. and Blauberger, M. (2017). 'Enter at Your Own Risk: Free Movement of EU Citizens in Practice', *West European Politics*, 40(6), pp. 1198–1217.

Heng, Y. K. and McDonagh, K. (2011). 'After the "War on Terror": Regulatory States, Risk Bureaucracies and the Risk-Based Governance of Terror', *International Relations*, 25(3), pp. 313–329.

Herzfeld, M. (1992), *The Social Production of Indifference: Exploring the Symbolic Roots of Western Bureaucracy*. New York: Berg.

Hess, S., Kasparek, B., Kron, S., Rodatz, M., Schwertl, M., and Sontowski, S. (eds.) (2016), *Der lange Sommer der Migration* (The Long Summer of Migration). Berlin and Hamburg: Assoziation A.

Hoesch, K. (2018). *Migration und Integration*. New York: Springer.

Holgersson, H. (2011). *Icke-medborgarskapets urbana geografi* (The Urban Geography of Non-Citizenship). Gothenburg: Glänta produktion.

Hosper, K., Nierkens, V., Nicolaou, M., and Stronks, K. (2007). 'Behavioural Risk Factors in Two Generations of Non-Western Migrants: Do Trends Converge towards the Host Population?' *European Journal of Epidemiology*, 22(3), pp. 163–172.

Ireland, P. R. (2004). *Becoming Europe: Immigration, Integration, and the Welfare State*. Pittsburgh: University of Pittsburgh Press.

Isotalo, R. (2009) 'Politicizing the Transnational: On Implications for Migrants, Refugees, and Scholarship', *Social Analysis*, 53(3), pp. 60–84.

Jackson, M. (2008). The Shock of the New: On Migrant Imaginaries and Critical Transitions. *Ethnos*, 73(1), pp. 57–72.

Johannesson, L. (2017). *In Courts We Trust: Administrative Justice in Swedish Migration Courts*. Su.diva-portal.org. Available at: http://su.diva-portal.org/smash/record.jsf?pid=diva2%3A1072557&dswid=7548 (Accessed 4 May 2017).

Joormann, M. (2017). A Temporary Asylum Law and Secret Legal Cases: The Swedish Migration Bureaucracy and its Exceptions. Oxford Border Criminologies Blog, 10 May 2017. Oxford, UK. www.law.ox.ac.uk/research-subject-groups/centre-criminology/centreborder-criminologies/blog/2017/05/temporary-asylum (Accessed 9 May 2020).

Joormann, M. (2018). 'Asylstafetten: A Longitudinal Ethnographic Study of Protest Walks Against the Detention of Asylum Seekers in Sweden', *Justice, Power and Resistance*, 2(2), pp. 335–356.

Joormann, M. (2019). *Legitimized Refugees: A Critical Investigation of Legitimacy Claims within the Precedents of Swedish Asylum Law*. PhD, Lund University.

Kentikelenis, A., Karanikolos, M., Williams, G., Mladovsky, P., King, L., Pharris, A., Suk, J. E., Hatzakis, A., McKee, M., Noori, T., and Stuckler, D. (2015). 'How do Economic Crises Affect Migrants' Risk of Infectious Disease? A Systematic Narrative Review', *The European Journal of Public Health*, 25(6), pp. 937–944.

Khosravi, S. (2014), 'Waiting – Keeping Time', in Anderson, B. and Keith, M. (eds.) *Migration: A COMPAS Anthology*. Oxford: COMPAS, pp. 66–67.

Lacroix, M. (2004). 'Canadian Refugee Policy and the Social Construction of the Refugee Claimant Subjectivity: Understanding Refugeeness', *Journal of Refugee Studies*, 17(2), pp. 147–166.

Lewis, R. and Mills, S. (2003) *Feminist Postcolonial Theory: A Reader*. New York: Routledge.

Lindberg, A. (2017). 'Svenska modellen är ingen gränsvakt' (The Swedish Model is not a Border Patroller). *Aftonbladet*. Available at: www.aftonbladet.se/ledare/a/yLeqE/svenska-modellen-ar-ingen-gransvakt. (Accessed 30 November 2017).

Lipsky, M. (1980). *Street-Level Bureaucracy: Dilemmas of the Individual in Public Services*. New York: Russell Sage Foundation.

Malkki, L. (1992). 'National Geographic: The Rooting of Peoples and the Territorialization of National Identity among Scholars and Refugees', *Cultural Anthropology*, 7(1), pp. 24–44.

Malkki, L. H. (1995). 'Refugees and Exile: From "Refugee Studies" to the National Order of Things', *Annual Review of Anthropology*, 24(1), pp. 495–523.

Mallardo, A. (2017). *Humanitarian Corridors: A Tool to Respond to the Refugees' Crisis*. Oxford Border Criminologies Blog. Available at: www.law.ox.ac.

uk/research-subject-groups/centre-criminology/centreborder-criminologies/blog/2017/05/humanitarian (Accessed 17 August 2017).
Maroufi, M. (2017). 'Precarious Integration: Labour Market Policies for Refugees or Refugee Policies for the German Labour Market?' *Refugee Review*, 3, pp. 15–33.
Massey, D. (1993). 'Power-Geometry and Progressive Sense of Place', in Bird, J. (ed.) *Mapping the Futures: Local Cultures, Global Change*. London: Routledge, pp. 280–288.
McKinnon, S. (2008). *The Discursive Formation of Gender in Women's Gendered Claims to U.S. Asylum*. PhD, Arizona State University.
Meier-Braun, K. (2017). *Die 101 wichtigsten Fragen* (The 101 Most Important Questions). Munich: C. H. Beck.
Mitchell, T. (1991). *Colonizing Egypt*. Berkeley: University of California Press.
Myrberg, G. (2014). 'Organizing Refugee Reception: The Case of the Swedish Introduction Reform'. Paper presented at the ECPR Joint Sessions Conference in Salamanca, Spain. https://ecpr.eu/Filestore/PaperProposal/82ea46f5-1443-44de-beee-a8be145d48a0.pdf (Accessed 11 February 2020).
Myrberg, G. (2017). 'Local Challenges and National Concerns: Municipal Level Responses to National Refugee Settlement Policies in Denmark and Sweden', *International Review of Administrative Sciences*, 83(2), pp. 322–339.
Navaro-Yashin, Y. (2012). *The Make-Believe Space, Affective Geography in a Postwar Polity*. Durham: Duke University Press.
Nobel, P. (1988). 'Refugees and Other Migrants Viewed with the Legal Eye – or how to Fight Confusion', in Petersen, K. H. and Rutherford, A. (eds.) *Displaced Persons*. Sydney: Dangaroo Press, pp. 18–31.
Noll, G. (2005). 'Salvation by the Grace of State? Explaining Credibility Assessment in the Asylum Procedure', in Noll, G. (ed.), *Proof, Evidentiary Assessment and Credibility in Asylum Procedures*. Leiden: Martinus Nijhoff, pp. 197–214.
Öberg, N. (1994). *Gränslös rättvisa eller rättvisa inom gränser? Om moraliska dilemman i välfärdsstaters invandrings- och invandrarpolitik*. (Borderless Justice or Justice Within Borders? About Moral Dilemmas in Welfare States' Immigration and Immigration Policies). Uppsala: Acta Universitatis Upsaliensis.
Odugbesan, A. and Schwiertz, H. (2018) '"We Are Here to Stay": Refugee Struggles in Germany Between Unity and Division', in Rosenberger, S., Stern, V., and Merhaut, N. (eds.) *Protest Movements in Asylum and Deportation*. New York: Springer, pp. 185–203.
Pardo, I. and Prato, G. B. (eds.) (2011). *Citizenship and Legitimacy of Governance: Anthropology in the Mediterranean Region*. London: Routledge.
Pedersen, O. K. (2011). *Konkurrencestaten* (The State of Competition). Copenhagen: Hans Reitzels forlag.
Rogaly, B. (2015). 'Disrupting Migration Stories: Reading Life Histories through the Lens of Mobility and Fixity', *Environment and Planning D: Society and Space*, 33(3), pp. 528–544.
Rytter, M. (2018). 'Made in Denmark: Refugees, Integration and the Self-Dependent Society', *Anthropology Today*, 34(3), pp. 12–14.
Sager, M. and Öberg, K. (2017). 'Articulations of Deportability: Changing Migration Policies in Sweden 2015–2016', *Refugee Review*, 3, pp. 2–14.
Schmidt, G. (2013). '"Let's get Together": Perspectives on Multiculturalism and Local Implications in Denmark', in Kivisto, P. and Wahlbeck, Ö. (eds.) *Debating*

*Multiculturalism in the Nordic Welfare States*. London: Palgrave Macmillan, pp. 197–218.

Sköld, J. (2013). 'Historical Abuse – A Contemporary Issue: Compiling Inquiries into Abuse and Neglect of Children in Out-of-Home Care Worldwide', *Journal of Scandinavian Studies in Criminology and Crime Prevention*, 14 (sup1), pp. 5–23.

Spivak, G. (1990). 'Can the Subaltern Speak?' in Grossberg, C. and Grossberg, N. L. (eds.) *Marxism and the Interpretation of Culture*. Urbana: University of Illinois Press, pp. 271–313.

Strathern, M. (ed.) 2000). *Audit Culture: Anthropological Studies in Accountability, Ethics and the Academy*. London: Routledge.

Swedish Social Insurance Agency (2018). 'När du har sökt asyl i Sverige' (When You Have Sought Asylum in Sweden). Forsakringskassan.se. Available at: www.forsakringskassan.se/privatpers/flytta-till-arbeta-studera-eller-nyanland-i-sverige/nyanland-i-sverige/asylsokande-i-sverige/nar-du-har-sokt-asyl-i-sverige (Accessed 21 May 2018).

Sydow Mölleby, M. et al. (2011). *Samers rättigheter: Motion 2011/12:K210* (The Rights of Sami People: Motion to the Swedish Parliament). Riksdagen.se. Available at: www.riksdagen.se/sv/dokument-lagar/dokument/motion/samers-rattigheter_GZ02K210 (Accessed 24 November 2019).

Söderström, O., Ruedin, D., Randeria, S., D'Amato, G., and Panese, F. (2013). *Critical Mobilities*. London: Routledge.

Turner, B. S. (2007). 'The Enclave Society: Towards a Sociology of Immobility', *European Journal of Social Theory*, 10(2), pp. 287–303.

UNHCR (2017). Global Trends: Forced Displacement in 2016. Available at: http://file://uwfpcluster01.uw.lu.se/socl-mtj$/Desktop/DISS/UNHCR%20Global-Trends-2016.pdf (Accessed 30 November 2017).

Valenta, M., and Bunar, N. (2010). 'State Assisted Integration: Refugee Integration Policies in Scandinavian Welfare States: The Swedish and Norwegian Experience', *Journal of Refugee Studies*, 23(4), pp. 463–483.

Walzer, M. (1983). *Spheres of Justice*. Oxford: Martin Robertson.

Waters, J. (2014). 'Mobilities', in Lee, R., Castree, N., Kitchin, R., Lawson, V., Paasi, A. Philo, C., Radcliffe, S., Roberts, S., and Withers, C. (eds.) *The SAGE Handbook of Human Geography*. London: SAGE, pp. 22–44.

Weber, M. (2009). 'Bureaucracy', in Gerth, H. H. and Wright Mills, C. (eds.) *From Max Weber: Essays in Sociology*. New York: Routledge, pp. 196–244.

Whyte, Z. (2011). 'Enter the Myoptican: Uncertain Surveillance in the Danish Asylum System', *Anthropology Today*, 27(3), pp. 18–21.

Wodak, R. (2019). 'Entering the "Post-Shame Era": The Rise of Illiberal Democracy, Populism and Neo-Authoritarianism in Europe', *Global Discourse: An Interdisciplinary Journal of Current Affairs*, 9(1), pp. 195–213.

Zetter, R. (1991). 'Labelling Refugees: Forming and Transforming a Bureaucratic Identity', *Journal of Refugee Studies*, 4(1), pp. 39–62.

# PART I

# Governing refugees

# 2  Martin Joormann

# Social class, economic capital and the Swedish, German and Danish asylum systems

This chapter starts by problematizing the politico-legal distinction between 'economic migrant' and 'refugee' in the Swedish and wider European contexts. It goes on to discuss the procedural similarities and differences of the Swedish, German and Danish asylum systems, their different appeal instances and their implications regarding the question of who can be granted (refugee) protection status. Drawing on insights from my PhD thesis (Joormann, 2019) and building on its analysis of semi-structured interviews, which I conducted from 2015 to 2017 with judges at Sweden's Migration Courts, I develop the discussion against the backdrop of a literature review of other relevant studies. Besides legal procedures, the discussion focuses on social class. With a close look at some classed aspects of the Swedish, German and Danish asylum systems, the chapter argues that international migration marks – and is marked by – the border crosser's access to social, cultural and, in particular, economic capital. Hence, relying on Pierre Bourdieu's (1984) conceptualization of classed distinctions rooted in these three forms of capital, the chapter shares the following understanding. Migration and indeed human mobility in general 'cannot be analysed without reference to class and capital [ … while] mobility in asylum seeking is both socially stratified and socially stratifying' (Ihring (2016) cited in Scheinert, 2017, p. 133).

### Sweden's migration bureaucracy and access to (economic) capital

Political scientist Livia Johannesson (2017, p. 1) stresses the assessment of many legal scholars, finding that 'asylum determinations constitute the most complex decision-making in contemporary Western societies.' While understanding law as part of society, I first need to problematize hegemonic definitions of who 'the refugee' is. Embedded in dominant discourses about 'deserving refugees' (see also chapter 8) there is the (often implicit) demand that an armed conflict and/or the persecution of an asylum-seeking individual must be evidenced so that the person in question can be eligible for (full) refugee status. In contrast, when individuals or families escape from economic hardship, this is not accepted as a reason to be granted any international protection status. In this context, I give an excerpt from an interview I recorded in 2017 with a judge at Sweden's Migration Court of Appeal (hereafter MCA). The judge claimed that:

> those unaccompanied [asylum-seeking] minors, especially in Stockholm, have been the Moroccan[1] children on the street. I can say that I think that we have many LVU [cases that include the treatment of minors] which concern precisely unaccompanied minors, because they have a socially disintegrating behaviour, they are addicted to drugs, they roam around, as one talks about in the Social Service Act, they have not stayed in one place and so on. I think that, in the eyes of the people, this becomes a problem as well. So everything is affected by everything else in society, because it is connected. And it happens a lot – especially the Moroccan boys – that they do not get a residence permit, and then they don't get any housing or they get housing and then one is so aggressive (*utåtagerande*) that one cannot stay at the housing. And so they live at Sergels Torg [a square in central Stockholm], by selling drugs, and by prostitution. This is a vicious circle, because this does lower people's tolerance, and then, those who really need protection, they ride along in the same category. (Swedish judge, quoted in Joormann, 2019, pp. 28–29)

I asked the judge what was meant by 'category' in this context: 'if one looks at how they have come, then I think that many [are] actually *economic asylum seekers* – because they need to earn a living, they have already lived on the street, and then they have a perspective of getting a better life' (pp. 28–29, my emphasis).

When following this line of argumentation, 'economic asylum seekers' (pp. 28–29) cannot be considered refugees because they have not fled from war, other armed conflict or (fear of) persecution. Depending on the national context, in the respective legal texts often referred to as 'humanitarian grounds', certain migrants might not be granted full refugee status but 'subsidiary protection' (see e.g. Johannesson, 2017). If neither is deemed to be the case – or if, as currently in the Swedish context, a 'temporarily' more restrictive refugee policy is enforced (see also Introduction to this volume) – such people might not receive any protection status at all. Instead, the affected groups tend to be labelled 'economic' migrants who left their countries of origin due to material circumstances such as unemployment or poverty.

If we take a step back while looking at this problem, we see the classed aspects of it. The class background of groups facing material hardship does of course play a central role in the question of whether lack of employment in the country of origin will lead to lack of food on the table. In other words, while it is clear that a person's class position is crucial to assess the risk that this person will starve, become homeless or lack access to (physiological and psychological) health services, coming from a lower class position is in general not considered to be a legitimate reason for cross-border migration that 'deserves' protection (see Khosravi, 2010, p. 111; De Genova, 2015, pp. 192ff.). Illustrating this hegemonic discourse about 'undeserving economic migrants', the Swedish office of the United Nations High Commissioner for Refugees (hereafter UNHCR) uses the term 'economic migrant' (*ekonomisk migrant*) on its webpages:

> As a rule, an economic migrant leaves a country voluntarily to seek a better future somewhere else. If the person would choose to return home, they would benefit from the protection of the home country. Refugees flee because of war, conflict or threat of persecution and they cannot return safely to their homes under prevailing circumstances. (UNHCR Sweden, 2018)

Free will and individual, rational choice characterize the travel of the 'economic migrant', this argument implies. On the other hand, as such discourse about 'deservingness' propagates, the 'refugee' had to leave, they were forced, had no alternative. The term 'economic migrant' is of central discursive importance here. It becomes the binary opposite of 'refugee'. The 'economic migrant' choses actively, as UNHCR Sweden (2018) argues in the definition cited above.

From a critical discourse-analytical perspective (Fairclough, 2003), the reader's attention is drawn to 'voluntarily' and 'choose'. Linked to 'economic migrant', these terms contribute to the construction of the '(un) deservingness' problematized above. On the other side of this discursive binary, refugees 'flee'. Yet they are supposed to 'flee' not in order 'to seek a better future' (see chapter 10), but 'because of war, conflict or threat of persecution' (UNHCR Sweden, 2018). UNHCR Sweden's refugee definition, as exemplified by the excerpt above, is thereby in line with how 'the refugee' is produced as a politico-legal category with its roots in the 1951 UN Refugee Convention. Based on the Convention and its 1967 Protocol, this category emerged during the Cold War and contributed significantly to the framings of today's international refugee regime (Barnett, 2002; Mayblin, 2014; McAdam, 2017).

While refugee migration is as much gendered and racialized as it is a classed social process (Holm Pedersen, 2012; Wikström, 2014; see also chapter 6), we need to pay attention to the classed selectivity of 'Fortress Europe' (Odugbesan and Schwiertz, 2018). Due to this selectivity, people who are socio-economically disadvantaged in their countries of origin face certain class-based obstacles when aiming to reach a European country of destination. To put it simply, there are (almost) no legal ways[2] to apply for refugee status without first having to reach the country of destination. Many asylum seekers aiming for European countries need to pay for smugglers and forged identity papers (Khosravi, 2010). Humanitarian visas to enter countries like Germany are the exception (Scheinert, 2016), while

UNHCR-organized 're-settlement' programmes to countries like Sweden have in recent years concerned not much more than a couple of thousand refugees annually (Swedish Migration Agency, 2017). Denmark has recently decided to restart its resettlement programme – for about 500 'quota refugees' a year (DR, 2019).

Taking into consideration the circumstances in many refugee-sending countries, as Khosravi (2010, p. 111) aptly reminds us, forced displacement has not only an economic but also a political dimension:

> In most refugee sending societies, the boundary between politics and the economy is blurred. Not even forced displacement due to environmental disaster can be defined as completely 'natural' and 'non-political'. Famine, for example, is a political as well as an economic phenomenon (supranote: Turton 2003). While drought is a natural condition, famine is a consequence of political circumstances. People who starve in a famine in fact suffer from insufficient entitlement to food; they do not starve because no food is available (supranote: Sen, 1981). They simply do not 'deserve' to have food.

The deservingness not to be exposed to hunger is, in this sense, not only classed but also dependent on the political circumstances that lead to certain groups being forced into displacement – and being or not being entitled to food. To give a well-known historical example, Jews were deliberately exposed to starvation and other of the Nazis' necropolitics (see Mbembe, 2003). Many of the people who were murdered in the Third Reich's ghettos and concentration camps were indeed from middle-class backgrounds.

In contemporary Europe, refugees are frequently pushed into lower-class positions after their migration and asylum determination processes have been completed (Mulinari and Neergaard, 2004; Schierup et al., 2006; Holm Pedersen, 2012; see also chapter 9). In spite of the omnipresent, catch-all phrase of integration (Loch, 2014; cf. Wieviorka, 2014), social inclusion is often a very difficult and lengthy process for many newly arrived refugees (see e.g. chapter 4 in this book). An important aspect that shapes this difficulty is structural violence[3] (Galtung, 1969), which, in today's Europe, is oftentimes rooted not only in racism, orientalism and Islamophobia (see Holm Pedersen, 2012) but also in those classed processes of social exclusion which I will further problematize below.

We see that an (upper) middle-class background can be advantageous when it comes to passing through not only the unauthorized (Carling, 2007) border-crossing into Europe[4] (Scheinert, 2016) but also through the asylum process itself. To be legally recognized as a refugee, Europe's different national systems of asylum determination all include the possibility to pay for lawyers who have specialized in immigration and refugee law (see e.g. Eule et al., 2019; Gill and Good, 2019). In certain countries (including Denmark and Sweden), the state provides publicly paid legal aid for asylum seekers. In other countries (for instance Germany, see Schittenhelm, 2018), there is no guarantee that asylum seekers will be legally represented or at least receive support from a legal professional. So, how much does it matter if someone can or cannot pay for a lawyer who has specialized in asylum cases? Regarding the legal aid paid by for by the Swedish state, a judge told me:

> unfortunately, this business, if one speaks from the side of the lawyers, is not so lucrative. It is quite a limited number of hours that the public counsels get [paid for], so how one [as a public counsel] writes an application for leave to appeal[5] becomes, maybe, not so stringent, because it is indeed still like this. For us to process this [as an appeal], we need to get help from the [legal] parties, who stress that this question is of interest for a legal precedent. And not only say – sometimes when we get applications for leave to appeal at the Migration Court of Appeal, they [the legal party of the asylum seekers] say that there are reasons to grant leave to appeal, there is importance for the application of law, or there are special reasons, and then they don't develop it. Instead, one must write indeed why there is importance for the application of law, which specific legal question it is that has importance for the application of law and lends itself to pick up precisely this [legal] case. And we would wish that they were better at highlighting the questions of interest for a precedent. (Swedish judge, quoted in Joormann, 2019, pp. 31–32)

In line with Johannesson's (2017) findings, this part of my data adds to previously published criticism of the Swedish asylum system (Stern, 2014; Wikström, 2014; Martén, 2015; Wettergren and Wikström, 2014). Legal aid provided by public counsels is no guarantee that the power imbalance between asylum seekers and the Swedish Migration Agency (hereafter SMA) is affected. When decided at a Migration Court, asylum cases entail that the SMA becomes the legal party that opposes the asylum applicant(s) in court. In 'normal' (more than 99 per cent of)[6] asylum cases, a judge then decides based on claims presented by the two legal parties that represent a) the applicant(s) and b) the SMA (Johannesson, 2017). Given several important details not illustrated in the image below – for example, the possibility that a unanimous decision of the three 'lay judges' (*nämdemän*, recruited from the political parties) can overrule the presiding judge's verdict (Johannesson, 2017) – the Swedish migration bureaucracy's layout is explained in figure 2.

When it comes to cases in which decisions are appealed to the MCA as the highest legal instance, I was told the following:

> The SMA often has better applications for leave to appeal, because they stress precisely that which is of interest for a precedent, and it is not so many cases that they appeal. So, often, they [the lawyers of the SMA] indeed get – what can one say – a little bit of cream on top, because they appeal so seldom. So, one looks a little bit more carefully into this [kind of appeal], maybe there is something in it. (Swedish judge, quoted in Joormann, 2019, p. 32)

# Swedish Migration Board — Migration Court — Migration Court of Appeal

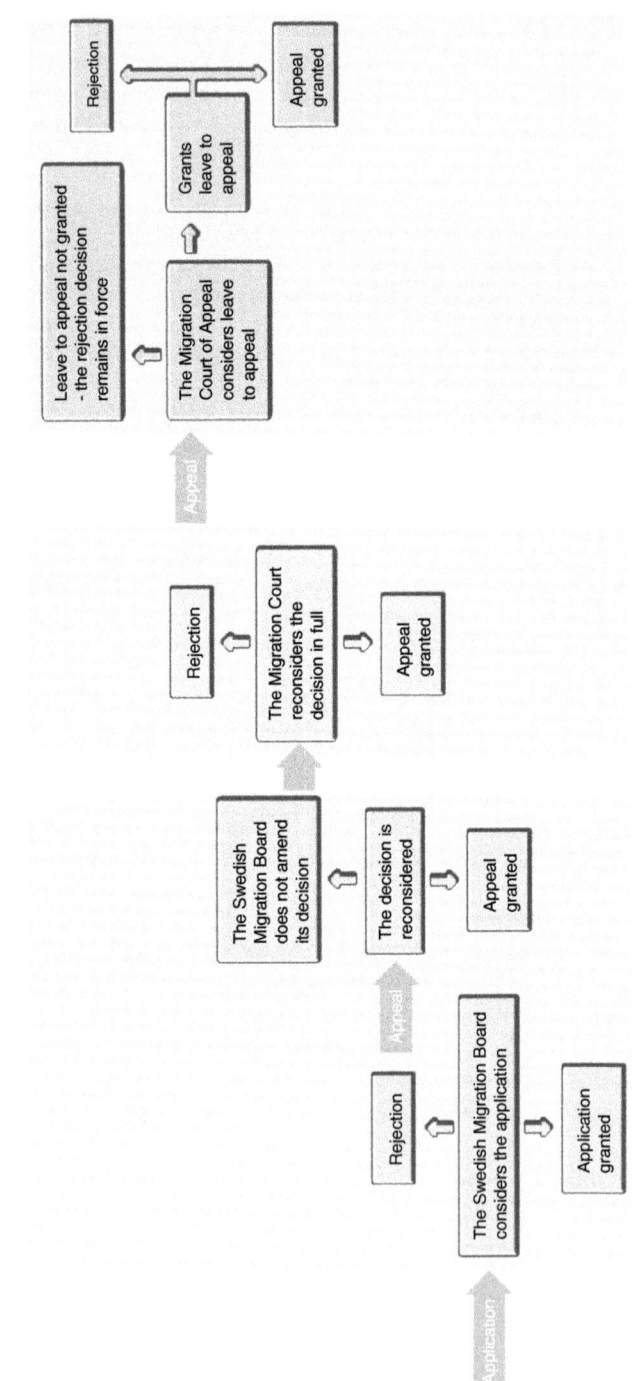

2 Swedish migration bureaucracy

In this excerpt from an interview with an MCA judge, the interviewee confirmed that the power imbalance between the legal parties also persists at the highest legal instance. The judge compared the public counsels' applications for leave to appeal with those of the SMA and stressed that providing legal aid to an asylum seeker is 'not so lucrative'. In addition to that, the SMA files fewer appeals, which tend to be, according to the judge, 'better applications'. As illustrated above, if an asylum case is decided at court, the SMA, which is the decision-making state agency in the first legal instance, finds itself in the position of opposing the asylum seeker as the other legal party. This is due to the adversarial principle of two legal parties opposing each other in administrative courts. Johannesson (2017, p. 98) refers to this as the 'dual role' of the SMA: the first instance being an 'expert agency on asylum' (p. 98); in the second instance, becoming one of the two legal parties. Meanwhile, as the MCA judge quoted above claimed, the SMA's applications are often 'better applications'. In other words, when asylum seekers and their public counsels write an appeal to the MCA, their formulations are often not as legally convincing as those crafted by the immigration law specialists of the state agency. The judge identified one main source of this problem. Providing legal aid as a public counsel was 'not so lucrative' for a Swedish lawyer. My research thereby identified an *institutionalized power imbalance* that is built into the Swedish migration bureaucracy and its asylum system (Joormann, 2019). I base this finding on the observation that the *procedural power imbalance* between the asylum applicant and the SMA – given the SMA's 'dual role' (Johannesson 2017: 98) as, first, decision-making state agency and, then, the opposing legal party in the appeal instances – shifts yet persists throughout all three instances. To pay privately for a legal professional who has specialized in immigration law is a possibility to balance this disadvantage. The problem is that not every asylum seeker has the money to do so. This strengthens the link between the ability to successfully claim asylum and one's access to economic resources.

### (The business of) bordering Europe

In *Illegality Inc.*, Ruben Andersson (2014, p. 273) writes about the business of bordering Europe. I understand this business as, primarily, a complex and multi-dimensional process of accumulating capital, from which various social actors profit. There is, of course, the business of smugglers, which is indeed an economic activity based on the fact that, for asylum seekers, there are, as mentioned above, almost no 'legal ways' to Europe (Scheinert, 2017). This being noted, residence permits – and sometimes citizenship – can be bought entirely legally in many countries of the Global North (see e.g. Barbulescu, 2014; Boatcă, 2016; Keshavarz, 2016, pp. 136ff.; Farolfi et al., 2017). To give an example, London-based Henley & Partners is one of the law firms that have specialized in providing their wealthy clients with legal advice when 'investing' in an EU country in order to gain citizenship. In the case of Malta, they advertise such citizenship-by-investment as follows:

> The Malta Individual Investor Program (IIP), which Henley & Partners was contracted in 2014 by the Government of Malta to design and implement, is the most modern citizenship-by-investment program. The IIP is one of the most exclusive citizenship-by-investment portfolios worldwide. It offers clients the opportunity to acquire citizenship in a country that has one of the strongest, most stable economies of the EU and Eurozone. ... The combined upfront financial requirement, including applicable government charges and citizenship application fees, is just under EUR 900,000. These costs will increase slightly depending on the family size. (Henley & Partners, 2019)

At the time of writing, there are no IIPs for gaining residency in Sweden. In other words, there are no schemes through which wealthy people can use their economic capital to buy a Swedish residence permit or citizenship. However, as Vanessa Barker (2018) has observed, since the late 1980s, the 'walls' of the Swedish welfare state have opened up to a certain extent based on (neo)liberal ideas of attracting investment and labour. For individual migrants, earning more than SEK 13,000 (approx. EUR 1,300) per month throughout the year is currently the legally defined minimum to receive a Swedish residence permit based on employment. That said, starting a business as 'self-employed' (*egen företagare*) in Sweden can be grounds for granting residence permits – if the applicants 'have enough own money to provide for [their] livelihood and, if applicable, that of [their] family during the first two years (equivalent of SEK 200,000 for [the main applicant], 100,000 for [the] spouse and 50,000 for every child)' (Swedish Migration Agency, 2019). The Swedish state, therefore, defines either a minimum monthly income (SEK 13,000), or a minimum of financial assets in cash (SEK 200,000 for individuals without family members) as needed to be eligible to apply for a Swedish residence permit based on (self-)employment.

In the context of refugee migration, such regulations have significance. As legal professionals whom I interviewed explained (Joorman, 2019), many asylum cases are not only concerned with the question of whether the application is 'in need of protection' but also with the applicant's *ties*[7] to Sweden (including family, study, work and Swedish language skills). In certain cases, when asylum seekers who are already in Sweden apply for residence, legal decisions can therefore justify a permit based on such ties, thus making an 'exception to the rule that residence permits must be arranged prior to entry' (MCA precedent MIG 2011, p. 27, cited in Joormann, 2019, p. 201).

Social class, economic capital and asylum systems                                    39

**The largest total number of refugees in the EU: Germany**

During 2015's long summer of migration (Odugbesan and Schwiertz, 2018), Germany and Sweden received the largest total and, respectively, per capita number of asylum applications in the EU (see UNHCR, 2016). In both countries, as exemplified with the description of the Swedish migration bureaucracy above, these asylum claims are in the first legal instance processed by a state agency (Germany: *Bundesamt für Migration und Flüchtlinge* (*BAMF*); Sweden: *Migrationsverket*), where case officers take decisions on the asylum seekers' residence permit applications (Hinger et al., 2016; Parusel, 2016). In 2017, 56 per cent and 59 per cent of all first instance applications for international protection were rejected in Germany and Sweden, respectively (BAMF, 2018; Migration Agency, 2018).

If leave to appeal these decisions is granted, and if the case reaches the second legal instance, in both Germany and Sweden it is an administrative court that takes the second-instance decision (Schittenhelm, 2018). Thus, asylum appeals move the legal case from the inquisitorial setting of a state agency (case officer takes top-down decision on applicant's asylum claim) to the adversarial setting of an administrative court. Compared with the Swedish context described above, there are no 'lay judges' deciding on asylum applications at German administrative courts; in Germany, the judge adjudicates and takes the second-instance decision (Arndt, 2015).

Another difference, which one can identify when comparing the two national contexts, is that the Swedish court system designates, as visualized in the image above, certain administrative courts (*Förvalningsrätt*) as Migration Courts (*Migrations-domstol*). Moreover, in the first instance of the migration bureaucracy, the Swedish system already tends to employ caseworkers with (some) legal training. As Karin Schittenhelm (2018) puts it, when comparing the Swedish and German asylum systems, many of 'the [caseworkers] interviewed in Sweden were university graduates, primarily holding law degrees, while administrative and vocational training have been more common in Germany'. In Germany, migration cases are '*Ländersache*', which means they fall under the authority of the sixteen Federal States (*Bundesländer*), while the largest (*Migrationsdomstolen vid Förvaltningsrätten i Stockholm*) and the most authoritative (*Migrationsöverdomstolen*) of Sweden's Migration Courts are both located in Stockholm (Arndt, 2015; Johanesson, 2017).

To summarize, in Germany asylum applications are in the first legal instance submitted to the local branch of the *BAMF*. When rejected – which in 2017 applied to more than half of all asylum claims – the decision can be appealed. In the second legal instance, then, the decision is taken by a judge at one of Germany's administrative courts. One important difference in comparison with Sweden is that asylum seekers in Germany are not necessarily represented by a lawyer. In Schittenhelm's (2018, p. 7) words, 'legal assistance is funded by the Swedish state and covers both legal advice and representation during the personal interview and all subsequent steps in the regular procedures ... The absence of such free, institutionalized legal assistance by professional lawyers in the German asylum system is a critical difference' (Schittenhelm, 2018, p. 7). This means that, while in Sweden asylum seekers can benefit from (the limited amount of) legal aid provided by public counsels (see above), in Germany they are largely dependent on their own access to economic capital when seeking professional advice and legal representation in court.

### Temporary humanitarian admission programmes in Germany

Before the numbers of asylum applications peaked in 2015, the German government had established reception programmes, particularly for Syrian citizens (Scheinert, 2016). Outside the general rules of the asylum system, in which applicants must file their claims with the *BAMF* in one of the Federal States as described above, Germany implemented Temporary Humanitarian Admission Programmes (THAPs). As part of this initiative at the national level, the government had promised to receive 20,000 Syrian refugees in Germany. Syrians were invited to apply to UNHCR for re-settlement to Germany, meaning that they did not have to enter Germany as 'unauthorized border crossers' (see above; Carling, 2007). In order to be selected for one of these programmes, however, the applicants had to fit into one of the following categories:

1) humanitarian criteria (special protection needs of children, sick persons, women, religiously persecuted persons);
2) ties to Germany (family ties, previous sojourns, language skills, receptive Syrian religious minority institutions);
3) ability to make a special contribution to rebuilding the country after the end of the conflict (possibility to expand existing qualifications in Germany). (Scheinert, 2017, p. 130)

In this way, until 'mid-2015, around 35,000 admission visas had been granted and just over 26,000 people reached Germany' (Scheinert, 2017, p. 129). Conceptually speaking, two of the categories listed above demonstrate the importance of economic, social and cultural capital in Bourdieu's terms. The second and third categories make clear that refugees with a certain amount of social ('ties'), cultural ('skills') and economic capital ('contribution') were high on the German authorities' wish list. THAPs thereby looked for an ideal type of refugee whom Scheinert calls 'the classed refugee' (Scheinert, 2017, p. 132). In the context of her study, this term refers to people who had sufficient access to capital to deserve the right to reside in Germany. In Scheinert's analysis, it was required of refugees to have the financial resources to be able to pay for protection. Hence, 'the admission programmes are highly selective' (Scheinert, 2017, p. 132). To

# Social class, economic capital and asylum systems

take up a term that is particularly problematic ethically, family members of Syrian refugees were in this way asked to *sponsor* (Scheinert, 2017, p. 132, emphasis added) the residence permits of their loved ones. In a similar vein as Sweden's permits for the self-employed and other European countries' more straightforward 'Immigrant Investor Programmes', a look at Germany's THAPs thereby makes clear that, at least from a sociological perspective, the binary distinction between 'economic migrant' and 'refugee' does not make much sense.

## One of the most restrictive asylum systems in Europe: Denmark

In Denmark, seeking asylum begins with the first interview, in many cases at a police station, where an officer takes the applicants' fingerprints. Alternatively, people can file their asylum claims directly with the Immigration Service (*Udlændingeservice*) at Centre Sandholm, which is the largest reception facility for asylum seekers in Denmark (see also chapter 12 below). This first interview separates applicants according to three categories: 'Dublin', 'manifestly unfounded', and 'regular procedure' (Canning, 2019).

Persons sorted into the first category are to be expelled to the country where they were registered as having entered Europe, as defined by the Dublin system (currently Dublin III, officially called EU Regulation 604/2013). The second category, 'manifestly unfounded', means that protection is denied. These decisions can be appealed by a veto of the Danish Refugee Council (DRC), which is 'an umbrella organisation consisting of members broadly representing civil society organisations in Denmark committed to the refugee cause' (DRC, 2019). Such a veto moves the case to the category of 'regular procedure'.

In this regular procedure, cases are once more separated and either processed according to the normal procedure or categorized as manifestly well-founded. Such well-founded applications are directly granted due to obvious reasons for asylum. In normal cases, which are the clear majority of asylum applications processed in Denmark, the Immigration Services conduct a second interview. The outcome of this interview can either be that asylum is granted or a preliminary rejection (DRC, 2019). In cases of rejection, the appeal 'automatically goes to [the Danish] Refugee Appeal Board' and the state 'provides [a] lawyer' (Canning, 2019, p. 14). Given this aforementioned detail that Denmark also provides publicly paid legal aid to asylum seekers, the Refugee Appeal Board (*Flygtningenævnet*)[8] then takes the final decision, which is either some form of projection status or a definite rejection.

To summarize, in clear contrast to both Sweden and Germany, the Danish asylum system does not make use of administrative courts. Compared with Sweden, in Denmark there are no special migration courts (or Tribunals as in the UK, see Canning, 2019, p. 11) and neither is there the possibility to file an appeal to a local administrative court as in Germany (Arndt, 2015). Instead, the Immigration Service is the first of two legal instances in Denmark. Its initial rejections based on manifestly unfounded claims can only be vetoed by the Danish Refugee Council. When vetoed by the DRC, manifestly unfounded asylum claims become normal procedure, which leads to a second interview by the Immigration Service. Rejections after this second interview can be appealed to and reviewed by the Refugee Appeal Board as the highest legal instance.

### The Jewellery Law: a Border Spectacle against the 'classed refugee'?

In spite of the news that, by January 2019, 'three years after Denmark's infamous "jewellery law" hit world headlines, not a single piece [of jewellery had] been confiscated' (The Local Denmark, 2019), the regulation became quite well known throughout Europe and the world over. From February 2016, refugees in possession of belongings worth more that DKK 10,000 (about EUR 1,300) were to have their belongings confiscated upon entry to Denmark. Meanwhile, Danish police were 'told not to take wedding rings or engagement rings and individual officers [were] left to determine the sentimental value of other items' (The Local Denmark, 2019). Until 24 January 2019, precisely 'one car and 186,000 kroner in cash have been seized – and no jewellery' (The Local Denmark, 2019). Clearly, measures like the Jewellery Law were not really there to be implemented but, instead, to be talked about, in order to deter and to reduce the incentives of coming to Denmark. In a word, that law should make Denmark (even) less attractive for migrants. In line with a now notorious photograph of former Danish Minister for Immigration, Integration and Housing, Inger Støjberg, cutting a cake to celebrate the '50th amendment to tighten immigration controls' (Pasha-Robinson, 2017), this specific legal norm about jewellery was thereby highly symbolic (see also chapter 5).

Echoing Nicholas De Genova, the Jewellery Law is a good example of a 'Border Spectacle'. As a scene of exclusion, 'it affirms the obscene fact of a kind of subordinate inclusion' (De Genova, 2013). This subordinate inclusion was directed at all 'deserving refugees'. Asylum seekers with less than DKK 10,000 of valuables should immediately be granted access to the procedures, while people with more than that (arguably modest) amount of personal belongings should first pay for their right to have their claim processed. Hence understandable as a form of De Genova's Border Spectacle, the law implied at least three messages with rather straightforward claims, yet addressed at different audiences:

1) Many asylum seekers have more than DKK 10,000 on them and they are not supposed to have 'so much money' (audience is mainly the Danish public);

# Social class, economic capital and asylum systems

2) Refugees are a cost to Danish society and we will make them pay, if they are rich (audience is mainly the Danish public);
3) Denmark is not a welcoming country; they will take your savings from you when you get there. Therefore, do not seek asylum in Demark (audience is mainly the potential asylum seeker outside Denmark).

Understood as a Border Spectacle, as De Genova conceptualizes it, the Jewellery Law is in this sense first of all a speech-act within domestic politics and only of secondary importance as a measure of deterrence directed against unwanted migrants. Now, if one understands such policies as communication primarily geared to harvest anti-immigration votes, one sees that they function to

a) maintain the dichotomy between economic migrants and refugees, and
b) convince the domestic public that no, 'classed refugees' (in Scheinert's (2017) usage of the term, so defined by their secured access to capital, see above) will be allowed to enter Denmark without first having to 'pay' for their reception.

Firstly, thus, the Jewellery Law as a Border Spectacle gives an obscene but clear message: If people come here to make money (or to seek a better life, see above, UNHCR Sweden, 2018), they will have to start without any cash. In De Genova's terms, asylum seekers are thereby subjected to victimization (they are constructed as deserving if they have less than DDK 10,000 on them), while some are exploitable (if they have more than DKK 10,000 they must pay for the hospitality). Secondly, in this context, the ideal type that Scheinert (2017, p. 132) describes with the term classed refugee – who were relatively well-off and were therefore wanted migrants in the context of Germany – is an image that is applicable in a different fashion in the Danish case. With the spectacle of introducing the possibility (rather than the practice) of confiscating valuables, it is claimed that

1) there are classed refugees (relatively well-off migrants), at the same time as,
2) the Danish state will make sure that these people (with more than DKK 10,000 of valuables on them) will cease to be classed refugees as soon as they decide to enter Denmark.

In brief, the Border Spectacle of the Danish Jewellery Law instrumentalizes the fear of (or hatred against) 'undeserving' refugees. More than anything else a spectacle for domestic politics – a race to the bottom for the toughest stance on migration – the law reifies the hegemonic discursive construction of the refugee as a passive victim who can only be welcomed if they did not leave 'their country voluntarily to seek a better future' (UNHCR Sweden, 2018, see above).

A look at the Danish context thereby highlights that, while migration regimes in general favour asylum seekers with more capital (as I have exemplified above in the cases of Sweden and Germany), the very same regimes rest on the imagination that refugees must be destitute victims without any access to (economic) capital. In other words, the refugee regime becomes a Catch-22. This Catch-22 illustrates the violence built into the political discourse and the legal practices that define national asylum systems and the international migration regime at large.

## Conclusion

The Danish, German and Swedish asylum systems are similar and yet rather different. From the viewpoint of procedural (rather than substantive) law, the three countries' processes of appealing a first-instance decision are organized quite differently. In all three countries, initial applications are processed by a state agency (Denmark's *Udlændingeservice*, Germany's *Bundesamt für Migration und Flüchtlinge*, and Sweden's *Migrationsverket*) according to the inquisitorial procedures of administrative law. In Germany, then, asylum appeals are decided by judges at the local administrative courts (*Verwaltungsgerichte*) under the authority of the sixteen Federal States (*Bundesländer*). In Sweden, appeals are adjudicated by a judge and three lay judges (*nämdemän*, that is, individuals recruited from Sweden's political parties) who take the decision at one of Sweden's four second-instance migration courts (*Migrationsdomstolar*). In Denmark, the initial rejection of manifestly unfounded asylum claims can be vetoed by the civil-society-based Danish Refugee Council, while rejection decisions of the Immigration Service (*Udlændingeservice*) can be appealed to Denmark's Refugee Appeal Board (*Flygtningenævnet*). To put it briefly, Germany uses its local administrative courts under the authority of the Federal States to process asylum appeals, while Sweden established distinct migration courts in 2006. Denmark does not involve any of its administrative courts. Instead, similar to how the system worked in Sweden until 1 April 2006 (Johannesson, 2017), the Danish Refugee Appeal Board processes appeals. At this board, asylum cases are heard by three members: an appointed judge, an official appointed by the Ministry of Refugee, Immigration and Integration Affairs, and a member nominated and appointed by the Council of the Danish Bar and Law Society (Flygtningenævnet, 2019). Given these procedural differences across the three countries, all of which are part of the Common European Asylum System (CEAS) operating within the overall legal framework of international refugee law, it is remarkable that the three national systems display this extent of procedural differences. This is important because it illustrates different institutional settings in which asylum applicants must make their case. If one compares, for instance, Germany with Denmark, the Danish Refugee Appeal Board – where a judge and another legal professional must decide together with an appointee of the Immigration Ministry

(Flygtningenævnet, 2019) – is clearly a more politicized appeal instance than a German administrative court (Arndt, 2015).

Given such differences, a class background marked by a secured access to economic capital can be a significant advantage for migrants who aim to reside in either Sweden, Germany or Denmark. Within all three asylum systems, paying privately for a professional immigration lawyer strengthens the applicant's position (the two Nordic countries here do provide some hours of publicly paid legal aid for all asylum seekers, see above). Outside the asylum system, larger amounts of economic capital – for Maltese citizenship, EUR 900,000 – open up mobility corridors for the ultra-rich (Barbulescu, 2014). This exclusiveness and, consequentially, the social exclusion that these potential and direct advantages of access to economic capital imply, is indeed a classed form of structural violence (Galtung, 1969).

With a closer look at the asylum systems of welfare states such as Sweden, Germany and Denmark, which are arguably still strong, it becomes clear that, similar to other social processes, even asylum determination procedures are classed. Embedded within the European migration regime, the asylum systems analysed here do not mitigate the disadvantages that migrants without sufficient amounts of (economic) capital must deal with. This chapter has shown that, firstly, there is the difference of the German asylum system not guaranteeing state-sponsored legal aid. Secondly, the Danish migration bureaucracy does not include any formal courts but a politicized appeal board, at the same time as Sweden's migration courts are settings of administrative law where a judge decides together with three 'lay judges' recruited from the political parties. That said, to pay privately for a specialist lawyer is an opportunity to profit from economic capital that asylum seekers in Germany, Denmark and Sweden can make use of – if they have the money.

## Notes

1 At the time, there was a moral panic (see chapter 7) in much of Swedish mainstream media about these unaccompanied minors – often presenting them as 'undeserving' (or 'bogus', see chapter 8) asylum seekers.
2 Carling uses 'unauthorized entry' for those border crossings that are completed without any state official checking the traveller. Conversely, he defines an 'authorized entry' as the border crossing during which the traveller is checked and allowed to enter (regardless of whether a forged or invalid passport or similar has been used). In relation to people seeking asylum, Carling writes as follows: 'Unauthorized entry is legitimate under the 1951 Geneva Convention when it is done for the purpose of seeking asylum. Migration can therefore be "unauthorized" without being illegal' (Carling, 2007, p. 6).
3 Going back to Johan Galtung's *Violence, Peace, and Peace Research* (Galtung, 1969), structural violence can be defined as social structures and institutions

that cause different forms of violence, which harm people due to, for example, institutionalised classism, ethnocentrism, nationalism, racism and/or sexism.
4  Here referring to those (relatively) wealthy countries whose bureaucracies operate with the European migration regime defined by the Schengen Agreement, the Dublin Regulation(s) and the Common European Asylum System (CEAS).
5  To have an appeal processed at Sweden's Migration Court of Appeal, the court must grant leave to appeal, i.e. it must recognize that the case is (legally) interesting enough to decide it and thereby turn it into a precedent. Such precedents will be guiding for the lower legal instances, i.e. the second-instance Migration Courts and the first-instance Migration Agency.
6  One notable exception to this setup would be a 'security case' (*säkerhetsärende*, see Joormann, 2017), which is an immigration case deemed to be of importance for national security. In such cases, the Swedish Security Police (*Säkerhetspolisen*) become the first legal instance (UtlL 2005:716, Chapter 16 § 6).
7  In Swedish legal terms, such 'ties' are called *anknytning*.
8  On the Board's homepage in Danish, *Flygtningenævnet* is described as an 'independent, collegial, administrative body that resembles a court' (*uafhængigt kollegialt domstolslignende forvaltningsorgan*, Flygtningenævnet, 2019)

## References

Andersson, R. (2014). *Illegality, Inc.: Clandestine Migration and the Business of Bordering Europe*. Palo Alto: University of California Press.
Arndt, S. (2015). Ambivalente Rechtssubjektivität. Zur Position Asylsuchender in der gerichtlichen Interaktion (Ambivalent Legal Subjectivity. The Position of Asylum Seekers in Court Interaction). *Zeitschrift für Rechtssoziologie* 35(1), pp. 117–142.
BAMF (2018). Jahresgerichtsstatistik 2017: Klagezahlen gegen Asylentscheidungen des Bundesamts für Migration und Flüchtlinge (Annual Statistics 2017: Number of Appealed BAMF Decisions). Available at: www.bamf.de/SharedDocs/Meldungen/DE/2018/20180223-klagezahlen-gegen-asylentscheidungen.html (Accessed 10 February 2020).
Barbulescu, R. (2014). Global Mobility Corridors for the Ultra-Rich. The Neoliberal Transformation of Citizenship. In Shachar, A. and Baubock, R. (eds.) *Should Citizenship Be for Sale?* Robert Schuman Centre for Advanced Studies Research Paper No. 2014/01.
Barker, V. (2018). *Nordic Nationalism and Penal Order – Walling the Welfare State*. London: Routledge.
Barnett, L. (2002). Global Governance and the Evolution of the International Refugee Regime. *International Journal of Refugee Law* 14 (2&3), pp. 238–262.
Boatcă, M. (2016). Globale Ungleichheiten und gekaufte Staatsbürgerschaft. Zum Mechanismus eines knappen Gutes (Global Inequalities and Purchased Citizenship: To the Mechanism of a Scarce Good). In Robertson von Trotha, C. (ed.), *Die Zwischengesellschaft*. Baden-Baden: Nomos.
Bourdieu, P. (1984). *Distinction: A Social Critique of the Judgement of Taste* (1st ed.). Cambridge, MA: Harvard University Press.

Canning, V. (2019). *Reimagining Refugee Rights: Addressing Asylum Harms in Britain, Denmark and Sweden.* Bristol: Migration Mobilities Bristol, University of Bristol. Available at: www.statewatch.org/news/2019/mar/uk-dk-se-reimagining-refugee-rights-asylum-harms-3-19.pdf (Accessed 18 July 2019).

Carling, J. (2007). Unauthorized Migration from Africa to Spain. *International Migration* 45(4), pp. 3–37.

De Genova, N. (2013). Spectacles of Migrant 'Illegality': The Scene of Exclusion, the Obscene of Inclusion. *Ethnic and Racial Studies* 36(7), The Language of Inclusion and Exclusion, pp. 1180–1198.

De Genova, N. (2015). The Otherness of Citizenship. In Anderson, B. and Hughes, V. (eds.), *Citizenship and Its Others.* London: Palgrave Macmillan.

DR [Danish Radio] (2019). *Regeringen til FN: vi vil igen modtage kvoteflygtninge* (The Government to the UN: We Want to Receive Quota Refugees Again). Available at: www.dr.dk/nyheder/politik/regeringen-til-fn-vi-vil-igen-modtage-kvoteflygtningeorganisation (Accessed 28 August 2019).

DRC [Danish Refugee Council] (2019). *The Organisation.* Available at: https://drc.ngo/about-drc/facts-about-drc/the-organisation (Accessed 30 July 2019).

Eule, T., Borrelli, L., Lindberg, A. and Wyss, A. (2019). *Migrants Before the Law: Contested Migration Control in Europe.* London: Palgrave Macmillan, Cham.

Fairclough, N. (2003). *Analysing Discourse: Textual Analysis for Social Research.* London: Routledge.

Farolfi, S., Pegg, D. and Orphanides, S. (2017). Cyprus 'Selling' EU Citizenship to Super Rich of Russia and Ukraine, *The Guardian.* Available at: www.theguardian.com/world/2017/sep/17/cyprus-selling-eu-citizenship-to-super-rich-of-russia-and-ukraine (Accessed 3 October 2017).

Flygtningenævnet (2019). *General Information Regarding the Danish Refugee Appeals Board.* Available at: www.fln.dk/da/English/General_information_regarding_fln (Accessed 30 July 2019).

Galtung, J. (1969). Violence, Peace, and Peace Research. *Journal of Peace Research* 6(3), pp. 167–191.

Gill, N. and Good, A. (eds.) (2019). *Asylum Determination in Europe: Ethnographic Perspectives.* London: Palgrave Socio-Legal Studies.

Henley & Partners (2019). *Malta Citizenship-by-Investment Overview.* Available at: www.henleyglobal.com/citizenship-malta-overview/ (Accessed 8 February 2019).

Hinger, S., Schäfer, P. and Pott, A. (2016). The Local Production of Asylum. *Journal of Refugee Studies*, 29(4), pp. 440–463.

Holm Pedersen, M. (2012). Going on a Class Journey: The Inclusion and Exclusion of Iraqi Refugees in Denmark. *Journal of Ethnic and Migration Studies* 38(7), pp. 1101–1117.

Ihring, D. (2016). Human Mobility as a Resource in Conflict: The Case of Syria. *RSC Working Paper Series 115.* March 2016.

Johannesson, L. (2017). *In Courts We Trust: Administrative Justice in Swedish Migration Courts.* PhD, Stockholm University.

Joormann, M. (2019). *Legitimized Refugees: A Critical Investigation of Legitimacy Claims within the Precedents of Swedish Asylum Law.* PhD, Lund University.

Keshavarz, M. (2016). *Design-Politics: An Inquiry into Passports, Camps and Borders.* PhD, Malmö University.

Khosravi, S. (2010). *'Illegal' Traveller: An Auto-Ethnography of Borders*. London: Palgrave Macmillan.
Loch, D. (2014). Integration as a Sociological Concept and National Model for Immigrants: Scope and Limits. *Identities*, 21(6), pp. 623–632.
Martén, L. (2015). *Political Bias in Court? Lay Judges and Asylum Appeals*. Working paper 2015:2, Department of Economics. Uppsala: Uppsala University.
Mayblin, L. (2014). Colonialism, Decolonisation, and the Right to be Human: Britain and the 1951 Geneva Convention on the Status of Refugees. *Journal of Historical Sociology* 27(3) pp. 423–441.
Mbembe, A. (2003). 'Necropolitics'. *Public Culture* 15(1), pp. 11–40.
McAdam, J. (2017). The Enduring Relevance of the 1951 Refugee Convention. *International Journal of Refugee Law* 29(1), pp. 1–9.
Migration, Agency (2018). Avgjorda asylärenden beslutade av Migrationsverket, förstagångsansökningar, 2017 (Asylum Cases Decided by the Swedish Migration Agency, First-Instance Applications, 2017). Available at: www.migrationsverket.se/download/18.4100dc0b159d67dc6146d1/1514898751014/Avgjorda%20asyl%C3%A4renden%202017%20-%20Asylum%20decisions%202017.pdf (Accessed 12 March 2019).
Mulinari, D. and Neergaard, A. (2004). *Den nya svenska arbetarklassen: rasifierade arbetareskamp inom facket* (The New Swedish Working Class: Racialised Labour Struggles Within the Union). Umeå: Boréa.
Odugbesan, A. and Schwiertz, H. (2018). 'We Are Here to Stay': Refugee Struggles in Germany Between Unity and Division. In Rosenberger, S., Stern, V. and Merhaut, N. (eds.), *Protest Movements in Asylum and Deportation*. London: Springer Open.
Parusel, B. (2016). *Sweden's Asylum Procedures*. Available at: www.bertelsmannstiftung.de/fileadmin/files/Projekte/28_Einwanderung_und_Vielfalt/IB_Studie_Asylum_Procedures_Sweden_Parusel_2016.pdf (Accessed 7 April 2018).
Pasha-Robinson, L. (2017). Danish minister sparks furious backlash after celebrating tougher immigration laws with cake. *Independent*. Available at: www.independent.co.uk/news/world/europe/danish-integration-minister-inger-stjberg-furious-backlash-celebrating-tougher-immigration-laws-a7632161.html (Accessed 7 May 2020).
Scheinert, L. (2016). Sichere Einreise. Deutschlands Aufnahmeprogramme für syrische Flüchtlinge 2013–2015 und ihre Folgen für Asylpolitik und Flüchtlingszuwanderung. *Bundeszentrale für politische Bildung. Kurzdossiers* (Safe Entry: Germany's Reception Programmes for Syrian Refugees 2013–2015 and Their Consequences for Asylum Policy and Refugee Immigration. Federal Agency for Civic Education. Briefs). Available at: www.bpb.de (Accessed 7 April 2018).
Scheinert, L. (2017). Collapsing Discourses in Refugee Protection Policies Exploring the Case of Germany's Temporary Humanitarian Admission Programmes. *movements* 3(1). Available at: https://movements-journal.org/issues/04.bewegungen/09.scheinert–collapsing-discourses-refugee-protection-policies.html (Accessed 10 February 2020).
Schierup, C-U., Hansen, P. and Castles, S. (2006). *Migration, Citizenship, and the European Welfare State: A European Dilemma*. Oxford: Oxford University Press.

Schittenhelm, K. (2018). Implementing and Rethinking the European Union's Asylum Legislation: The Asylum Procedures Directive. *International Migration* 57(1), pp. 229–244.
Sen, A. (1981). *Poverty and Famines: An Essay on Entitlement and Deprivation*. Oxford: Oxford University Press.
Stern, R. (2014). "Our Refugee Policy is Generous": Reflections on the Importance of a State's Self-Image. *Refugee Survey Quarterly* 33(1), pp. 25–43.
Swedish Migration Agency (2017). *Avgjorda asylärenden beslutade av Migrationsverket, förstagångsansökningar 2017* (Decided Asylum Cases by the Migration Agency, First Time Applications 2017). Available at: www.migrationsverket.se/download/18.4100dc0b159d67dc6146d1/1501583467948/Avgjorda+asyl%C3%A4renden+2017+-+Asylum+decisions+2017.pdf (Accessed 19 October 2017).
Swedish Migration Agency (2019). *Uppehållstillstånd för den som har eget företag* (Residence Permit for Those Who Have their Own Firm). Available at: www.migrationsverket.se/Privatpersoner/Arbeta-i-Sverige/Eget-foretag.html (Accessed 12 March 2019).
The Local Denmark (2019). *Three Years After Denmark's Infamous 'Jewellery Law' Hit World Headlines, Not a Single Piece Has Been Confiscated*. Available at: www.thelocal.dk/20190124/three-years-after-denmarks-infamous-jewellery-law-hit-world-headlines-not-a-single-piece-has-been-confiscated [Accessed 10 February 2020).
Turton, D. (2003). Conceptualising Forced Migration. *Working Papers No. 12*. Refugee Studies Centre. Oxford: University of Oxford.
UNHCR (2016). *Global Trends: Forced Displacement in 2015*. Available at: https://s3.amazonaws.com/unhcrsharedmedia/2016/2016-06-20-global-trends/2016-06-14-Global-Trends-2015.pdf (Accessed 22 June 2016).
UNHCR Sweden (2018). *Vem är flykting?* (Who is a Refugee?). Available at: www.sydsvenskan.se/2005-05-26/utlanningsnamnden-avvecklas-nasta-ar (Accessed 24 August 2018).
UtlL (2005:716) *Utlänningslag (2005:716)* (The Alien Act). Available at: www.riksdagen.se/sv/dokument-lagar/dokument/svensk-forfattningssamling/utlanningslag-2005716_sfs-2005-716 (Accessed 30 November 2017).
Wettergren, Å. and Wikström, H. (2014). Who is a Refugee? Political Subjectivity and the Categorisation of Somali Asylum Seekers in Sweden. *Journal of Ethnic and Migration Studies* 40(4), pp. 566–583.
Wikström, H. (2014). Gender, Culture and Epistemic Injustice: The Institutional Logic in Assessment of Asylum Applications in Sweden. *Nordic Journal of Migration Research* 4(4), pp. 210–218.
Wieviorka, M. (2014). A Critique of Integration. *Identities*, 21(6), pp. 633–641.

# 3 Admir Skodo

# Lesson for the future or threat to sovereignty? Contesting the meaning of the 2015 refugee crisis in Sweden

Following the entry of 162,877 asylum seekers in 2015, Sweden introduced border controls in November of that year. These were followed by new laws in 2015–2016 that curtailed the possibility of being granted permanent residence, family reunification, and the social rights of asylum seekers. Such measures were necessary, according to the Swedish government, because the large number of entries triggered a refugee crisis. These were far-reaching changes in a country that has long prided itself on welcoming asylum seekers. But, far from threatening Swedish state sovereignty, as the Swedish national government and mainstream media claimed, I show that this perceived crisis has both justified, asserted, and extended it by recourse to national and international law on the one hand, and an associative chain link between asylum seekers, illegal immigration, terrorism, and crisis, on the other. At the same time, I reveal how the perceived crisis has exposed rifts between different levels of Swedish governance, where the municipalities, in particular, have opposed the national government's portrayal of 2015 as a fundamental threat to Swedish sovereignty and domestic governance. Indeed, the municipalities sought to portray 2015 as a difficult but valuable lesson for scaling up services and capabilities to help people fleeing persecution.

In this chapter, I problematize this dynamic primarily by analysing an official government report (*Statens Offentliga Utredningar*) on the refugee crisis. My analysis additionally rests on news articles and interviews I conducted in 2017 with a Swedish Migration Agency Executive Officer and a local civil servant in the southeast of Sweden. The report, published in 2017, is entitled 'Att ta emot människor på flykt: Sverige hösten 2015' ('Receiving Refugees: Sweden during the Fall of 2015' – hereafter 'Receiving Refugees'), and is the final product of a Swedish government commission formed in 2016. The government directed the commission to describe the sequence of events that comprise the refugee crisis on the one hand, and to map how the national government, national state agencies, counties, municipalities, and civil society organizations managed it, on the other. Gudrun Antemar, a lawyer and chief district judge of the Stockholm district court, led the commission, which was composed of academics, heads of state agencies, UNICEF representatives, and government officials.

Such government reports are an excellent source for the study of the powers, political imaginary, ideas, and discourses that shape Swedish politics and governance. They document Swedish politics both synchronically, as a condensed snapshot of a particular moment in history, and diachronically, as source for tracing continuities and changes since 1922, when the first such report was published.[1] Some are preparatory works for legislation, and as such they reveal processes of social and political inclusion and exclusion, normalization and stigmatization, of issues ranging from the legalization of homosexuality, to cheating at national university entrance exams, to the re-organization of the police academy. They are also a convenient way to either frame or 'bury' (or both) an issue to which a popular political solution seems unlikely, as is the case with the report studied here. The historian Lars Trägårdh captures well the ambiguous political role of Swedish government commissions which produce these reports, when he writes that they 'have in fact been seen both as the epitome of deliberative democracy and, more cynically, as a quasi-corrupt and secretive system whereby a cabal of insiders representing privileged organizations have been able to strike favourable deals with agents of the state' (Trägårdh, 2010, p. 237). A similar ambiguity permeates the report discussed in this chapter, as it presents conflicting viewpoints, and challenges and criticizes certain government assumptions and actions, but nonetheless narrows its investigation and structures its findings in accordance with the government directive.

Since 'Receiving Refugees' documents a contestation over the meaning and appropriate response to the events of 2015, I have found it methodologically useful to analyse the report as an expression of the 'official public theories' of Swedish government and state agencies.[2] The study of official public theory examines executive decisions, laws, bureaucratic practices, official reports, and policies through their explicit and implicit theoretical justifications and assumptions (Silverman, 1992; Favell, 1998; Thomas, 2011). According to the sociologist Adrian Favell (1998), political or policy documents, such as reports, decrees, orders, laws, and directives, are theoretical insofar as they contain statements on the following three interweaving and interconnected conceptual levels:

1) *Epistemological level.* Statements on this level describe and conceptualize the 'basic facts' of a social situation, such as a crisis or structural ethnic discrimination.
2) *Methodological or explanatory level.* Statements on this level theorize the means and applications of any political intervention and contain claims about the causality of political and social processes.

3) *Normative level*. Statements on this level describe core values and goals of practices and policies on the one hand, and provide a justification for such values and goals on the other.

Although interrelated in practice, I separate these levels in this chapter for the purpose of analytical clarification.

**Ideas and theorizing matter in politics and in public administration**

The value of the approach just outlined is that it allows us to discern the nuances within and differences between how different parts of a state or government think about certain issues, and how that thinking imbues decisions, orders, actions, and policies. In the case of analysing 'Receiving Refugees', this approach leads to two significant findings. The first is that the statements provided to the commission by the government, state agencies, and municipalities imply a significant difference in the official theory of the national government and the national state agencies on the one hand, and that of the municipalities on the other. While the government and the state agencies saw 2015 as an existential threat to Swedish sovereignty and bureaucracy, the municipalities saw it as a strain on the bureaucracy that was successfully managed, the lessons and resources of which were lost on the government and the state precisely at the moment when new practices were established that could effectively deal with another mass entry. The second finding is that the municipalities were able to contest the sovereign power of the government only to a limited extent, since the national government used its theory of crisis to curtail the autonomy of the municipalities.

The national government's use of the concept of crisis in this manner follows a well-established historical trajectory. Indeed, in the nineteenth century, historians and philosophers imagined crisis as a litmus test of national character and institutions (O'Connor, 1981). Nations' response to a crisis, such intellectuals opined, would determine whether the nation would be reinvigorated, reinvented, strengthened, weakened, or destroyed. The historical theorist Reinhart Koselleck has shown that the concept of crisis took on a key role in the language of politics even before the nineteenth century. Starting with the political thought of the French Revolution, Koselleck argues, crisis takes its place as a fundamental concept on par with equally fundamental but not necessarily compatible concepts, such as human rights and citizenship. However, because the emergence of the concept of crisis dovetails the compression of space and time through new travel and communication technologies, it begins a global journey from its local origins and is put to a variety of different, both conflicting and complementing, uses. As such, the concept of crisis has come to serve as a pivotal point for interpreting the past, offering diagnoses of and remedies for the present, and making predictions for the future in diverse contexts (Koselleck, 2002, pp. 14–15). In this sense, crisis is not an innocent descriptive term, but rather a contested and politicized concept that can be used to generate, structure, or re-structure social and political relationships. That is precisely what happened to Swedish asylum law and the political landscape following 2015, where immigration has cut across the left and right divide and created some unholy alliances.

The following three sections spell out the theory of the national government and the state agencies, followed by a section that describes the theory of the municipalities. In light of these findings, I conclude by discussing the dangerous consequence of successfully casting immigration in general, and asylum seekers in particular, as a fundamental threat to sovereignty or national security, or both – namely the rise of immigration alarmism. I discuss how immigration alarmism made visible the power imbalances between local, regional, and national governance.

### Epistemological statism: the 'basic fact' of the crisis and its contexts

> There is extensive historical research on what an event is and how it can be explained. Regardless of the philosophy of history one adheres to, there are few today who claim that events happen randomly or spontaneously. There are, however, different conceptions of whether events can be explained by individuals' actions, by economic and material conditions, by the intellectual development of societies, or by repeating patterns of change – or perhaps by all these forces, and more. The concept of event and series of events can in other words be interpreted differently and *we have interpreted the events according to the descriptions in our [government] directive. It is clear that the directive does not emphasize an examination of the underlying causes of why so many people made their way to Sweden in 2015.* ('Receiving Refugees', p. 289; emphasis added)[3]

This passage from the report under scrutiny barely veils the fact that the experts of the commission were unhappy with the government's directive *not* to look at the underlying causes of the crisis or place it in broader contexts, and to only focus on describing the unfolding of events for the purpose of improving crisis management. At least from the perspective of history and refugee studies, one can see why the authors of the report did not take too kindly to the government's injunction. The entry of 162,877 asylum seekers to Sweden in 2015 is unprecedented. It dwarfs the previous record from 1992 when 84,018 people, mainly from former Yugoslavia, sought asylum in Sweden (Swedish Migration Agency, n.d.).[4] Neither the government nor the Swedish Migration Agency expected this many to enter in 2015. One would think that such a dramatic change would spontaneously give rise to questions of why, when, how, and not least whether the mass flight to Sweden could have been predicted or at least anticipated.

Yet, as the report makes clear, the way the government and state agencies conceptualized the basic facts of this unprecedented situation betrays not only an utter disregard for global socio-economic and political developments, but also the perspective of asylum seekers. Instead, for the government and the state, *the* basic fact of the entry of a large number of asylum seekers was that it caused a crisis for the Swedish state. The context of this fact thus exclusively becomes the Swedish state. Consequently, for the state and the government, this basic fact attains meaning in the context of Swedish legal and bureaucratic norms, rules, laws, and institutions that manage migration. I call this perspective epistemological statism. In the report, epistemological statism is most clearly expressed in statements on the law and the bureaucracy, respectively.

### The basic fact in its legal context

The first context through which the government and the state interpreted the basic fact of the refugee crisis is Swedish law. This, the report makes clear, is comprised of the following components: Sweden's adherence to international human rights law, the rule of law (*legalitetsprincipen*), EU directives and regulations, and due process ('Receiving Refugees', p. 15, p. 41). The government found support in both EU regulations and international human rights law, and thereby Swedish law, for a violation by the government of those same regulations and laws because of the basic fact of crisis. For example, in the case of the Geneva Convention and the Declaration on Territorial Asylum, which informs Swedish asylum law, the report states:

> In the Declaration on Territorial Asylum (GA Res. 2312 on December 14 1967) [ ...] there is a ban on returning or removing a person who has the right of asylum in a country [the *non-refoulement* principle], to a country where he or she risks persecution (article 3). *Exceptions may only be made on account of pressing national security concerns or to protect the general population. As examples are mentioned 'a mass invasion of refugees'.* ('Receiving Refugees', p. 307; emphasis added).

'Mass invasion of refugees' is a term that is conveniently left undefined. Such inexact constructions of terms can be found in both national and international law and government decisions, since at least the Cold War. We also find a transnational family resemblance in the powers that national governments confer upon themselves in response to the perceived threat posed to national security by mass immigration. In 1981 the Reagan administration, to take an example, issued a Declaration of Emergency following the unwanted entry of large numbers of Haitian asylum seekers. The 'triggering criteria' for an emergency, the Declaration states, must remain 'necessarily inexact'. The emergency (sovereign) powers, on the other hand, must be precise ('Immigration Control (2)', 1981). In the case of the Haitians, to the outcry of civil rights groups and immigration attorneys and numerous US Senators, these powers include intercepting asylum seekers outside of US territorial waters, followed by camp internment; sending new arrivals back to Haiti after 'mass, closed-door hearings from which even lawyers have been barred' (Thomas, 1981); and 'expedited adjudications' by the Attorney General on a case-by-case basis ('Immigration Control (2)', 1981). Much like the US in 1981 (or the ongoing inhumane treatment of Central American asylum seekers on the US southern border for that matter), Sweden in 2015 worded the crisis in imprecise terms as it fashioned a response with precision. The report describes one such precise move, where Sweden applied and was allowed to perform border controls by the EU:

> The European Council decision (EU) 2016/894 of May 12, 2016 [ …] decided that Sweden, for a maximum period of six months, can perform border controls [ …] The decision makes evident that Sweden ought to be allowed to continue performing such controls because 'it is an appropriate method for managing a serious threat against public order and internal security which is tied to the secondary movements of irregular migrants'. ('Receiving Refugees', p. 109)

The Swedish government claimed that it perceived the mass entrance of asylum seekers as a national security threat against Sweden's sovereignty and the very bureaucracy that allows it to function as a welfare state *and* uphold its commitments to human rights. Sweden's sovereignty was threatened, thereby justifying, *on the very basis of Swedish and international law*, both the violation of Sweden's commitments to the right of asylum and the imposition of highly restrictionist measures (among those border controls) between November 2015 and July 2016. Paradoxically, although the universal right of asylum does allow for mass entry as an abstract possibility, as an empirical reality mass entry is discursively constructed by the Swedish government as a threat to Sweden's ability to offer international protection to persecuted people. Or, in the words of Elisabeth Abiri, in her discussion of Swedish refugee policy during the 1990s: 'a generous refugee policy can only be so when its generosity is not put to the test' (Abiri, 2000, p. 25). Sweden, like the US and all other nation states, upholds non-territorial universal rights only insofar as they do not threaten perceived territorial sovereignty and the state's privilege to accept or reject anyone seeking to exercise their universal human rights. The granting of asylum rests on the condition of an imagined sovereign power with absolute control over immigration issues, whether real or imagined.

Such a condition is, to use Hegelian terminology, an expression of abstract universality. Abstract universality – a commitment to ensuring human rights for all, for instance – conceives of itself as complete and therefore threatened by unexpected concrete events and 'irregular' people, such as those who entered in 2015. The government abides by universal human rights only insofar as the concrete events that trigger them, an influx of asylum seekers in this case, fall within the regulated sphere of migration. As long as the possibility of a large number of asylum seekers finding their way to Sweden remained abstract, Sweden remained committed to accepting them. It is as a champion of this abstract universality we must decipher the Swedish Prime Minister Stefan Löfven's speech of September 2015 where he famously said: 'My Europe accepts people who are fleeing war. My Europe doesn't build walls', and his subsequent statement there is no ceiling for how many asylum seekers Sweden can accept ('Receiving Refugees', p. 13). But it is in that very same context that we must also read Löfven's speech from November 2015, in which he spoke of the need for 'breathing space' from the large numbers of asylum seekers and the changed policies that followed.

### The basic fact in its bureaucratic context

The second context in which the government and state agencies interpreted the basic fact of the refugee crisis is the Swedish bureaucracy. The Swedish migration bureaucracy divides the reception and management of asylum seekers between state (*stat*), municipality (*kommun*), and county (*landsting/ region*). The primary responsibility for receiving asylum seekers falls on the Migration Agency and the municipalities, which means that 'people who arrive to Sweden and apply for asylum are registered and provided with housing in an asylum seeker compound, as well as the possibility of working and of economic aid according to the regulations of the law (1994:137) of reception of asylum seekers and others (LMA)' ('Receiving Refugees', p. 43).

The government and the Migration Agency saw the municipalities as unable to understand the basic fact of a bureaucracy in crisis and manage the crisis accordingly. An interview that I conducted with an Executive Officer at the Migration Agency in 2017 offers a glimpse into state reasoning on this issue. I was told that it has 'been a constant problem getting the municipalities to follow [the laws], or to take their responsibility'. The officer was referring to a situation in 2015 when finding housing for asylum seekers became a critical issue. Although it is the responsibility of the municipalities to find housing for asylum seekers after they are assigned to a municipality by the Migration Agency, when it became clear that more and more asylum seekers were arriving,

> the municipalities said that we can't accept them. Initially there was a voluntary aspect built into the system where the counties and municipalities would

sign these agreements. But they respond: '[we'll take] girls in this age, or boys in this', you know. As a result, the housing needs of asylum seekers were not being met, according to this interviewee. At that point, *the government came in and said, now it's compulsory to take on certain numbers based on various parameters*. Whether it turned out well, I don't know, but it got better. However, there are no sanctions in the law [emphasis added].

Because there were no sanctions to enforce the law, municipalities were able to contest the government compulsion to accept designated numbers of asylum seekers. According to the officer, it was not uncommon for municipalities to agree on a plan, but then make an excuse for not implementing it on time. 'Then they blame it on the politicians in the municipalities, or the civil servants.' Although it is clear that the municipalities were able to contest the state and the government to some extent, it is difficult to assess the efficacy of such a contestation, especially since the compulsion to accept specific numbers of asylum seekers was ratified in a law which states that municipalities cannot appeal the government's decision (*Dagens Juridik*, 2016). And, as we will see below, the municipalities saw the government as significantly limiting the municipalities' activities.

## Methodological statism: explaining the crisis

'There seems to be no significant migration episode, past or present, in which states have not had an active, rather than reactive, hand' and yet the nation state 'conceives of immigration as an externally motivated event, with states as passive receivers who are forced to respond' (Joppke, 1998, pp. 6–7). Sweden in 2015–2016 is no exception. As stressed above, the report does not make or cite any positive or substantive statements on how and why many asylum seekers made their way to Sweden in those particular years. As a matter of internal statist coherence, this makes perfect sense. The government directive for the authors of the report was, after all, to only stick to the facts and not look for underlying causes. Hence there is no need to consider a comparative or transnational methodology, contextualization, social and economic causes, or how states have had a decisive role to play in creating the conditions for migration patterns. The very concept of the state has what Liisa Malkki (1992) calls an inbuilt territorial 'sedentary bias' (see also the Introduction in this volume). It therefore makes perfect sense that statist explanations of essentially mobile and global phenomena would conceptually wrest them precisely of their mobility and global nature.

It also makes perfect sense, from the statist perspective, that unwanted mobile people by default serve as indirect explanations of existential threats to an imagined normal condition of territorially limited sedentariness. The report cites explanatory statements from the national government and various state agencies in which the asylum seekers are described as a national security threat, and as a collective actor which brought on a major breakdown in the bureaucratic capacity of the Swedish asylum system ('Receiving Refugees', p. 17). For example, the Migration Agency referred to the conscious and informed choices of a large number of migrants to come to Sweden when discussing what 'simply' preceded the crisis, which implicitly acts as an explanation of the crisis ('Receiving Refugees', p. 73, p. 291).[5] There is for instance no reference to an earlier Swedish decision from 2013 that grants all asylum-seeking Syrians permanent residency – a policy that might have been a 'pull' factor for many Syrians forced to flee their homes (Ruist, 2015).

The Swedish Civil Contingencies Agency, the police, and the Migration Agency all described the crisis in a way that implies that essential social institutions and functions – such as housing, health care, and schools – were existentially threatened by the mass influx of migrants. For instance, in the words of the Migration Agency, the situation was 'entirely out of control' ('Receiving Refugees', p. 110). Needless to add, these agencies did not contemplate other possible descriptions or explanations.

**Normative statism: restoring public order**

It was fully in line with the statist epistemological and explanatory logic that Prime Minister Löfven made a normative leap when he spoke in November 2015 of the need for 'breathing space', which necessitated a strong state response to restore public order ('Receiving Refugees', pp. 18–19). How was order restored, and how was that restoration justified? Drawing on the explanations of the police, the Migration Agency, and the Swedish Civil Contingencies Agency:

> [the] government on November 12, 2015 made the comprehensive assessment that 'conditions are now such that from a broad perspective there is a threat against general order and internal security' and said that since 'other measures have been deemed insufficient to counter this threat, inner border control will be effected in accordance with article 25 of the Schengen Border Code'. ('Receiving Refugees', pp. 109–110)

The Migration Agency, in fact, had written a letter to the Ministry of Justice on 11 November 2015 urging the enforcement of border controls. In this letter, the Migration Agency pointed to the importance of maintaining the official Swedish policy of 'managed migration and the police authority's responsibility for internal border control'. Managed migration had come under threat, not least because of the housing crisis, when 'people who

# Lesson for the future or threat to sovereignty? 59

cannot find their own housing are thrown out on the street'. A particularly vexing problem, according to the Migration Agency, which called for border controls was the existence of asylum seekers who did not intend to seek asylum in Sweden but wanted to travel onwards to Norway or Finland, and who were in Sweden without a visa or residence permits – in other words, they were unauthorized border-crossers travelling through Sweden 'illegally' (see also chapter 2). The Migration Agency, then, conflated the concept of asylum seeker with the concept of illegal immigrant, a description which served to justify the imposition of border controls.[6] On a more general level, the Migration Agency argued that border controls would be conducive to a restoration of order:

> The Migration Agency has not assessed whether border controls would lead to more or less asylum applications in Sweden. However, there are reasons to believe that border controls could contribute to an increased orderly reception of asylum seekers and better control of the great number of people who travel into the country with other reasons that seeking asylum. ('Receiving Refugees', p. 115)

The border controls have been extended far beyond the maximum six months allowed by the Schengen Border Code. In an extension of the border controls in September 2017, Sweden cited the threat of terrorism as justification for continued border controls (Lönnaeus, 2017). The extension came not long after the rejected Uzbek asylum seeker Rakhmat Akilov carried out a terrorist attack in Stockholm in April 2017. The government used the same justification in its six-month long extension of border controls in May 2019 (Fritze, 2019). By extending, justifying, and timing the extension of border controls in this manner, the government has effectively conflated the image of the asylum seeker with that of the terrorist. Indeed, in response to the Akhilov attack, Löfven stated: 'We need to improve the ability to deport people', implying that if only failed asylum seekers are deported, terror attacks can be avoided (Habib and Witte, 2017).

The restoration of public order began with border controls and ended with the passing of restrictive asylum laws. In November 2015:

> The government announced the need for a 'breathing space' and that Swedish asylum law temporarily needed to be adjusted to the minimum standards of international law so that the right to residence became temporary and the right to family reunification was restricted. ('Receiving Refugees', pp. 18–19)

Since July 2016 there has been a temporary law 'that limits the possibilities for asylum seekers and their family members to be granted permanent residence permits in Sweden' (see also chapter 5 below). Another law states that 'an asylum seeker does not have a right to assistance' if the 'asylum seeker has received a refusal of entry or expulsion order that has entered into force'.[7] Nor is an asylum seeker entitled to assistance if the deadline for voluntary return, which is four weeks, has expired. This means that the asylum seeker loses their free housing and daily allowance.

**Contesting the statist theory: the municipalities**

Apart from mapping the state's response, the report also emphasized a deep tension between the state on the one hand and counties and municipalities on the other. The municipalities, in particular, criticized in no uncertain terms what they perceived as a mischaracterization of the situation in 2015 and how it was managed by the government and state agencies. Re-described in terms of an official public theory, the municipalities offered an alternative theory along epistemological and normative axes. In regard to epistemology, many municipalities countered the view of 2015 as a crisis. For example:

> the city of Mölndal[8] did not want to use the word 'crisis' and claims that it is a word used by the state, and not by the municipalities. The municipality experienced a strained situation, not a crisis. And everything happened in the municipalities, not, for example, in the Swedish Association of Local Authorities and Regions. The state was all about calculations and assessments, but the municipalities were all about people. The city of Mölndal believes that the state pushed the problems over to the municipalities. The city of Malmö[9] asked why state-owned buildings could not be used for housing. The municipality of Norberg[10] believes that the fact that the military could not make their stored beds available was strange in the eyes of the municipalities. ('Receving Refugees', p. 265)

These observations echoed in an interview I conducted in 2017 with a civil servant in the municipality of Simrishamn, located in the southeast of Sweden. The civil servant, charged with the reception of unaccompanied minors, stated: 'the Migration Agency basically only provides housing and food. There are big gaps to be filled there. Voluntary associations [and the municipality] fill those gaps'. The voluntary associations, according to the civil servant, have been 'invaluable' because they befriended the asylum seekers, drove them to medical appointments or schools, donated clothes and other everyday items, helped them with their asylum cases, and so much more. Decision-makers from all parties – except the far-right populist party the Sweden Democrats – and civil servants in the municipality of Simrishamn approached the reception of asylum seekers not as a problem, and certainly not as a crisis, but as a way to help those in need with resources that are available. The civil servant I interviewed told me that he had personally greeted every unaccompanied minor assigned to Simrishamn, listened to their story, informed them about the Swedish school system, informed them about their options, and continuously checked in on them once they were enrolled in school. And because there was cross-party and cross-ideological agreement on this approach, the Sweden Democrat's anti-immigrant discourse was effectively excluded.

Another scathing critique from the municipalities in the report concerned the state's assessment that the situation was entirely out of control:

> Several municipalities describe how the situation with a lot of people suddenly ended with the border controls in November. Yet, at that point the municipalities had found routines and scaled their operations for a large number of people, who then never came [ …]. The municipality of Trelleborg[11] describes how many processes were started during the autumn, such as processes of obtaining permits for building housing for unaccompanied minors. When these processes were completed, there were no more minors. The resources of the municipalities had thus been wasted. ('Receiving Refugees', p. 263)

Because the municipalities offered a radically different perspective on the basic facts presented by the state they were led to different normative conclusions. Indeed, multiple municipalities stated that the 'greatest difficulty was not to come up with practical solutions at short notice, but rather to interpret different regulatory frameworks or the fact that these frameworks were contradictory'.[12] The choice for local civil servants was to either 'follow the regulations or try to solve the problems, and most chose the latter' ('Receiving Refugees', p. 256). Ultimately, the demands of the sovereign prevailed.

## Conclusion

The most surprising, and arguably the most important, result in this chapter is the discovery that not all authorities responded to the events of 2015 in the alarmist mode sounded by the mainstream media and the national government. The municipalities contested the national government's conceptualization of 2015 as a crisis, while showing that they were more than capable of helping asylum seekers in a way that would improve their capacity to receive large numbers of people fleeing from persecution in the future. And, equally importantly, some municipalities were able to form a consensus across party divides, which successfully resisted the discourse of the anti-immigrant far-right. Their voice, and the lessons learned from their practices, is important since such a future seems likely, given that the number of people fleeing from various types of persecution and extreme life-threatening conditions in the Global South will keep rising due to neo-colonial and neoliberal economic policies whose exploitative political, military, and economic practices propel people to flee in the first place. Their voice is also important because the social dislocation of neoliberal policies in Western countries will probably continue creating fertile ground for nationalist anti-immigrant political parties, movements, and discourses.

Theorists of the relationship between bureaucracy and sovereignty, from Hegel (1991) to Weber (1978), have noted that in a nation state, the bureaucracy is either tacitly or overtly subordinated to the demands of sovereign power (president, monarch, national government, and so on). In times of peace or 'normal' conflicts (such as jurisdictional conflicts, political rivalry, contested appointments of bureaucrats, corruption, or conflicts over policy), such a subordinate role is barely noticeable. However, in times of perceived crisis, such as war or perceived social disintegration, this subordination becomes explicit. And in times of an imagined crisis, one might add to better understand Sweden in 2015, the subordination oscillates between tacit and overt, reflecting the ambiguity and contradictions inherent in the political imaginary.

The shrill cry of the government's immigration alarmism has drowned out the, by comparison, measured voice of the municipalities in public discourse and national decision-making. This immigration alarmism, clearly documented in 'Receiving Refugees', apart from its obvious opportunism on the electoral successes of the far-right, bears a disconcerting resemblance to climate change denialism. Climate science deniers falsely deny climate change, when there is overwhelming evidence for the unfolding of this process and its effect on the natural and human environment. Immigration alarmists falsely assert what we might call catastrophic immigration change, despite a clear lack of evidence that immigration leads to social, cultural, or economic catastrophe. We are already seeing two detrimental consequences of immigration alarmism in Sweden and other Western countries:

1) The rule of law and the division of power, fundamental to democracy and human rights, are undermined in favour of sovereign power, that is, an immigration system in which the executive makes decisions unaccountable to any other branch, for reasons that need no justification or discussion. This development finds concrete expression in the deeply flawed legal protections afforded to asylum seekers in Migration Court hearings (Johannesson, 2017; Skodo, 2018; see also chapter 2 above), and in the prevalence of extra-legal criteria such as 'judgment, political considerations, foreign policy, or national security' (Coutin, Richland and Fortin, 2012).
2) Research results from various academic disciplines, including sociology, history, political economy, and migration studies, are undermined. We see this in the denial of research which shows that immigration is a highly patterned socio-historical process and rarely, if ever, an overwhelming crisis (e.g. Sassen, 1999). We also see it in the denial of research which shows that the state investment in welfare goods and services during and after 2015 meant that the Swedish economic growth

after 2015 was four times greater than that of its Nordic neighbours (Rothstein, 2017).

It is difficult to remain optimistic in light of these developments, especially since they dovetail the near complete normalization of the far right across the globe. However, as history instructs us, contingency and unpredictability lurk behind even the mightiest traditions, structures, and paths. We cannot know what the future holds for human affairs, but we can and should commit to a globalized democracy which is thoroughly equal, inclusive, and open to change and examination from within and from without. This mountain will not come to us, we will have to go to it.

## Notes

1 An excellent diachronic study of these government reports is Edenheim (2015).
2 Sovereignty has again been raised as an altar in European politics, from Brexit to the re-imposition of national borders between EU member states during 2015. The question over whether state sovereignty has been buckling under the pressure of increased transnational migration continues to be a major issue in Migration Studies. There are three main interpretive strands. First, there are those who hold on to the nation state paradigm, arguing that state sovereignty and national trajectories ultimately determine the shape of today's citizenship and immigration policies (Brubaker, 1992; Favell, 1998). Second, there are those who argue that migration policies and practices exhibit a paradoxical development. Although an erosion of state sovereignty through global capitalism and the international human rights regime, which benefits wealthy persons and transnational corporations, is occurring, a parallel process is unfolding where wealthy nations are tightening their borders and practising highly restrictive and punitive measures against poor and marginalized migrants (Sassen, 1996; Benhabib, 2004). Third, there are those who argue that while there are transnational, internal, and global pressures on state sovereignty, these are addressed within the nation state paradigm through partisan politics, 'client politics', 'shared governance', pressure from big business, and civil society; in short, what Joppke calls 'self-limited sovereignty' (Joppke, 1999). Although all three theories contain truths, in the case of Sweden's response to 2015, Joppke's approach seems to yield the best interpretive framework.
3 All translations from Swedish are the author's.
4 State and government perceptions of the refugee crisis of 1992 were in some ways remarkably similar to perceptions of the 2015 crisis. For example, the 1992 crisis was seen as overstretching the capacity of the Swedish bureaucracy, the need to restore order was voiced, and countries like Poland and Hungary were seen as not sharing the burden of accepting a fair share of the refugees (Abiri, 2000).
5 The Migration Agency further invoked the dysfunctional EU asylum regulations and the self-interest of member states as explanations. These ensured that the 'country of first asylum' regulation (the Dublin Regulation) was simply

ignored by most states that did not want to accept any asylum seekers. The Migration Agency stated that by autumn 2015 Sweden was effectively bordering Turkey when it came to asylum seekers ('Receiving Refugees', p. 292).
6   For more on the criminalization of immigrants in Sweden see Khosravi (2009).
7   This refers to Law (2016: 752).
8   A suburb of Sweden's second largest city, Gothenburg.
9   Sweden's third largest city and the first city encountered when crossing by train from Denmark.
10  In north central Sweden.
11  In the south region of Skåne and the entry point for ferries crossing from Germany.
12  For more on the reception, during 2015, of asylum seekers by municipalities see Lidén and Nyhlén (2015).

## References

Abiri, E. (2000). 'The Changing Praxis of "Generosity": Swedish Refugee Policy During the 1990s', *Journal of Refugee Studies*, 13(1), pp. 11–28.
Brubaker, R. (1992). *Citizenship and Nationhood in France and Germany*. Cambridge MA: Harvard University Press.
Benhabib, Seyla (2004). *The Rights of Others: Aliens, Residents, and Citizens*. Cambridge: Cambridge University Press.
Coutin, S., Richland, J., and Fortin, V. (2012). 'Routine Exceptionality: The Plenary Power Doctrine and the Indigenous Under U.S. Law', *UC Irvine Law Review*, 4(1), pp. 97–120.
Dagens Juridik (2016). 'Staten Får Tvinga Kommuner att ta Emot Flyktingar – Riksdagen Klubbade Lagen' (The State Allowed to Force Municipalities to Receive Refugees – Parliament Passed the Law), 28 January. Available at: www.dagensjuridik.se/2016/01/staten-far-tvinga-kommuner-att-ta-emot-flyktingar-riksdagen-klubbade-lagen (Accessed 8 December 2017.)
Edenheim, S. (2015). 'Äktenskapet, Sexualmoralen och Barnets Bästa som Samhällsorganisatörer i Två Statliga Utredningar: Kommentar till Texter om Äktenskap' (Marriage, Sexual Morality and What's Best for Children as Social Organizers in Two Official Government Reports: Comments on Texts on Marriage), in Arnberg, K., Laskar P., and Sundeval, F. (eds.) *Sexualpolitiska nyckeltexter*. Stockholm: Leopard, pp. 317–325.
Favell, A. (1998). *Philosophies of Integration: Immigration and the Idea of Citizenship in France and Britain*. Basingstoke: Palgrave Macmillan.
Fritze, G. (2019). 'Gränskontrollerna Förlängs Ett Halvår Till' (Border Controls Extended Another Six Months), *SVT Nyheter*, 19 May. Available at: www.svt.se/nyheter/lokalt/skane/granskontrollerna-blir-kvar-i-ett-halvt-ar-till (Accessed 13 July 2019).
Habib, H. and Witte, G. (2017). 'Swedish Police Say Stockholm Truck-Attack Suspect Was Failed Uzbek Asylum-Seeker', *Washington Post*, 9 April. Available at: www.washingtonpost.com/world/swedish-police-say-stockholm-truck-attack-suspect-was-failed-uzbek-asylum-seeker/2017/04/09/65b5e7d6-1d1b-11e7-a0a7-8b2a45e3dc84_story.html (Accessed 4 December 2017.)

Hegel, G. W. F. (1991). *Elements of the Philosophy of Right*. Cambridge: Cambridge University Press.
'Immigration Control (2)' (1981). Ronald Reagan Presidential Library, Kenneth Cribb Files. Available at: https://reaganlibrary.gov/archives/digital-library (Accessed 15 June 2017).
Johannesson, L. (2017). *In Courts We Trust: Administrative Justice in Swedishe Migration Courts*. PhD, Stockholm University. Available at: https://su.diva-portal.org/smash/get/diva2:1072557/FULLTEXT01.pdf (Accessed 23 July 2019).
Joppke, C. (1998). 'Immigration Challenges to the Nation-State', in Joppke, C. (ed.) *Challenge to the Nation-State: Immigration in Western Europe and the United States*. Oxford: Oxford University Press, pp. 6–47.
Joppke, C. (1999). *Immigration and the Nation-State: The United States, Germany, and Great Britain*. Oxford: Oxford University Press.
Khosravi, Shahram (2009). 'Sweden: Detention and Deportation of Asylum Seekers.' *Race & Class*, 50(4): 38–56.
Koselleck, R. (2002). 'Some Questions Concerning the Conceptual History of "Crisis"', in Witoszek, N. and Trägårdh, L. (eds.) *Culture and Crisis: The Case of Germany and Sweden*. New York: Berghahn Books, pp. 12–24.
Lidén, G. and Nyhlén, J. (2015). 'Reception of Refugees in Swedish Municipalities: Evidences from Comparative Case Studies', *Migration and Development*, 4(1), pp. 55–71.
Lönnaeus, O. (2017). 'EU Ger Klartecken till Sverige att Fortsätta med Gränskontroller' (EU Gives Green Light to Sweden to Continue Border Controls), *Sydsvenskan*, 27 September. Available at: www.sydsvenskan.se/2017-09-27/eu-ger-klartecken-till-sverige-att-fortsatta-med-granskontroller (Accessed 15 December 2017.).
Malkki, L. (1992). 'The Rooting of Peoples and the Territorialization of National Identity Among Scholars and Refugees', *Cultural Anthropology*, 7(1), pp. 24–44.
O'Connor, J. (1981). 'The Meaning of Crisis', *International Journal of Urban and Regional Research* 5(3), pp. 301–329.
Rothstein, B. (2017). 'Immigration and Economic Growth: Is Keynes Back?' *Social Europe* (blog), 20 June 2017. Available at: www.socialeurope.eu/immigration-and-economic-growth-is-keynes-back (Accessed 19 December 2017).
Ruist, J. (2015). 'The Fiscal Cost of Refugee Immigration: The Example of Sweden', *Population and Development Review* 4(41), pp. 567–581.
Sassen (1996). *Losing Control? Sovereignty in an Age of Globalization*. New York: Columbia University Press.
Sassen, S. (1999). *Guests and Aliens*. New York: The Free Press.
Silverman, M. (1992). *Deconstructing the Nation: Immigration, Racism and Citizenship in Modern France*. London; New York: Routledge.
Skodo, A. (2018). 'A Populist Myth About Immigration Courts and Public Opinion', *openDemocracy*, 3 March. Available at: www.opendemocracy.net/en/can-europe-make-it/populist-myth-about-immigration-courts-and-public-opinion-evidence-from-us-and-sweden/ (Accessed 19 July 2019).
Swedish Migration Agency (n.d.). 'Asylsökande till Sverige 1984–1999' (Asylum Seekers to Sweden 1984–1999). Available at: www.migrationsverket.se/downloa d/18.2d998ffc151ac3871598171/1485556079445/Asyls%C3%B6kande+till+Sverige+198 4-1999.pdf (Accessed 4 December 2017.)

Thomas, E. R. (2011). *Immigration, Islam, and the Politics of Belonging in France*. Pittsburgh: University of Pennsylvania Press.

Thomas, J. (1981). 'Haitians' Plight Frustrating to All Sides', *The New York Times*, 28. June. Available at: www.nytimes.com/1981/06/28/us/haitians-plight-frustrating-to-all-sides.html (Accessed 24 July 2019).

Trägårdh, L. (2010). 'Rethinking the Nordic Welfare State through a Neo-Hegelian Theory of State and Civil Society', *Journal of Political Ideologies*, 15(3), pp. 227–239.

Weber, M. (1978). *Economy and Society: Volume 2*. Berkeley: University of California Press.

# 4  Martin Bak Jørgensen

# Representations of the refugee crisis in Denmark: deterrence policies and refugee strategies

When (then) Prime Minister Lars Løkke Rasmussen gave his New Year's Address on 1 January 2016 he focused particularly on the high number of refugees and asylum seekers who came to Europe and Denmark in 2015.[1] The number both pressed and challenged Denmark, he said and then continued:

> Let us be honest with each other – we are challenged: it challenges our economy when we have to spend many more billions on asylum seekers and refugees. Money that could otherwise go to health, education and several private jobs. … It challenges our cohesion when many come from very different cultures. Strangers to the unwritten rules and norms that are so obvious to us. Because we have grown up in a tradition of freedom and equality. … And it basically challenges our values and image of who we really are. (Statsministeriet, 2016)[2]

These statements offer a particular framing of the encounter between the Danish state and the refugees arriving at the Danish borders. There are different themes at stake here. The encounter is framed as having both economic, cultural, and democratic implications. It even becomes a challenge to Danish self-identity as the Prime Minister claimed.

Prem Kumar Rajaram (2015) argued that the refugee crisis must be understood as a representation: 'The refugee crisis in Europe is fabricated'. When we seek to understand the crisis and its particular consequences, we need to investigate the crisis as a particular framing that works to construct an idea of the refugee. This framing can be compared and contrasted with one which has outward aims, a framing which reduces the complexities of the situation to an abstracted understanding, allowing policy-makers and commentators to treat it as an exceptional condition. The first aim of this chapter is to investigate how the crisis was represented and framed in the case of Denmark. The refugee crisis arrived in Denmark the first Sunday of September 2015. Before that particular day, the crisis was understood as taking place on Greek islands, in Eastern Europe or at German train stations. It had little to do with Denmark. That perception changed abruptly during the early days of September. During the following week, 1,500 refugees entered the country. The second aim of this chapter is to provide an analysis of the deterrence policies set up by Danish authorities from 2015 and to investigate the rationale behind them. The third aim is to illustrate how civil society and refugees reacted to the deterrence policies. This third part provides short examples of civil society responses as well as examples of strategies used by refugees individually and collectively to cope with the (policy) regime.[3] In these analyses, I focus on three main concepts, which I unpack in the different parts of the chapter: deterrence policies, institutional uncertainty, and deportable populations.

The main findings of this chapter are as follows. The refugee crisis legitimised an even more restrictive policy shift than experienced during the previous decades. The new approach, termed as a paradigmatic shift, has the support of both the previous government and the present Social Democratic government. Besides creating extreme institutional uncertainty caused by continuous policy changes, it also extended the category of deportable populations to a degree where integration from both a policy perspective and from the perspective of the refugees becomes pointless, as the refugee is, with the recent policy change, always at risk of being forced to leave the country. The paradigmatic shift in this way becomes an example of bureaucratic violence legitimised through the refugee crisis (see also the Introduction of this volume).

The method used in this chapter is based on a mix of participant observation, informal interviews, desk research, and textual analysis. The material used in the third section is part of broader ethnographic fieldwork. I have been working with asylum seekers both as an activist and as a militant researcher (Jørgensen, 2019; Lindberg et al., 2018). Militant research connects to Nancy Scheper-Hughes' (1995) call for a militant anthropology and the primacy of the ethical, and for anthropologists to become morally and politically engaged. My own approach and work draw on this normative point of departure. Here, I mainly use it to provide short examples of responses to the Danish policy regime and the strategies used by refugees to navigate these policies. Moreover, some observations stem from the ongoing data collection for a project on migrants' digital practices (the DIGINAUTS project), where we focus particularly on anti-deportation and return strategies among migrants in Denmark and Germany.[4]

**Framing the crisis – encounters**

What made politicians, policy-makers, and, to some degree, academics construct what has since been called the refugee crisis in 2015? Migrants had been crossing the Mediterranean for years with grave humanitarian consequences. Manuela Bojadžijev and Sandro Mezzadra (2015) claim that the 'geography of the current crisis is significantly different' from the years before. Three events in 2015 can be said to inaugurate what has since been described as the refugee crisis (Agustin and Jørgensen, 2019b). The first happened on 19 April 2015, when a ship transporting over eight hundred migrants and refugees capsized *en route* from Tripoli to Italy and all but twenty-seven persons drowned or went missing (Bonomolo and Kirchgaessner, 2015). The second incident was the image of the drowned Syrian child Alan Kurdi, whose body was washed ashore on 3 September near Bodrum in Turkey, after his family's failed attempt to reach the Greek island of Kos. The third event, which gave way to the narrative of the refugee crisis, happened the day after that on 4 September. Thousands of migrants and refugees had been encamped at the Budapest Keleti railway station, and Hungarian police had started denying them access to the trains and were beginning to reroute them towards detention camps outside the city (De Genova, 2016a). More than a thousand migrants and refugees then self-mobilised and started chanting 'freedom!' and soon took to the road, heading towards Vienna in what was soon called 'the March of Hope'. The Hungarian authorities changed tactics and with opportunistic motivations assisted the marchers towards Austria and Germany who then declared their borders to be open (Agustin and Jørgensen, 2019b).

However, the crisis narrative is not only situated fluidly in time but also spatially constructed. For instance, for South Eastern and Central Eastern European countries, a triggering event was the closure of the Hungarian border on 15 September 2015. In Italy, the shipwreck outside Sicily on 19 April 2015 was another triggering event. In Greece, a critical event was the closure of the Balkan route on 18 February 2016 and the debate over excluding Greece from Schengen. All these examples are given by Triandafyllidou (2017, p. 199), who argues that 'there is an interactive relationship between specific events that take place and their coverage and de-/re-construction through media and political discourse. In other words there is an interactive link between factual events and related representations and speech events'. We can continue from this premise and argue that a particular framing and coverage of an event (or encounter) can and will have material effects beyond the representation and speech event as it informs policy-making and political initiatives, as we shall see from the Danish case.

In terms of policy developments, the refugee crisis caused a domino effect when the migrant and refugee flows advanced from the southern and southeastern part of Europe towards Central and Northern Europe. Within a very short time, most of the EU member states claimed that they were unable to cope with the situation and found themselves in a state of emergency, which called for – and also allowed for – exceptional measures. In reality, these exceptional measures breached the principle of free mobility for citizens and legally tolerated non-citizens within most of the EU according to the Schengen Agreement. This free mobility was de facto cancelled, at least in the south-to-north direction. Tensions arose around specific internal borders within the EU where border controls were re-installed, such as between France and Germany, Germany and Austria, Slovenia and Austria, Germany and Denmark, and Denmark and Sweden (Agustin and Jørgensen, 2019b).

**The refugee crisis in Denmark**

As mentioned above, the refugee crisis came to Denmark the first Sunday of September 2015. The Sunday encounter had its own timeline and spurred different reactions from both the public and the authorities. That afternoon, the first large group of refugees and migrants arrived at the small town of Rødby on the island of Lolland some 150 kilometres south of Copenhagen. They came by ferry from Germany, but fled beyond the nearby fields at Rødby Ferry Station for fear of being registered and forced to apply for asylum in Denmark. A larger group started to walk on the E47 motorway towards Sweden (Agustin and Jørgensen, 2019b). Five hundred refugees crossed the border within twenty hours and the situation was described as chaotic and out of control (Róin, 2016). The long summer of migration had come to Denmark. In the media, the group of pedestrians were termed both migrants and refugees (e.g. TV2, 13 September 2015).

The following Wednesday night, the police gave up detaining the hundreds of refugees who refused to cooperate or be registered. As some refugees had blocked trains, the Danish police gave safe passage to all the refugees who stayed in the towns of Padborg and Rødby, both close to the German border. They were allowed to move onwards to Sweden, which was, as mentioned, the initial destination for the vast majority of them. Interestingly, this decision was praised by both the (then) Prime Minister and the Minister of Justice (at the time). While the number of asylum applications Denmark received over the course of 2015 was much lower than in Sweden,[5] the increase in asylum applications – over 40 per cent higher than the preceding year – was noticeable (Agustin and Jørgensen, 2019b). During the peak of the 'crisis' in November 2015, Danish police[6] estimated that between 7,500 and 11,000 people were crossing into Denmark from Germany each week (Jørgensen, 2016).

The decision of many refugees to use Denmark mainly as a transit-country rather than a destination paradoxically caused mixed feelings among the Danish public. In a way, this should not come as a surprise. Only months before, the Danish Ministry of Immigration and Integration had paid for an advert in four Lebanese newspapers informing readers about the conditions of asylum seekers in Denmark and restrictions in terms of family reunification, halving of social benefits, and so on. The advert begins: 'Denmark has decided to tighten the regulations concerning refugees in a number of areas' (BBC, 2015). Although the adverts must be seen as also being a highly symbolic act, as it is difficult to assess if any of the incoming refugees had heard of these particular restrictions, the Danish authorities were claiming it to be a success when refugees chose not to apply for asylum in Denmark. Some of the reasons given by refugees crossing through Denmark for moving on to Sweden have to do with the restrictive Danish policy regime. Many refugees stated that temporary residence permits, the negative rhetoric about refugees, and especially the restrictions for family reunification (in Denmark a minimum one year of waiting before reunification, compared to a few months in Sweden and Finland at the time) made them travel onwards (Christensen and Bolvinkel, 2015). Likewise, existing networks and the lowering of social benefits targeting asylum seekers played a role in deciding where to go and where to apply for asylum (Christensen and Bolvinkel, 2015). Among the public this caused reactions. Some people thought the refugees were ungrateful. Although many did not want them to apply for asylum in Denmark, the fact that they did not wish to was also seen as a problem (Jyllands-Posten, 11 September 2015). Some of the political opponents of the then Minister of Integration, Inger Støjberg, blamed her for having given Denmark a bad name (Politiken, 8 September 2015). Others were upset that Denmark did very little to actively help solve the refugee crisis and claimed that the Danish authorities should accept many more refugees than they had done at the time (DR, 2015). The decision to offer the Sweden-bound refugees safe-conduct to pass through the country led to criticism from other EU member states. The Swedish Prime Minister Stefan Löfven (from the Social Democrats) was heavily critical of the Danish response, and the chairperson of the Swedish Left Party (*Vänsterpartiet*) termed Denmark 'Hungary Light' (Expressen, 10 September 2015).

**Policy encounters – deterrence over welcoming**

In outlining the ways the refugee crisis has been framed and how the Danish state encountered the 'crisis' once people started crossing the borders, my argument is that a particular framing has particular implications and consequences for how policy initiatives are developed to solve the alleged problems. The response of the Danish state can be analysed as comprising a number of different actions: re-bordering practices, the strengthening of deterrence policies, motivating enhancement measures to make (rejected) asylum seekers leave the country, and increasing bureaucratisation (see also the Introduction of this volume). The crisis was framed as something out of control, something creating insecurity for the Danish population (as in discussions of the growth of terrorism or terrorists hiding among refugees) and something that would mean a blow to the Danish welfare state. The refugee crisis was thus framed as challenging Danish security. The efforts introduced would be means to maintaining security, order and welfare.

### Border control: re-bordering practices

The Danish government followed the path set by other European countries when it strengthened border controls on 4 January 2016, due to an 'exceptional' situation which allowed for suspending the Schengen Agreement on freedom of movement (Agustin and Jørgensen, 2019b). The decision was made the same day as Sweden announced that it would introduce strengthened (*förstärkta*) border controls in the direction from Denmark to Sweden. However, already before this, six other countries (Austria, Finland, France, Germany, Malta and Norway) had implemented similar forms of border controls. According to the Danish Prime Minister, in early January 2016, 91,000 refugees entered Denmark. Thirteen thousand of those applied for asylum, while the rest were expected to have entered Norway or Sweden (Kofoed, 2016). When most of the incoming refugees were only passing through Denmark, the situation was perceived as less grave, but with the de facto border closures directed against unwanted migrants on their way to the neighbouring Nordic countries, the perception changed.

Since then, the temporary border controls have been extended several times with the approval of the EU due to the alleged state of emergency. Across the Danish political landscape – with the exception of the most leftist parties, the social liberals, and *Alternativet* (a party resembling Green parties in other countries) – there has been a consensus on the need to limit the number of asylum applicants. Numerous political actors inside and outside the government welcomed the legislative changes with reference to the state of emergency the country was believed to be in (Jørgensen, 2016). Most political parties deemed the new measures to be fair and appropriate, considering the exceptional circumstances. A framing of the 'crisis' as being a challenge to security and welfare unfolded, which legitimised exclusivist, restrictive practices and policies. In October 2018, the government managed to get the border controls extended for another six months. The EU Parliament was against this development and, in the spring of 2018, a majority within the EU parliament issued a report stating that the border controls were damaging the EU in terms of the economy and mutual trust between member states. However, the Minister of Integration at the time, Inger Støjberg, and the rest of the Danish government showed no intention of changing the extended control and prioritised what they believed to be the interest of Denmark.

## Deterrence policies

Alongside the physical control at the external borders and the re-bordering practices, we also find more implicit measures, which had the purpose of deterring people by decreasing the alleged attractiveness of Denmark as a destination for asylum seekers. The former government implemented a number of initiatives aimed to decrease the number of arriving refugees and thereby the number of people being granted asylum in Denmark. I have already mentioned highly symbolic acts such as the adverts in Lebanese newspapers as one example of what we can term deterrence policies. While some were overt measures to reduce flows, such as of temporary controls at the border with Germany, others, as mentioned, were intended instead to decrease the attractiveness of Denmark. The most contentious of these has been labelled the Jewellery Law (see also chapter 2), which was adopted in January 2016. This bill introduced additional limitations on access to permanent residency, extended waiting periods for family reunification, and legalised the confiscation of valuables worth more than DKK 10,000 (approximately EUR 1,300) from arriving refugees.

While different governments have, since the turn of the century, made it more difficult to obtain permanent residence, these conditions were further restricted as a response to the refugee crisis. Previously, refugees who had been in the country for eight years and shown what is described as a will to integrate, but not yet met specific goals pertaining to what is perceived as active citizenship, level of income, higher level of Danish proficiency, and employment (which are taken to signify integration and commonly referred to as integration criteria) could get easier access to permanent residency. This possibility was removed in the wake of the proclaimed crisis. Instead, a combination of residency duration and so-called integration criteria is currently required to obtain permanent residency. This follows a long list of attempts by different governments to restrict immigrants' rights to welfare citizenship since 2001 (see also chapters 5 and 12).

Deterrence has clearly been a primary motivation behind these and other initiatives. Across the political landscape – with the exception of the most leftist parties, the social liberals, and *Alternativet* – there has been a consensus on the need to limit the number of refugees applying for asylum. As highlighted above, numerous political actors inside and outside the government have welcomed the legislative changes with reference to the state of emergency the country is claimed to be in. Most political parties deemed the new measures to be fair and appropriate, considering the circumstances. For instance, the Social Democrats' spokesperson for Integration at the time, Nicolai Wammen, stated that 'We are in an extraordinary situation where up to 200 asylum seekers arrive on a daily level to Denmark and that calls for extraordinary decisions' (quoted in Drachmann, 2015).

The cornerstone of the government's reforms in 2015 was the reintroduction of the integration benefit.[7] This is an allowance given to newly arrived refugees that is purposefully low, as it is intended to encourage integration by incentivising work, but according to the Minister of Integration at the time, Inger Støjberg, it also has an outspoken deterrence goal. When introducing the regulations, she stated, 'We must tighten up, so we can control the inflow of asylum seekers coming to Denmark ... This is the first in a line of restrictions which the government will implement to get the foreigners issue [fremmedesagen] under control again' (Beskæftigelsesministeriet, 2015). The lowering of the social benefit was thus meant to reduce the number of people being interested in applying for asylum in Denmark. However, it is difficult to assess if the integration benefit had the direct effect the government was hoping for, as the numbers of asylum seekers entering other European member states also dropped after 2016. Other countries implemented different forms of deterrence policies. Nevertheless, we can also see that the number of asylum seekers entering Denmark is historically low. New statistics from February 2019 shows that only 5 out of 1,000 asylum seekers entering Europe apply for asylum in Denmark. During the last twenty years the rate was between 10 and 15 out of 1,000 (Andersen and Larsen, 2019).

Despite the acclaimed success of the restrictions mentioned above and the very few people actually applying for asylum in Denmark, the Conservative government, supported by the Danish People's Party, used the Finance Bill in 2019 to introduce a number of further restrictions targeting refugees having obtained asylum: 'Now, the immigration policy is being further expanded with a number of significant initiatives to ensure that the temporary protection in Denmark does not become permanent when the need for protection ceases' (Finansministeriet, 2019, p. 25). Moreover, 'rules and practices need to be adapted so that an asylum permit no longer has to be considered as an admission ticket to live in Denmark when you no longer have a need for protection' (Finansministeriet, 2019, p. 26). In concrete terms, this entailed reducing welfare benefits even more. NGOs already point to the damaging effects of the previous benefit level and foresee increased and protracted levels of poverty. The lowering of the allowance is meant both to have a deterrence effect, making it less favourable to apply for asylum in Denmark, as well as sending a signal of a hard demand for self-sufficiency to the people already living in Denmark. The lowering of the benefit is only one among a number of new restrictions. They are part of a paradigmatic shift in immigration policy. The Social Democrats support this shift, which makes change difficult (Agustin and Jørgensen, 2019a). As emphasised in the quotation above from the Finance Bill, this shift entails a focus on return and deportation. The integration benefit, for instance, was renamed as the return benefit (hjemrejseydelse), which sends an unmistakable message to the recipient about their stay being temporary. Other policy measures include further restrictions on access to permanent residency and access to family reunification. In sum, the new restrictions make temporariness the central concern in the policy framework. Refugees, regardless of their achievements and time of residency in Denmark, are expected to leave. Consequently, integration (as it is portrayed in the Finance Bill) is basically not possible, and refugees remain deportable populations. Nicholas De Genova (2016, p. 2) argues that 'within any given regime of immigration-related conditionalities ... and contingencies, migrants always remain more or less deportable' and describes this as an "economy" of deportability: even if all non-citizens are potentially subject to deportation, not everyone is deported, and not everyone is subject to deportation to the same degree' (2016, p. 2).

Another set of measures are the 'motivation enhancement measures', which target rejected asylum seekers who cannot be deported, as well as immigrants living in Denmark on tolerated stay (that is, immigrants with a criminal record and/or a deportation order which cannot be executed because their country of origin is not safe or will not receive them (see Freedom of Movement Research Collective, 2018). The conditions in the deportation centres Kærshovedgaard and Sjælsmark, where these people on tolerated stay live, are extremely harsh and offer little possibility of an autonomous everyday life. The immigrants living there receive only a minimal allowance, are not allowed to cook for themselves, and have to register their whereabouts (e.g. Canning, 2019; see also chapter 12). These provisions seem to have had the desired effect for the government. New numbers show that 328 out of 447 people placed at Kærshovedgaard have disappeared without the authorities knowing where they are (Ibfelt and Skov-Jensen, 2019). While such disappearances may pose a security threat or be taken as a sign that the government is unable to achieve the desired control of the unwanted population, they have been used to explain the government's ultimate desire, which is to expel refugees without breaking the Geneva Convention. When interrogated about the disappearances, Inger Støjberg responded: 'The idea is of course that they have to go home to the country they came from. But I have always been aware that some are trying [to get asylum] in other countries'. The Danish People's Party's spokesperson on integration gave a similar response: 'This is a small success. Understood in the sense that they leave and travel to another European country and stay there rather than stay in Denmark. So in this way it is of course good' (Ibfelt and Skov-Jensen, 2019).

### Extreme bureaucratic and legal uncertainty

Since June 2015, the Ministry of Foreigners and Integration introduced more than 100 restrictions pertaining to non-citizens. Of these, more than half relate directly to asylum seekers. With the change of government and the appointment of a new minister, this development could change but it is too early to tell if this will be the case. The more or less constant changes in immigration policy make it very difficult to navigate the system. Refugees, especially, experience a system that can change overnight and where the procedure is never set. A new report by the Danish Refugee Council shows that people with a refugee background experience stress, dissatisfaction, depression, and anxiety because of the constant legal changes (Dansk Flygtningehjælp, 2019).

In her work on irregular migrants, Bridget Anderson (2010, p. 300) claims that the methodical making of 'institutional uncertainty' helps 'produce "precarious workers" over whom employers and labour users have particular mechanisms of control'. In this context, immigration controls function both as 'a tap regulating the flow of labour' and as 'a mould shaping certain forms of labour' (2010, p. 301). There is an inter-play of entrant categories, employment relations and construction of institutionalised uncertainty steered by immigration controls to form particular types of labour and relations to employers and the labour market (2010, p. 301). The legal status of the migrant is produced by immigration control, which at the same time produces other types of illegality.

There is a parallel between Anderson's analysis and the situation for refugees in the Danish context. Even when people with refugee status have found employment or education, they are never safe from deportation, as the principle of temporariness trumps other concerns. With the newest restrictions, 25,000 people who have recognised refugee statuses are at risk of being deported if the situations in their home countries are deemed to be safe, which illustrates how deportable populations are constructed within the policy framework. Of these, 8,700 people are now in paid employment and do what is expected of them in terms of integrating into the labour market (Andersen and Larsen, 2019). The decision to declare a country safe can seem quite arbitrary, as it results more from bilateral agreements with economic gains than a genuine assessment of security risks. As an example, Somalia is now considered a safe country by the Danish authorities despite the ironic fact that Danish civil servants from the Foreigners' Service who negotiated the return agreement with the Somali government never dared to leave the airport in Mogadishu as it was not deemed safe enough for them (Ottesen, 2017). The Danish civil servants trusted the assessment of the Institute for Economics and Peace that the country is not considered a dangerous place despite its ranking as the fifth most dangerous country in the world.[8] As a result of the agreement, hundreds of Somalis with refugee statuses living in Denmark now face deportation.

At the same time as the new restrictions were launched, existing practices such as family reunification were subjected to increased bureaucratisation. A lack of transparency (for example, rights being conditional on other policy measures such as the strategy against 'parallel societies' in social housing schemes or the discretionary power of civil servants assessing

# Representations of the refugee crisis in Denmark

the applications) indirectly serves as an exclusionary mechanism and as a deterrence measure. It can be argued that the Danish state is establishing an extreme version of bureaucratic and legal uncertainty for both asylum seekers and people with refugee statuses. In addition, despite the many public concerns for refugees' lack of integration, the current restrictive policies (emphasised also by the Finance Bill) seem to make integration pointless or impossible.

## Civil society and refugees responding to the politics of deterrence and uncertainty

In this section, I provide some examples of how civil society and refugees (individually and collectively) have reacted to the Danish policy developments.

### Welcoming over deterrence

The visibility of the crisis generated a myriad of solidarity initiatives and created/reactivated networks seeking to help and assist refugees. Thousands of people became involved in solidarity work within a very short period. Many people acted in civil disobedience and became criminalised 'humanitarian smugglers' by offering transportation to refugees wanting to go to Sweden. Some sailed groups of refugees over the Öresund to Sweden, whereas others crossed the bridge with refugees hidden in their cars (Agustin and Jørgensen, 2019b). These acts presented a dilemma to the government. On the one hand, the people in solidarity solved a problem for the state by moving an unwanted population away from Denmark; on the other hand, the authorities were also concerned that such acts in themselves could be an incentive for refugees to come to Denmark. It is in this political landscape that *Venligboerne* (literally friendly neighbours) emerged. The network dates back longer than 2015, though. The movement was not originally aimed at doing solidarity work with refugees, but was developed as an initiative in a social centre in Northern Jutland. The *Venligboerne* groups have a number of shared aims, such as: providing legal aid, practical help, medical support, language training, job-seeking assistance and everyday donations; creating broad alliances including both experienced activists and people new to solidarity work; setting up social centres; making the problems of the asylum process and integration into Danish society visible; practising a humanitarian approach different from the exclusivist and restrictivist approach characterising the state; and articulating the commonalities between people, refugees, and Danes alike (Jørgensen and Olsen, 2020). *Venligboerne* is one of the groups welcoming refugees which were active during the 'long summer of migration' and after (Jørgensen and Olsen, 2020). With the arrival of a large number of refugees, the *Venligboerne* initiative grew rapidly when it was introduced as an alternative way of meeting refugees. From here, the initiative spread across Denmark (and even outside the country) and received increasing attention as a way to counter the state's deterrence policies (Jørgensen and Olsen, 2020). The refugee crisis is, without doubt, a defining moment in explaining the strengthening and spread of civic solidarity, but it also links in with previous solidarity networks (Agustin and Jørgensen, 2019b). *Venligboerne* provide many roles in the encounter between civil society and migrants. The local groups have been vital in creating a space of inclusion where newcomers are received as peers. The power of *Venligboerne* lies firstly in its ability to forge alliances between different civil society organisations, networks, and refugee groups, and secondly in its flexibility and ability to adapt to the policy developments. When the government tightened aspects of the Foreigners' Law and regulations for asylum seekers, *Venligboerne* responded not only with a critique (of the asylum regime) but also with concrete actions.

While a strong welcoming culture may be important in the lives of individuals, it does not necessarily hold the power to change existing policies. *Venligboerne* has had an internal discussion regarding the politics it performs. Some members – including the original founder – regard it as a non-political organisation, whereas other members regard it as a non-formal political organisation (Agustin and Jørgensen, 2019b). Although *Venligboerne* has not been able to change the general political direction (towards increased restrictions and worsening conditions for refugees) it has been able to challenge the system by legal means. For instance, the government has made it more difficult to actually use refugees' right to family reunification. Even when all conditions for bringing one's family to Denmark are fulfilled, the criteria that the person applying for family reunification must bear all costs makes it de facto impossible. This is particularly the case for unaccompanied minors. To deal with this situation, *Venligboerne* created the group *Venligboerne samler ind til flygtninge* (friendly neighbours collect [donations] for refugees), which collects money to pay for these costs. The donations come from art shows, book sales and so on, and the organisation has created a very professional infrastructure to make the process efficient. In August 2018, the organisation had reunited more than 138 refugees and family members (BT, 2018). It has managed to uphold a high level of mobilisation and continuity. In 2018, three years after the initial mobilisation, the various *Venligboerne* chapters counted more than one hundred local groups and had more than 150,000 members (Fenger-Grøndahl, 2017).

### Refugee activism and initiatives

One strategy used by refugees is empowerment through knowledge sharing. An example is *visAvis*, which is a publication put together by migrants.

*visAvis* describes itself as: 'a magazine on asylum and migration, the movement of people across borders and the challenges connected to this. We work to improve the debate on asylum and migration, among other things by publishing texts that people seeking asylum want to share' (*visAvis*, nd.). The description of the background for producing the magazine continues: '*visAvis* is produced by people with or without citizenship living in Denmark. From our point of view the policies regarding migration and asylum are repressive. People seeking refuge are made suspect and migrants are made illegal' and '[i]n this precarious situation we wish to raise the level of debate, enhance the quality of information, and create a space where it is possible for people seeking asylum to express what is on their mind' (*visAvis*, nd.). It represents a type of citizen journalism with the peculiar fact that it is produced (primarily) by non-citizens; that is, people excluded from the protectionist framework of citizenship. What we see here are people claiming a presence and a public voice. Engin Isin (2008) regards such events as constituting acts of citizenship. Investigating acts of citizenship entails 'focus[ing] on those moments when, regardless of status and substance, subjects constitute themselves as citizens – or, better still, as those to whom the rights to have rights is due' (Isin, 2008, p. 18). Reviving political conflict, here in problematising the authorities' handling of asylum seekers and treatment of rejected asylum seekers, is a mode for making asylum seekers visible as political subjects. Refugees are active agents in constructing and disseminating an intrinsic knowledge about conditions, struggles and political claims in Denmark.

Another strategy has been acts of disobedience. The conditions in the deportation centres Sjælsmark and Kærshovedgaard have spurred varying actions and confrontations. Right now, there is a network of actors protesting in different ways against children growing up at Sjælsmark (demonstrations, solidarity events, occupations, etc.). The network unites a very diverse range of actors and has received considerable attention. So far, the government and parts of the opposition (the Social Democrats) have not reacted, but there are small signs of a change in opinion as the media (both national and international) keep highlighting the conditions in Sjælsmark. The rejected asylum seekers living in Kærshovedgaard tried another tactic by initiating a hunger strike in 2017 (see Lindberg et al. 2018). The strike also drew the media's attention, and the parliamentary Ombudsman visited the facility. In the end, however, nothing changed and the people forced to live in Kærshovedgaard have to deal with worse conditions than before.

Rejected asylum seekers have started leaving Denmark but not returning to their home countries. For some, being able to stay in Denmark against all the odds has not seemed possible. From the refugees I have been in contact with at asylum centres and one deportation centre, life, especially in the deportation centre, causes anxiety, depression, and a profound sense of powerlessness. Families started leaving at night without the employees of the centres knowing. Some people with the status of rejected asylum seekers have sought church asylum in Germany, which has turned out to be a second chance for some. German churches grant protection to refugees facing difficult situations, called hardship cases. The churches then present a request to the Federal Office for Migration and Refugees in Germany for further examination. *Venligboerne samler ind* has also supported these actions. The organisation, for instance, helped finance an Afghani family to reach Germany, where they sought church asylum and obtained the right to stay. People with Afghani background have travelled to France at times when the country started re-assessing the claims of Afghani asylum seekers (Ibfelt and Aaberg, 2019). However, the journeys are all towards the unknown, and some of my interlocutors are now living as irregular migrants in European countries with no chance of either returning to their home countries or obtaining asylum under the current regime(s). It is not only rejected asylum seekers, who for obvious reasons live in extremely precarious conditions facing forced deportation, but also asylum-seeking families and individuals staying on temporary residence permit who have started to leave Denmark.

## Conclusion

What does the future look like for refugees in Denmark? The discussion in this chapter has firstly posed the question of how the Danish authorities framed the refugee crisis and, secondly, how a framing of the situation as a sustained and protracted emergency legitimised a long series of restrictions for both new asylum seekers and refugees (and migrants) already residing in the country. The previous government introduced a number of immediate policy measures to face the 'crisis'. This included reinstatement of border controls and, more importantly, the introduction of deterrence measures. The overall policy goal has been to create a migration regime deterring potential asylum seekers from applying for asylum in Denmark. However, the policy measures not only target potentially arriving refugees but also the ones who have been in Denmark for years. The refugee crisis was thus used to expand the category of deportable populations. Whereas this category previously included rejected asylum seekers and migrants residing in Denmark on 'tolerated stay' (see above), the category has been expanded to also include refugees who had their claim for asylum accepted, who were re-united with their families, and who are in paid employment, learning Danish and so on. The politicisation of the question of who can hold the right to stay in Denmark created enormous insecurity. The government described the new policy approach as a paradigmatic shift – basically seeking to solve the refugee issue outside the EU's (or at least Denmark's) external borders, and which stresses temporality as a main factor (Frelick, Kysel, and Podkul, 2018). This approach aligns with the discussions within the EU of externalising the asylum procedures and establishing asylum application centres outside EU territories. The refugee crisis was used to legitimise this shift. As shown, it created extreme bureaucratic and legal uncertainty due to constant policy changes and to the expansion of the category of deportable populations. The approach bases itself on policy mechanisms and serves to make life unliveable in Denmark. A final consequence of the shift is that, in practice, it makes integration an impossible task, as having arrived as a refugee will always make you prone to deportation (see also De Genova, 2016b). In June 2019, Denmark inaugurated a new government when the Social Democrats won the election and, supported by the social liberal and the leftist parties, formed a minority government. It is too early to say if this will lead to any substantial policy changes, but everything seems to point away from a reversal of the restrictive policies. The Social Democrats support the paradigmatic shift and won the elections through promises of keeping the strict course on immigration (Agustin and Jørgensen, 2019a). However, the new Minister of Integration promised to improve conditions for children living at Sjælsmark, and recently suggested that it was time to slow down the restrictive policies, which could reduce the feeling of uncertainty to an extent. The government also opened up the possibility for allowing refugees to enrol in education, as was the case in the past. The main message is the same, however, and the foundation for restrictive policies continues to be the assumption that Denmark needs to be made less attractive to those wishing to re-establish their lives within its borders. For example, former Prime Minister Løkke Rasmussen explained that he understood the reasons Somalis prefer to live in a welfare state compared to life in Mogadishu and that he intends to follow existing rules.[9]

The restrictive policy regime has polarised Danish society. On the one hand, we see an organisation such as *Venligboerne* gaining popularity and being able to uphold a high level of mobilisation and engagement over time. On the other hand, we see continued support, not only for right-wing parties, but also for the restrictive position taken by the Social Democrats. Deterrence policies are likely to mark the future of the Danish political reality, and uncertainty may destroy the groundwork that strengthens the integration of migrants, including refugees. In the final part of this chapter, I have sketched out some of the nascent tendencies including the departure of the unwanted ones. In the end, people may decide not to stay in Denmark against all the odds.

**Notes**

1   When I mention government in this chapter I refer to the Liberal Party (*Venstre*)-led governments in power from June 2015 to June 2019. In June 2019 a Social Democratic government took power.
2   All translations from Danish to English are by the author.

3  In this chapter, I use both 'refugee' and 'migrant'. Although I prefer the term migrant to cover all mobile populations and thus underline their agency, several of the people I talked to during participant observation termed themselves refugees, so in order to respect this categorical self-identification I use both terms.
4  See www.en.cgs.aau.dk/research/projects/diginauts/. Accessed 12 February 2020.
5  Denmark received nearly 21,000 applications or 1.5 per cent of the EU total, while Sweden received approximately 160,000 or 11.7 per cent of the EU total.
6  'Skønsmæssig vurdering af indrejste udlændinge', Politi, published (last updated) 13 June 2016, www.politi.dk/da/aktuelt/nyheder/skoensmaessig_vurdering_af_indrejste_udlaendinge.htm. Accessed 12 February 2019.
7  The Liberal-Conservative governments from 2001–2011 implemented a lower social benefit, the 'Start Allowance', targeting newcomers who had lived in Denmark for the last seven out of eight years (i.e. including Danish citizens who had lived abroad). The Social Democratic-led government (2011–2015) abolished this benefit.
8  www.atlasandboots.com/most-dangerous-countries-in-the-world-ranked/. Accessed 12 February 2020.
9  *P1 Morgen*, DR, 7 August.

## References

Agustin, Ó. G. and Jørgensen, M. B. (2019a). 'Danes First, Welfare Last', *Jacobin*, 31 January. www.jacobinmag.com/2019/01/denmark-social-democrats-immigration-welfare (Accessed 13 March 2020).

Agustin, Ó. G. and Jørgensen, M. B. (2019b). *Solidarity and the 'Refugee Crisis' in Europe*. Cham: Palgrave Macmillan.

Anderson, B. (2010). 'Migration, Immigration Controls and the Fashioning of Precarious Workers', *Work, Employment and Society* 24(2), pp. 300–317.

Andersen, T. K. and Larsen, S. (2019). 'Danmark løfter en mindre del af flygtningebyrden', *Mandag Morgen*, 19 February.

BBC (2015). 'Denmark places anti-migrant adverts in Lebanon newspapers', *BBC*, 7 September. www.bbc.com/news/world-europe-34173542 (Accessed 13 March 2020).

Beskæftigelsesministeriet (2015). 'Straksindgreb på asylområdet. Ny integrationsydelse til nytilkomne udlændinge'. Press Release, 1 July.

Bojadžijev, M. and Mezzadra, S. (2015). '"Refugee crisis" or crisis of European migration policies?' www.focaalblog.com/2015/11/12/manuela-bojadzijev-and-sandro-mezzadra-refugee-crisis-or-crisis-of-european-migration-policies/ (Accessed 13 March 2020).

Bonomolo, A. and Kirchgaessner, S. (2015). 'UN says 800 migrants dead in boat disaster as Italy launches rescue of two more vessels', *The Guardian*, 20 April. www.theguardian.com/world/2015/apr/20/italy-pm-matteo-renzi-migrant-shipwreck-crisis-srebrenica-massacre. (Accessed 13 March 2020).

BT (2018). '138 udlændinge familiesammenført på Venligboernes regning', 23 August. www.bt.dk/samfund/138-udlaendinge-familiesammenfoert-paa-venligboernes-regning (Accessed 13 March 2020).

Canning, V. (2019). *Reimagining Refugee Rights: Addressing Asylum Harms in Britain, Denmark and Sweden*. Migration Mobilities Bristol, University of Bristol. Available at: www.statewatch.org/news/2019/mar/uk-dk-se-reimagining-refugee-rights-asylum-harms-3-19.pdf (Accessed 13 March 2020).

Christensen, E. and Bolvinkel, M. (2015). 'Fem grunde: Derfor "flygter" flygtningene fra Danmark til Sverige', *TV2 Nyheder*, 10 September. http://nyheder.tv2.dk/2015-09-10-fem-grunde-derfor-flygter-flygtningene-fra-danmark-til-sverige (Accessed 13 March 2020).

Dansk Flygtningehjælp (2019). *'Vi tager jo drømme fra dem'. En undersøgelse af, hvordan frivillige i Dansk Flygtningehjælp oplever, at de seneste lovændringer på udlændinge- og integrationsområdet påvirker mennesker med flygtningebaggrund*. København.

De Genova, N. (2016a). 'The "Crisis" of the European Border Regime: Towards a Marxist Theory of Borders', *International Socialism* 150, pp. 31–54.

De Genova, N. (2016b). 'Detention, Deportation, and Waiting: Toward a Theory of Migrant Detainability', *Global Detention Project Working Paper* No. 18.

DR (2015). 'Måling: Danskerne vil gerne hjælpe flygtninge, men...'. *DR*, 13 September.

Drachmann, H. (2015). 'Beslaglæggelse: Asylansøgere får lov til at beholde armbåndsure, vielsesringe og 3.000 kroner', *Politiken*, 10 December. http://politiken.dk/indland/politik/ECE2968953/beslaglaeggelse-asylansoegere-faar-lov-til-at-beholde-armbaandsure-vielsesringe-og-3000-kroner/ (Accessed 13 March 2020).

Expressen (2015). 'Löfven: "Det finns en bred samsyn"', *Expressen*, 10 September.

Fenger-Grøndahl, M. (2017). *Venligboerne. Historien om en bevægelse*. København: Bibelselskabet.

Finansministeriet (2019). *Aftale mellem regeringen og Dansk Folkeparti: Finansloven for 2019* (30 November 2018). København: Finansministeriet.

Freedom of Movement Research Collective (2018). *STOP KILLING US SLOWLY. A Research Report on the Motivation Enhancement Measures and the Criminalisation of Rejected Asylum Seekers in Denmark*. Roskilde.

Frelick, B., Kysel, I. M., and Podkul, J. (2018). 'The Impact of Externalization of Migration Controls on the Rights of Asylum Seekers and Other Migrants', *Journal on Migration and Human Security* 4(4), pp. 190–220.

Ibfelt, J. and Aaberg, M. (2019). 'Khoshaw forlod Kærshovedgaard: Nu får han ny chance i Italien', *Information*, 13 February.

Ibfelt, J. and Skov-Jensen, M. (2019). 'Asylansøgere forsvinder ud i det blå: Mange rejser videre til andre EU-lande', *DR*, 12 February. www.dr.dk/nyheder/regionale/midtvest/asylansoegere-forsvinder-ud-i-det-blaa-mange-rejser-videre-til-andre-eu-0 (Accessed 13 March 2020).

Isin, E. (2008). 'Theorizing Acts of Citizenship', in Isin, E. F. and Nielsen, G. M. (eds.) *Acts of Citizenship*. New York: Zed Books, pp. 15–43.

Jyllands-Posten (2015). 'Støjberg om skuffede flygtninge: Utaknemmelige', *Jyllands-Posten*, 11 September 11.

Jørgensen, M. B. (2016). 'New Approaches to Facilitating Refugee Integration in Denmark', in *Transatlantic Council on Migration Meeting 'The Other Side of the Asylum and Resettlement Coin: Investing in Refugees' Success across the Migration Continuum'*. Washington.

Jørgensen, M. B. (2019). '"A Goat that is Already Dead is No Longer Afraid of Knives". Refugee Mobilisations and Politics of (Necessary) Interference in Hamburg', *Ethnologia Europaea* 49(1), pp. 41–57.

Jørgensen, M. B. and Olsen, D. R. (2020). 'Civil Society in Times of Crisis', in Norocel, O. C., Hellström, A., and Jørgensen, M. B. (eds.) *Hope and Nostalgia at the Intersection between Welfare and Culture*. Cham: IMISCOE Series Springer, pp. n/a.

Kofoed, J. (2016). 'Nu indfører Danmark midlertidig grænsekontrol', *DR*, 4 January. www.dr.dk/ligetil/indland/nu-indfoerer-danmark-midlertidig-graensekontrol (Accessed 13 March 2020).

Lindberg, A., Meret, S., Joaquin, J., and Jørgensen, M. B. (2018). 'Reclaiming the Right to Life: Hunger Strikes and Protests in Denmark's Deportation Centres', *Open Democracy*, 7 January. www.opendemocracy.net/can-europe-make-it/susi-meret-annika-lindberg-jose-joaquin-arce-bayona-martin-bak-j-rgensen/reclaimi (Accessed 13 March 2020).

Ottesen, K. (2017). 'Udlændingestyrelsen undersøgte Somalia fra lufthavnen', *DR*, 1 February. www.dr.dk/ligetil/indland/udlaendingestyrelsen-undersoegte-somalia-fra-lufthavnen (Accessed 13 March 2020).

Politiken (2015). 'Støjbergs flygtningeannoncer er en skamplet på Danmark', *Politiken*, 8 September.

Rajaram, P. K. (2015). 'Beyond Crisis: Rethinking the Population Movements at Europe's Border', *Focal Blog*, www.focaalblog.com/2015/10/19/prem-kumar-rajaram-beyond-crisis/ (Accessed 13 March 2020).

Róin, P. (2016). 'Da medborgere blev menneskesmuglere', *Information*, 13 May, section 3, p. 14.

Scheper-Hughes, N. (1995). 'The Primacy of the Ethical: Propositions for a Militant Anthropology', *Current Anthropology* 36(3), pp. 409–440.

Statsministeriet (2016). 'Nytårstale dem 1. januar 2016'. www.stm.dk/_p_14279.html (Accessed 13 March 2020).

Triandafyllidou, A. (2017). 'A Refugee Crisis Unfolding: "Real" Events and Their Interpretation in Media and Political Debates'. *Journal of Immigrant and Refugee Studies*, pp. 198–216.

TV2 (2015). '7 historiske øjeblikke: Da flygtningekrisen kom til Danmark', *TV2*, 13 September. http://nyheder.tv2.dk/2015-09-13-7-historiske-oejeblikke-da-flygtningekrisen-kom-til-danmark (Accessed 13 March 2020).

*visAvis* (nd). 'About visAvis'. www.visavis.dk/background-of-visavis/ (Accessed 13 March 2020).

# 5 Annika Lindberg

# Minimum rights policies targeting people seeking protection in Denmark and Sweden

> The temporary law changed the general view of Sweden in Europe. We used to be the generous country, and that affected us as a public agency, because this generous image has also characterized our approach. If you look around here in our office, the rooms are named after Malala, Raoul Wallenberg … all human rights advocates. We have the human rights convention framed on our walls … but now, we are supposed to adapt to an absolute minimum approach. We're now at the edge of the European Convention. It's a clear political signal, but we have to figure out what it means to us, this new focus on minimum levels and on return. (Richard, senior official at Swedish Migration Agency)

I interviewed Richard,[1] a senior official at the Swedish Migration Agency, in February 2017, approximately one year after the Social Democratic-Green coalition government had decided to close Sweden's borders and adopt the 'temporary law' (Lagen 2016:752). As Richard's reflection indicates, the law entailed a restrictive shift, designed to deter people from seeking protection in Sweden, and enhance the rate and speed of deportations. The law increased the hurdles in obtaining protection, introduced temporary rather than permanent residence permits for people who had obtained protection status, and circumscribed their right to family reunification (see also chapters 3 and 12 in this volume), and was accompanied by a political promise to enforce more deportations, expand migration-related detention, and increase the capacity of the border police. For Richard and his colleagues at the Swedish Migration Agency, it also implied a shift in how they approached their work.

Sweden had thus joined the so-called 'race to the bottom' in European asylum and migration policy (Slominski and Trauner, 2018). Meanwhile, across the Öresund, the Danish government was, at a higher speed than ever, issuing amendments to its Alien's Act with the explicit aim of rendering Denmark unattractive for people seeking protection (see also chapter 4). In 2018, the (now former) government declared a paradigm shift in the country's asylum regime, which would change the focus of the asylum system 'from integration to temporariness and repatriation' (Regeringen, 2018, p. 5). While having made certain concessions, the new Social Democratic-led coalition government has declared its intent to maintain the restrictive course in Denmark's asylum and migration regime.

The restrictive policy amendments have had drastic implications for people seeking protection in both Sweden and Denmark, and have severely circumscribed their access to protection as well as to welfare rights and services (Clante Bendixen, 2017). What is more, and as Richard's reflection illustrates, they signalled a shift in how border bureaucracies were supposed to approach people seeking protection – even though prior research has shown that restrictive and rigorous border regimes are constitutive of the Nordic states, rather than an anomaly (Barker, 2013, p. 2017). In this chapter, I address the question of how state officials at the forefront of border bureaucracies (Brodkin, 2012) have made sense of and enforced the restrictive policy regimes targeting people seeking protection in Denmark and Sweden. I focus in particular on what I call minimum rights approaches that limit or withdraw access to welfare services and that are designed to deter unwanted migrants from remaining in the countries. In Denmark, this logic has applied both to people in the asylum process and to those who have received a negative decision and are awaiting deportation; in the Swedish case, I focus on the policy measures targeting people whose asylum application has been rejected.

The chapter is based on qualitative research conducted in 2016 and 2017, including interviews with Danish and Swedish police officers, civil society organizations, social services, migration officials and legal advisors. Moreover, I conducted participant observation and interviews with staff in Danish so-called departure centres (*udrejsecenter*) and Swedish departure housing units (*återvändandeenheter*), the latter of which are open housing units (as opposed to locked detention centres) where people are accommodated prior to deportation. Denmark and Sweden have often been discussed as two very different cases with regard to migration and asylum policy (Green-Pedersen and Krogstrup, 2010), with Sweden being a self-proclaimed humanitarian great power (Parusel, 2015) and Denmark representing a more long-standing restrictive approach. In contrast, I focus on similarities in terms of how wealthy, bureaucratized welfare states produce an intricate web of exclusionary practices, which affirm the non-belonging of people who have been categorized as unwanted by the state. Tracing the implementation of the minimum rights approaches in the two countries, I demonstrate the particular forms of violence enabled through the intense presence of the state in the everyday life of (non)citizens (see Introduction to this volume).

In what follows, I first introduce the argument that the politics of deterrence and minimum rights can be understood as forms of necropolitical (Mbembe, 2003) state violence. Second, I outline practitioners' reactions to the deterrence policies justified by both governments' declarations of a crisis of asylum reception, and discuss how this political framing justified the adoption of policies which only aggravated the precarious condition of persons seeking protection. Third, I analyse the minimum welfare policies targeting rejected asylum seekers in Denmark and Sweden, and discuss their implications for the agents of enforcement as well as for those targeted. I conclude by arguing that these forms of violence, rather than being exceptional, are integral to the welfare states, and produce hierarchies of belonging, rights and humanity among populations. Importantly, I recognize that the perspective of state officials risks overlooking the ways in which people seeking protection navigate and challenge the minimum rights policies and how they partake in shaping border regimes from a disadvantaged position (Mezzadra and Nielsen, 2013). Acknowledging the partiality of the perspective offered in this chapter, I nevertheless maintain that the views of street-level bureaucrats may offer important insights into the exclusionary bordering mechanisms of bureaucratized welfare states.

## Minimum rights as necropolitics

Much literature on migration control regimes focuses on the coercive state powers they mobilize, such as practices of policing, detainment and forced deportation (Bosworth, Parmar and Vázquez, 2018), and how they inflict direct, physical violence and punishment on unwanted foreign nationals. Yet migration control also operates through welfare services, which can be mobilized as instruments of migration control: for instance, when states adjust foreign nationals' access to essential social rights and services to an absolute humanitarian minimum (Johansen, 2013) or render them conditional upon cooperation with authorities in asylum or deportation processes (Rosenberger and Koppes, 2018). These policy measures, which can be understood as a form of indirect violence (Valenta and Thorshaug, 2011), are the focus of this chapter.

Prior research has suggested an understanding of minimum welfare approaches as a form of minimalist biopolitics (Johansen, 2013), which denies people who are conceived as unwanted by the state equal access to basic rights and services, including work, health care, education and welfare. The aim of such policies is ultimately to expel them from the territory and/ or the social body (Walters, 2011). Compared to direct, coercive regulatory practices, minimum welfare policies are financially and legally less costly for states, while they enable governments to expose 'those physically and politically marginalized ... to very real bodily violence ... *while* fulfilling their legal obligations to those making an application for asylum' (Mayblin et al., 2019, p. 15, emphasis in original). Applying a postcolonial perspective in their writing on the lived experiences of poverty and marginalization among people seeking asylum in the UK, Mayblin et al. (2019, p. 2) argue that the minimum welfare approach should be understood as a form of bordering that produces a hierarchization of human life and rights. This hierarchization, in turn, follows a 'logical contemporary expression of historically embedded colonial/modern, racially hierarchical worldviews which have their roots in colonial enterprise'. The authors thus draw attention to how the political production of such abject 'necropolitical' (Mbembe, 2003, p. 21) conditions, where populations are 'kept alive, but in a state of injury', is ultimately rendered possible through the racialized identity of the Other (for example migrant). Beyond the study of Mayblin et al. (2019), the analysis of minimum rights approaches to people who migrate as a form of necropolitics has informed several contemporary studies of border and migration regimes in Europe and beyond (Weber and Pickering, 2011; Davies, Isakjee and Dhesi, 2017), which have shown how these policy regimes expose racialized migrant groups to slow suffering, enforced through neglect and deprivation.

While necropolitics is by no means a governing strategy confined to Northern Europe, strategies of radical exclusion arguably take particular forms, and differ in their effects, when deployed by highly regulated welfare states. As Davies, Isakjee and Dhesi (2017, p. 1269) argue:

> Advanced states such as those in northern Europe have ample resources with which to ensure those within its borders are protected from hunger, provided with shelter and given the security required to live without constant fear. Welfare systems are relatively well funded; but just as power can be activated by such states through distribution of provision, exclusionary power can be exerted through its withdrawal.

The authors conclude that the 'active inaction' on behalf of states that have the capacity and resources to provide for persons seeking protection, yet intentionally chose not to do so, constitutes a form of structural violence (see also chapter 2). Hence, minimum rights approaches enable states to produce the suffering of unwanted populations through wilful neglect and conscious withdrawal of support (Canning, 2018).

This chapter shows that policies which produce the foreseeable marginalization and exclusion of certain populations are often perceived as contradicting the discursive and ideological foundations of a universalist welfare state. In Denmark and Sweden, the narrative of an inclusive and protective welfare state is key to the social and political identity of the state (Brochmann and Hagelund, 2012). However, the welfare state is, to an equal extent, premised on the exclusion or subordinate inclusion (De Genova, 2013) of non-members, whose (gendered, racialised and classed) difference becomes constituted as threats to the welfare state and society (Tervonen et al., 2018). Hence, the subordinate inclusion and infliction of structural violence onto unwanted others is one of the ways in which the welfare state (re)constructs itself and consolidates its borders (Aas, 2013;

Minimum rights policies 89

Barker, 2017). Nevertheless, enforcing policies that inflict slow violence (Mayblin et al., 2019) onto those 'excepted' (Khosravi, 2010) from social, political, and legal membership causes dilemmas for the agents of enforcement within border-oriented welfare bureaucracies. These dilemmas, and the ways in which border bureaucrats make sense of and address them, are explored in the remainder of this chapter.

## The crisis of the welfare state and politics of deterrence

The 2015 summer of migration (Buckel, 2016) was followed by a restrictive turn in the asylum and migration policy across Northern European states. As detailed in other chapters in this volume (see chapters 3, 4 and also 12), the Danish and Swedish governments both declared a crisis of their asylum reception system and used it as justification for introducing a series of restrictive measures targeting people seeking protection. Many of the policy restrictions can be understood as a form of symbolic politics of deterrence (Lemberg-Pedersen, 2016; Whyte, Campbell and Overgaard, 2018) whereby the Swedish and Danish governments sought to send signals to people seeking protection that they were no longer welcome. The deterrence policies relied on the assumption that asylum seekers are attracted to Northern European states for their generous welfare benefits (Lemberg-Pedersen 2016). Accordingly, the very presence of people seeking protection was presented as a threat to the welfare state, with the rational response of governments being to limit their access to these rights and services. Such narratives also circulated among street-level officials tasked with enforcing the new restrictions within the asylum system.

For instance, on a chilly February morning in 2016, a month after Sweden had installed passport controls at the borders to Denmark, I arrived on the platform at Hyllie train station, the first station you reach when travelling from Denmark to Sweden. Hyllie station, which months earlier had been the site where many of the people who arrived in Sweden to seek protection had disembarked after a long journey through Europe, was now curiously empty. A police van stood parked next to the metal fence demarcating the Swedish border. I asked one of the police officers, who stood idle on the platform, what she thought of the border controls. While she acknowledged that there was not much work for the police to do at the station, as the number of arrivals had dropped significantly since the peak in September 2015, she still maintained that the border controls served a purpose:

> Many police officers were frustrated before, when asylum seekers were just allowed to pass us by and continue their journeys without applying for asylum. If you are really in need of protection, you wouldn't just walk through several safe countries on the way. You should apply for asylum in the first

country you arrive in ... if you don't do that, I think one should ask what's your real motivation. As a police officer, I wonder, the Refugee Convention ... if you come straight from the dangerous country and cross the border to a safe country ... the intention of the Convention is that people should stay there.

While there were no legal grounds for the police officer's statement (nowhere in international law is it specified that a person seeking protection must register their asylum claim in the first safe country they arrive in (Joormann, 2019)), the police officer had a clear, normative judgement of who deserves protection. In accordance with the Dublin Regulation (see Introduction above), signatory states do have the right (not the obligation) to expel people seeking asylum to the country where they are suspected to have entered Europe. Yet, in the police officer's view, the very fact that a person decided to travel further to Sweden demonstrates that their real motivation for seeking asylum was not to obtain protection, but something else.

During interviews, police and migration officials on both sides of the Öresund similarly voiced their opinion that people were making their way to Northern Europe for its supposedly generous welfare benefits. Accordingly, when reflecting on the purpose of their border enforcement tasks, Danish and Swedish border police officers explained that they saw their role not only as gatekeepers of the territorial border, but also as protectors of the welfare state against a perceived threat of abuse. Such narratives reflect a welfare chauvinist ideology, which portrays the welfare state as reserved uniquely for members of the national community, and depicts foreign nationals as potential threats to the welfare state and society (Careja et al., 2016; Keskinen et al., 2016). Politically, similar narratives were instrumentalized in order to justify further deterrence measures, which circumscribed access to rights and welfare for people seeking protection. Yet not all agents of enforcement were comfortable with the restrictions. Richard, the migration official quoted earlier, reflected in the following way on the Swedish government's temporary law:

> It was a decision made by a nervous government. They claimed that we – the Swedish Migration Agency – had asked them to install border controls but that's simply not true ... The temporary law was hastily and sloppily prepared. For instance, they completely forgot about Article 3 and 8 of the European Convention for Human Rights in their first draft, and we would simply have violated the human rights convention if we complied ... In the end, they added that restrictions should be applied 'as long as they do not breach Sweden's international commitments', which is a stupid formulation.

Richard emphasized that the law had attracted critique among several bureaucratic officials and legal experts, yet he also admitted that it had forced the Swedish Migration Agency to 'change their mindset' in a more restrictive direction. The shift to deterrence policies thus influenced the attitudes of border bureaucrats, and risked placing their practices in the grey zone of human rights conventions.

In Denmark, one of the deterrence measures adopted in early 2016 was the establishment of tent camps, designed to house people who were waiting for their asylum applications to be processed. Commenting on the tent camps, the (now former) Minister of Immigration, Integration and Housing stated, 'There is no doubt that the more debate there is regarding the tents and reception conditions, the more I believe asylum-seekers will think that Denmark is not the place where they should go' (Inger Støjberg, quoted in Jyllands-Posten, 2016). While encampment is a long-established feature of Danish asylum and migration control (Whyte, 2011; Syppli-Kohl, 2015), the tent camps were established to indicate a state of crisis in the reception system. Karsten, a legal advisor for people applying for asylum whom I interviewed in 2016, noted that the tent camps were opened 'despite the fact that there are 166,000 empty buildings in Denmark [at the time]. Just to show that Denmark doesn't want them'. Whyte, Campbell and Overgaard (2018, p. 2) have described the tent camps as 'emblematic of a wider turn in asylum policies in the Global North towards making host countries seem as unattractive as possible to would-be asylum seekers'. Yet, beyond their symbolic function, the tent camps, as well as the other restrictions in reception conditions for people seeking protection, also had tangible effects. Elmira, another legal advisor in Denmark, commented the following way on the ensemble of regulations designed to make people seeking protection feel unwelcome in Denmark:

> The border closure and the issue [about the Jewellery Law] completely dominated the public debate. But this has no real meaning – it's merely symbolic, not interesting or particularly important for refugees ... If we talk about humiliating policies, it is far more humiliating that they are splitting families, introducing more surveillance measures and harsher detention conditions, and the stricter conditions in asylum centres ... Like now they can no longer cook their own food. This way, people lose ... the power over their own body that cooking your own meals still entails. And, the asylum camps look more like detention camps now. This sends a signal that they are not welcome.

As Elmira notes, the regulations that had the most tangible effects on people's lives included the obstacles to family life, the deprivation of autonomy, and everyday degradation in the camps. These stories rarely made the headlines but could be understood as expressions of the indirect or 'slow violence' (Mayblin et al., 2019) of the deterrence regime. Similar to Sweden, not all officials in Denmark were comfortable with imposing this regime. When I interviewed staff in asylum centres in Denmark regarding how the new restrictions affected their work, some of them explained that they tried to find ways to 'weasel their way out' of the policy restrictions and minimize the harmful effects on people seeking asylum (Borrelli and Lindberg, 2018, p. 171).

The deterrence policy regimes developed in both Denmark and Sweden thus served, on the one hand, to convey a sense of crisis, which was portrayed as having been caused by the people seeking protection and thus justifying restrictions in their access to rights, protection and services. On the other hand, the policies aggravated the crisis for those seeking protection, by exposing them to intensified suspicion, marginalization, and everyday degradation. Still, the deterrence policies enabled the governments to go to the edge of human rights conventions without overtly breaching them (see also chapter 12). This was particularly true for the minimum rights policies targeting people whose asylum application has been rejected in Denmark and Sweden respectively, to which I now turn.

### Enforcing the politics of minimum rights

The Swedish and Danish governments' response to their declared crisis of asylum reception also entailed promises to enhance the speed and rate of deportations. Under the pretext of preserving the integrity of the asylum system, both governments increased their investments in migration-related detention, and introduced restrictions to the social rights and freedom of movement of people whose asylum applications had been rejected.

In Denmark, this regime of rights restrictions has materialized in the two departure or deportation centres, Sjælsmark and Kærshovedgård, inaugurated in 2013, yet only in operation since 2015. The centres house people whose asylum applications have been rejected, including families and children, foreign nationals having received a deportation order following a criminal conviction, and people on so-called tolerated stay. Tolerated stay refers to an open-ended status for people who have been excluded from international protection (§ 1F, §10 and §25 of the Danish Alien's Act) because of their involvement in serious crime, or because they are suspected of posing a risk to national security, yet cannot be deported due to the risk of refoulement (see Suárez-Krabbe et al., 2018). Geographically isolated, located in former prison and military facilities run by the prison and probation service, and surrounded by non-secure fences, the purpose of deportation centres is to isolate and marginalize these groups of non-deported persons in view of pressuring them to leave Denmark 'voluntarily' (Suárez-Krabbe and Lindberg, 2019; see also chapter 12). Residents are obliged to reside in the centres, but are not legally detained, and can therefore be held there indefinitely. Meanwhile, they have no right to work, and as their daily allowance or pocket money is withdrawn, they are left to have their meals during specific hours in the centres' cafeteria.

# Minimum rights policies

The conditions in the deportation centres, and the acute threat of detainment and deportation that residents are exposed to, generate significant uncertainty, experiences of loss of autonomy, degradation, isolation and criminalization (Suárez-Krabbe et al., 2018; Canning, 2019). Staff tasked with enforcing or supervising this 'intolerability regime' (Suárez-Krabbe and Lindberg, 2019) approached their work with certain discomfort and ambivalence. 'Here we have no responsibilities compared to prisons, or even to migration detention', Mikkel, one of the prison officers, remarked. 'There, we are supposed to enforce the imprisonment and make it as humane as possible ... but here we do not have the mandate for that'. Some prison officers enjoyed not having to take responsibility for residents' wellbeing or monitor their whereabouts, while others regretted lacking the ability to ameliorate the harsh conditions for those held in the centres. Jonas, a colleague of Mikkel, told me:

> They say we should make life intolerable for them, to make life shit. I find that appalling. They should get out here and see the reality. A colleague of mine said that one day we'll have to get a funeral undertaker out here, because what are we to do with them? ... This gets right to the long-term question: What do we do with them? They are unwanted here ... but it's not dignified to treat them like that. (Quoted in Lindberg et al., 2018)

Jonas, and many of his colleagues, emphasized that the rule of intolerability was enforced by the structure, architecture and rules of the centres – not by prison officers. Still, he admitted that he found the intolerability regime, which subjected residents to conditions that were intentionally designed to 'make their life shit', appalling. The deportation centres have attracted criticism from numerous human rights organizations and agents for amounting to de facto detention, and for deliberately exposing residents to physical and psychologically harmful conditions (Helsinki-Komitéen for Menneskerettigheder, 2017; Røde Kors, 2019). What is more, and as Jonas noted, the combination of the architectural and legal setup of the centres and their temporal indeterminacy risked leaving residents indefinitely stranded under these conditions. Indeed, the centres have not contributed to enhancing deportation rates but instead, as formulated by residents stranded in the centres, 'left them to die, slowly' at the margins of state and society (Suárez-Krabbe et al., 2018).

Residents' articulations correspond well with Mbembe's (2003) depiction of the necropolitical condition that exposes certain groups to slow suffering, enforced through neglect and deprivation (Davies et al., 2017; Mayblin et al., 2019). However, when I discussed the deportation centres with state officials and NGO representatives in Denmark, they maintained that 'it could be worse'. For instance, Mette, who worked at a large NGO providing legal support to rejected asylum seekers in Denmark, noted, 'They could have chosen to use homelessness as a motivation measure instead, and just thrown rejected asylum-seekers out on the streets ... at least we don't do that in Denmark'. She might have been unaware that such a policy had entered into force in Sweden in June 2016.

Sweden's amended Act (1994:137) on the reception of asylum seekers and others (hereafter LMA) came into force in June 2016. According to the law, people whose asylum application has been rejected and who fail to leave Sweden within the four weeks' stipulated timeframe for 'voluntary' departure, will have their daily allowance and access to accommodation withdrawn. Families with children, unaccompanied minors and persons in need of emergency healthcare are excepted from the rule, yet the law urges authorities to apply exceptions restrictively (Migrationsverket, SR 13/2016). As a result of the amendment, people are effectively deprived of access to basic social rights, including access to food and accommodation, once their asylum application has been rejected.[2] When I interviewed migration officials working with deportation processes at the Swedish Migration Agency, many of them thought of the law as being correct in principle, as it demonstrated consistency in asylum policies. Maria, who worked in a migration-related detention centre, argued: 'We cannot tolerate that once the state tells people they are not allowed to stay, we have people who remain in the system living off its support, or municipalities and other actors allowing for a parallel society to grow, and legitimating that people stay here without authorization.' In the quote from Maria, we can distinguish the same deterrence logic that underpinned the Swedish police officer's reasoning above, where the exclusion of those 'undeserving' of state protection (Chauvin and Garcés-Mascareñas, 2012) from welfare services is posited as a necessity for keeping the welfare state solvent for members. It also shows a strong identification and loyalty with the welfare state among the street-level bureaucrats (see also chapter 7). However, the amendment also caused dilemmas for state officials. Susanne, another migration official, told me:

> An option we have is to subject them to registration duties, make them register regularly with authorities. But with the new LMA, there is no point – they have no incentive to stay in the system when they are not even getting a place to stay. What should we tell them – 'ok we need your address, you say you live under the bridge over there?' That's just absurd! (Quoted in Lindberg, 2019, p. 127)

Susanne concluded that the LMA amendment, rather than obtaining the desired effect of deterring people from remaining in Sweden despite a deportation order, disincentivized them from remaining in touch with authorities, and consequently pushed them into illegality. As our conversation continued, Susanne mentioned that 'it feels like we are just pushing the problem and the costs around between different state agencies'. Indeed, the

Swedish Migration Agency has reported that the LMA amendment has not had any tangible effect on deportation rates (see Sellin, 2018); instead, reports suggest that a growing number of people have been pushed into destitution and have become dependent on the support of non-governmental actors for their survival (European Commissioner for Human Rights, 2018). Jan, a social worker, reflected on the amendment:

> We are talking about people who do not have the right to be anywhere in the world. Maybe their decisions are not even enforceable ... the law doesn't match the wider perspective, the dilemmas we encounter with this group. This is nothing new, it has gone on for a long time ... We can no longer shut our eyes and pretend that the system covers it.

Jan suggested that the cause of the problem was the result of a policy failure and a gap in social service provision. Yet the exclusion of people with precarious or no legal status from essential welfare services is, in this case, the direct result of a law that purposely produces their destitution. As such, this is nothing new; as argued by Könönen (2018, p. 53), immigration law invalidates 'the universalism of rights and a residence-based welfare system'. Yet the minimum rights policies discussed in this chapter cannot be understood as mere policy failures but are intentional, even integral, to the operation of deterrence policies that deliberately withdraw access to rights and services for those perceived as non-members, even though they evoke dilemmas and bewilderment among the agents of enforcement.

In line with findings from research on similar policy measures in other countries, including Germany (Ellermann, 2010), the Netherlands (Kalir and van Schendel, 2017) and Norway (Valenta and Thorshaug, 2011; Johansen, 2013), the minimum rights approaches used in Denmark and Sweden have had counterproductive effects on deportation rates. Yet they have also allowed governments to tacitly ignore the 'slow violence' of destitution, illegalization and degradation that is a direct effect of the deterrence policies (see Canning, 2018; Mayblin et al., 2019). The policies have further enabled state authorities to tacitly ignore (Kalir and van Schendel, 2017) those unwanted on their territory and push the responsibility for their basic social rights either onto civil society actors, or on other European states. Indeed, recent reports on trends in Dublin transfers suggest that the restrictive conditions in Denmark and Sweden have pushed more people to move on to other European countries, including Germany, France and Italy (EMN, 2017; Ibfelt and Skov-Jensen, 2019 see also chapter 4). While access to asylum and to essential welfare services might be equally restrictive in those countries, the lack of essential service provisions might be easier to navigate for people with precarious legal status than in the highly bureaucratized Nordic welfare states. The asylum applications of specific nationalities are also treated differently from country to country. Issa, who had his application for asylum rejected in Denmark and spent one year in a Danish deportation centre, explained:

> Maybe you stay in one place for a few years, then you leave to a new place, you have to change places and then come back again ... and from what I have understood that's what people do: they get frustrated in one place, they try their luck in another place. But when you are already in the position of being rejected here, it's not the same as in Greece, Italy, or Spain ... there, you are allowed to walk around freely without documents, because they cannot afford or organize your deportation. But in Sweden, Denmark, Germany, it's more difficult. ... The system is made to protect you but can also control you. That's why, when the economic situation was good, it was actually ok to be a refugee in Greece, Spain, Italy ... that's why it's so difficult to live underground or as rejected here. Then you are basically wasting your time, you will never fit in. All is regulated. (Lindberg, 2019, p. 61)

Issa suggested that it is more difficult to navigate exclusionary policies in bureaucratized welfare states than in Greece, Italy or Spain which, as prior research has highlighted, are characterized by weaker internal gatekeeping and larger informal economies (Sager, 2011; Triandafyllidou and Ambrosini, 2011; see also DeBono et al., 2015). Returning to the suggestion by Davies, Isakjee and Dhesi (2017) that the intentional exclusion or withdrawal of basic services practised by wealthy, Nordic welfare states constitutes a governing technique in its own right, Issa's observation suggests that the minimum rights policies practised by Denmark and Sweden do have severe, violent effects on people seeking protection. The regulated, bureaucratized nature of service provisions in these states may also present additional barriers, which exacerbate the subordinate inclusion of unwanted populations.

## Conclusion

In this chapter, I have discussed the implementation of minimum rights policies targeting people seeking protection in Denmark and Sweden with the aim of deterring them from arriving or staying. The examples I have focused on are policy measures adopted or implemented since 2015, which have been fuelled by the notion of a crisis of asylum reception, where migration was portrayed as a threat to the social and political order of the welfare state. Focusing on indirect (Valenta and Thorshaug, 2011) coercive measures, including restrictions or withdrawal of access to basic social rights for people deemed unwanted or non-belonging to the welfare state, I have discussed the way bureaucratic violence operates through everyday degradation and enforced destitution (Davies et al., 2017; Mayblin et al., 2019). I have argued that the logic of deterrence, which gradually circumscribes the rights of people seeking protection, and the deliberate production of abject conditions for those whose asylum application has been rejected amount to necropolitical violence (Mbembe, 2003). I have demonstrated how the enforcement of this governance logic has evoked confusion, discomfort and dilemmas for border bureaucrats, and resulted in aggravated marginalization, destitution and illegalization of people lacking legal authorization to remain. The dilemmas that border bureaucrats experience in enforcing state violence reflect the paradoxes inherent in the simultaneously caring and repressive welfare apparatus – notably when policies aggravate the crisis they were officially meant to address.

There remain important differences between the minimum rights approaches practised in Denmark and Sweden. In Denmark, the policies were a continuation of previous restrictive practices, whereas the temporary law in Sweden constituted a more drastic policy shift. Moreover, while the Danish government has been remarkably explicit in their unwelcoming approach (as illustrated by its promise to make life intolerable for residents of deportation centres), the intent behind the Swedish government's minimum rights approach is not as pronounced. This does not, however, mean that the Swedish government holds less responsibility for the harmful effects of the temporary law and the LMA amendment on people seeking protection; as Richard noted in his critique of the temporary law, its harmful effects were, if not foreseen, at least foreseeable (see also Canning, 2018).

Political differences aside, the reflection offered by Issa is instructive for understanding the specific hurdles encountering people seeking protection in bureaucratized Nordic welfare states. Getting by without support from state agencies and evading their intense regulative presence in the everyday is challenging, and access to alternative support structures might be conditional, partial and depend on kinship or other social networks, or on a person's ability to find work in the informal sector (Sager, 2011; Chauvin and Garcés-Mascareñas, 2012). Still, many people endure these conditions of constraint – or try their luck elsewhere in Europe. Their knowledge and experience are crucial to consider if we are to challenge the exclusionary power of bureaucratized states.

## Notes

1 Due to agreements on anonymity, all names of informants are fictive.
2 So far, other prior liberalizations of their social rights have not been revoked, notably the 2013 amendments, which granted people whose asylum application had been rejected, plus illegalized persons, the same right to healthcare as people who were in asylum procedures. Access to schooling for all children, including those lacking legal authorization to remain, is inscribed into national law.

## References

Aas, K. F. (2013). 'The Ordered and the Bordered Society: Migration Control, Citizenship, and the Northern Penal State', in Aas, K. J. and Bosworth, M. (eds.) *The Borders of Punishment: Migration, Citizenship, and Social Exclusion*. Oxford, New York: Oxford University Press, pp. 21–39.

Barker, V. (2013). 'Nordic Exceptionalism Revisited: Explaining the Paradox of a Janus-Faced Penal Regime', *Theoretical Criminology* 17(1), pp. 5–25.

Barker, V. (2017). 'Penal Power at the Border: Realigning State and Nation', *Theoretical Criminology* 21(4), pp. 441–457.

Borrelli, L. M. and Lindberg, A. (2018). 'The Creativity of Coping: Alternative Tales of Moral Dilemmas among Migration Control Officers', *International Journal of Migration and Border Studies* 4(3), pp. 163–178.

Bosworth, M., Parmar A. and Vázquez, Y (eds.) (2018). *Race, Criminal Justice and Immigration Control: Enforcing the Boundaries of Belonging*. Oxford: Oxford University Press.

Brochmann, G. and Hagelund, A. (2012). *Immigration Policy and the Scandinavian Welfare State 1945–2010*. Basingstoke: Palgrave Macmillan.

Brodkin, E. (2012). 'Reflections on Street-Level Bureaucracy: Past, Present, and Future', *Public Administration Review* 72(6), pp. 940–949.

Buckel, S. (2016). 'Welcome Management: Making Sense of the "Summer of Migration"'. *Near futures online*. Available at: http://nearfuturesonline.org/welcome-management-making-sense-of-the- summer-of-migration/ (Accessed 03 February 2019).

Canning, V. (2018). 'Border (Mis)Management, Ignorance and Denial', in Barton, A. and Davis, H. (eds.) *Ignorance, Power and Harm: Agnotology and The Criminological Imagination, Critical Criminological Perspectives*. Cham: Springer International Publishing, pp. 139–62.

Canning, V. (2019). *Supporting Sanctuary: Addressing Harms in the British, Danish and Swedish Asylum Systems*. Calverts Co-operative.

Careja, R., Elmelund-Præstekær, C., Klitgaard, M. and Larsen, E. (2016). 'Direct and Indirect Welfare Chauvinism as Party Strategies: An Analysis of the Danish People's Party'. *Scandinavian Political Studies* 39(4), pp. 435–57.

Chauvin, S. and Garcés-Mascareñas, B. (2012). 'Beyond Informal Citizenship: The New Moral Economy of Migrant Illegality', *International Political Sociology* 6(3), pp. 241–259.

Clante Bendixen, M. (2017). 'Long Waiting Times and Impossible Demands for Family Reunification.' Available at: http://refugees.dk/en/focus/2017/january/long-waiting-times-and-impossible-demands-for-family-reunification/ (Accessed 3 February 2019).

Davies, T., Isakjee, A. and Dhesi, S. (2017). 'Violent Inaction: The Necropolitical Experience of Refugees in Europe', *Antipode* 49(5), pp. 1263–1284.

DeBono, D., Rönnqvist, S. and Magnusson, K. (2015). *Humane and Dignified? Migrants' Experiences of Living in a 'State of Deportability' in Sweden*. Malmö: Malmo University.

De Genova, N. (2013). 'Spectacles of Migrant "Illegality": The Scene of Exclusion, the Obscene of Inclusion', *Ethnic and Racial Studies* 36(7), pp. 1180–1198.

Ellermann, A. (2010). 'Undocumented Migrants and Resistance in the Liberal State', *Politics & Society* 38(3), pp. 408–29.

EMN. (2017). 'EMN Annual Report on Migration and Asylum 2017 Sweden'. Available at: https://ec.europa.eu/home-affairs/sites/homeaffairs/files/17a_sweden_arm_part2_2017_en.pdf (Accessed 3 December 2019).
European Commissioner for Human Rights. (2018). *Report by Nils Muznieks Following His Visit to Sweden from 2 to 6 October 2017* (CommDH2018)4). Available at: https://rm.coe.int/commdh-2018-4-report-on-the-visit-to-sweden-from-2-to-6-october-2017-b/16807893f8 (Accessed 3 December 2019).
Suárez-Krabbe, J., Lindberg, A. and Arce, J. (2018). *Stop Killing Us Slowly: A Research Report on the Motivation Enhancement Measures and the Criminalization of Rejected Asylum Seekers in Denmark*. Roskilde University.
Green-Pedersen, C. and Krogstrup, J. (2010). 'Immigration as a Political Issue in Denmark and Sweden', *European Journal of Political Research* 5(47): pp. 610–634.
Helsinki-Komitéen for Menneskerettigheder. (2017). *Notat vedr. Udlændinge- og udrejsecentre i Danmark* (Notes about Centres for Foreigners and Deportations in Denmark). Available at: www.ft.dk/samling/20161/almdel/UUI/bilag/218/1774547/index.htm (Accessed 27 January 2018).
Ibfelt, J. and Jensen, M. S. (2019). *Asylansøgere forsvinder ud i det blå: Mange rejser videre til andre EU-lande* (Asylum Seekers Disappearing Out in the Blue: Many Travel Further to Other EU Countries). Available at: www.dr.dk/nyheder/regionale/midtvest/asylansoegere-forsvinder-ud-i-det-blaa-mange-rejser-videre-til-andre-eu-0 (Accessed 4 August 2019).
Johansen, N. (2013). 'Governing the Funnel of Expulsion: Agamben, the Dynamics of Force, and Minimalist Biopolitics', in Aas, K. F. and Bosworth, M. (eds.) *The Borders of Punishment: Migration, Citizenship, and Social Exclusion*. Oxford: Oxford University Press, pp. 257–272.
Joormann, M. (2019). *Legitimized Refugees: A Critical Investigation of Legitimacy Claims within the Precedents of Swedish Asylum Law*. PhD, Lund University.
Jyllands-Posten. (2016). *Inger Støjberg om ny kritik af teltlejre. 'Jo mere debat om teltene, desto bedre'* (Inger Støjberg on the New Critique on the Tent Camps: 'The More Debate on the Tents, the Better') 28 August. Available at: https://jyllands-posten.dk/indland/ECE8956371/inger-stoejberg-glaeder-sig-over-kritik-af-teltlejre/ (Accessed 15 February 2019).
Kalir, B. and van Schendel, W. (2017). 'Introduction: Nonrecording States between Legibility and Looking Away', *Focaal* (77), pp. 1–7.
Keskinen, S., Norocel, O. C. and Jørgensen, M. (2016). 'The Politics and Policies of Welfare Chauvinism under the Economic Crisis'. *Critical Social Policy* 36(3), pp. 321–329.
Khosravi, S. (2010). 'Sweden: Detention and Deportation of Asylum-seekers', *Race & Class* 50(4), pp. 438–456.
Könönen, J. (2018). 'Differential Inclusion of Non-Citizens in a Universalistic Welfare State', *Citizenship Studies* 22(1), pp. 53–69.
Lagen (2016:752) Om tillfälliga begränsningar av möjligheten att få uppehållstillstånd i Sverige (The Law (2016:752) on Temporary Restrictions in the Possibility to Receive Residence Permits in Sweden. Available at: www.riksdagen.se/sv/dokumentlagar/dokument/svenskforfattningssamling/lag-2016752-om-tillfalliga-begransningar-av_sfs2016752 (Accessed 5 December 2019).
Lemberg-Pedersen, M. (2016). 'European Deterrence Politics and the End of Humanitarianism'. Available at: http://refugees.dk/en/focus/2016/july/european-deterrence-politics-and-the-end-of-humanitarianism/ (Accessed 3 December 2019).

Lindberg, A. (2019). *Governing the Deportation Limbo: State Responses to Non-deported Migrants in Denmark and Sweden*. PhD, University of Bern.

Lindberg, A., Meret, S., Arce, J. and Jørgensen, M.B. (2018). 'Reclaiming the Right to Life: Hunger Strikes and Protests in Denmark's Deportation Centres.' Available at: www.opendemocracy.net/can-europe-make-it/susi-meret-annika-lindberg-jose-joaquin-arce-bayona-martin-bak-j-rgensen/reclaimi (Accessed 3 December 2019).

Mayblin, L., Wake, M. and Kazemi, M. (2019). 'Necropolitics and the Slow Violence of the Everyday: Asylum Seeker Welfare in the Postcolonial Present', *Sociology*. Available at: https://doi.org/10.1177/0038038519862124 (Accessed 3 December 2019).

Mbembe, A. (2003). 'Necropolitics'. *Public Culture* 15(1), pp. 11–40.

Mezzadra, S. and Neilson, B. (2013). *Border as Method*. Durham: Duke University Press.

Migrationsverket. (2016). 'Rättsligt ställningstagande angående innebörden av rekvisitet "uppenbart oskäligt" i 11 § i lagen (1994:137) om mottagande av asylsökande m.fl. – SR13/2016' (Legal Position Concerning the Content of the Condition of 'Apparently Unresonable' in 11 § in Law (1994:137) on the Reception of Asylum Seekers among Others – SR13/2016). Available at: https://lifos.migrationsverket.se/dokument?documentSummaryId=3745 (Accessed 3 December 2019).

Parusel, B. (2015). 'Sweden's U-Turn on Asylum', *Forced Migration Review*. Available at: www.fmreview.org/solutions/parusel.html (Accessed 5 August 2019).

Regeringen. (2018). 'Aftale om Finansloven for 2019' (Budget Agreement for 2019). Available at: www.regeringen.dk/nyheder/aftale-om-finansloven-for-2019/ (Accessed 3 December 2019).

Rosenberger, S. and Koppes, S. (2018). 'Claiming Control: Cooperation with Return as a Condition for Social Benefits in Austria and the Netherlands', *Comparative Migration Studies* 6(26). Available at: https://doi.org/10.1186/s40878-018-0085-3 (Accessed 3 December 2019).

Røde Kors (2019). 'Trivsel hos børn på Udrejsecenter Sjælsmark' (Wellbeing of Children at the Deportation Centre Sjælsmark). Available at: www.rodekors.dk/sites/rodekors.dk/files/201904/2019.03_Sjælsmark_V09_Final_1.pdf (Accessed 5 November 2019).

Sager, M. (2011). *Everyday Clandestineity: Experiences on the Margins of Citizenship and Migration Policies*. Lund: Lund University.

Sellin, B. (2018). 'Migrationsverket: "Syftet har inte uppnåtts"' (Migration Agency: 'The Aim Has Not Been Reached'. Available at: www.svt.se/nyheter/lokalt/vasternorrland/migrationsverket-syftethar-inte-uppnatts (Accessed 3 December 2019).

Slominski, P. and Trauner, F. (2018). 'How Do Member States Return Unwanted Migrants? The Strategic (Non-)Use of "Europe" during the Migration Crisis'. *JCMS: Journal of Common Market Studies* 56(1), pp. 101–118.

Suárez-Krabbe, J. and Lindberg, A. (2019). 'Enforcing Apartheid? The Politics of "Intolerability" in the Danish Migration and Integration Regimes', *Migration and Society* 2(1), pp. 90–97.

Syppli-Kohl, K. (2015). *Asylaktivering og Ambivalens. Forvaltningen af asylansøgere på asylcentre* (Asylum Activation and Ambivalence: The Management of Asylum Seekers at Asylum Centres). PhD, University of Copenhagen.

Tervonen, M., Pellander, S. and Yuval-Davis, N. (2018). 'Everyday Bordering in the Nordic Countries', *Nordic Journal of Migration Research* 8(3), pp. 139–142.

Triandafyllidou, A. and Ambrosini, M. (2011). 'Irregular Immigration Control in Italy and Greece: Strong Fencing and Weak Gate-Keeping Serving the Labour Market', *European Journal of Migration and Law* 13(3), pp. 251–273.

Valenta, M. and Thorshaug, K. (2011). 'Failed Asylum-Seekers' Responses to Arrangements Promoting Return: Experiences from Norway', *Refugee Survey Quarterly* 30(2), pp. 1–23.

Walters, W. (2011). 'Foucault and Frontiers: Notes on the Birth of the Humanitarian Border, in Bröckling, U., Krasmann, S. and Lemke, T. (eds.) *Governmentality: Current Issues and Future Challenges*, New York: Routledge, pp. 138–164.

Weber, L. and Pickering, S. (2011), *Globalisation and Borders: Death at the Global Frontier*. Basingstoke: Palgrave Macmillan.

Whyte, Z. (2011). 'Enter the Myopticon: Uncertain Surveillance in the Danish Asylum System. *Anthropology Today* 27(3), pp. 18–21.

Whyte, Z., Campbell, R. and Overgaard, H. (2018). 'Paradoxical Infrastructures of Asylum: Notes on the Rise and Fall of Tent Camps in Denmark', *Migration Studies*. Available at: https://doi.org/10.1093/migration/mny018 (Accessed 3 December 2019).

# PART II

# Disciplining refugees

# 6 Jelena Jovičić

# Images of crisis and the crisis of images: a visual analysis of four frames of representation of 'refugeeness' in Swedish newspapers

The period 2015–2016 in Sweden (and beyond) became largely known as the refugee crisis – a construct readily associated with a negative event or a destabilizing period of time, which can affect both individuals and larger groups and societies. The term crisis came alongside the word 'refugee' – a pairing which is particularly loaded and comes with highly problematic political impositions. For example, how did people fleeing come to embody the term crisis? Media coverage of the events has been vast. Images and video material of boats crowded with de-faced and de-named black and brown bodies, images of indignity such as precarious living conditions and police abuse, as well as death and mourning. A common photographic style found in newspapers is that of a bird's-eye view – *shots* taken 'from above', which create a link to National Geographic's style of capturing 'wild life' that is present before our eyes yet too dangerous to approach closely.

Importantly, these relationships are manifestations of power structures: the gaze of the photographer/film-maker directed at their subject, the counter gaze of the subject towards the photographer and the spectator of the image. There are also the gaze of the editors in charge of selecting the right image for publishing and, importantly, the gaze of the researcher while collecting and analysing these very images. Therefore, naming an event a refugee crisis is not only a matter of language, but also that of knowledge production and construction of specific realities. In relation to that, Rose (2016) argues that images offer worldviews – they are not innocent carriers of a message to the world, rather, they give us interpretations of the world that are carried out in very particular ways. In order to explore these worldviews, and as this chapter will further illustrate, I turn to study what I call the crisis of images in Swedish newspaper dailies *Dagens Nyheter* (DN) and *Svenska Dagbladet* (SvD). What I refer to as the crisis of images is embedded in the simplified, shock and threat inducing portrayal of the very complex issues of flight, whereby people on the move are often forced to embody stereotypical and violent imageries.

This chapter critically examines front-page photography in Swedish newspapers and aims to answer the question: How is refugeeness constructed as a part of the refugee crisis 2015–2016 in Swedish daily newspapers *Dagens Nyheter* and *Svenska Dagbladet*? In particular, I bring forward the knowledge of the visual construction of the refugee bodies and refugees' positioning in relation to the Swedish nation state. Finally, I go beyond the research fixation on the refugee as the only agent in the crisis discourses and point to the other actors playing a role in how we understand the question of flight. In the coming paragraphs I present the overview of literature that informs the present chapter.

**Visual construction of refugeeness**

Research investigating the matter of visual representation and social construction of the meaning of refugeeness commonly deals with aspects of the physical appearance of refugee bodies in photography and the environment in which they are caught – the interest being that of the intersecting issues of gender, racialization and class (Wright, 2002; Johnson, 2011; on class and economic capital, see chapter 2). Moreover, another common research interest is that of refugee bodies and the visual composition of numbers – are people who are fleeing captured as individuals, small and medium groups or as a mass exodus of people? And what kind of knowledge do these different compositions disseminate to the public (Wright, 2002; Bleiker et al., 2013; Zhang and Hellmueller, 2017; Jovičić, 2018)? In line with one important theme of this book – the construction of refugeeness and refugee crisis in the context of Nordic welfare states – I am guided by the major concerns of the aforementioned research, yet I also shift away from the fixation on the refugee body and consider other actors that play a role in the visual construction of flight in the case of Sweden (on media discourse about refugees, see chapter 7).

The visual construction of refugeeness most commonly depends on the technologies of othering, which commonly perpetuate ideas of difference and elicit discussions on deservingness and genuineness (Bhabha, 1983). Research consistently points to a clear dualism in the visual portrayal of flight and refugees – on the one hand the victimized refugee body in need of protection, on the other hand the welfare and security threat – a crisis posed to the nation state (Malkki, 1995; Wright, 2002; Mannik, 2012; Bleiker et al., 2013; Jovičić, 2018). Aforementioned discussions are imbedded in the Western understanding of who is a 'genuine' refugee and how refugees are imagined and represented. Visual representation, therefore, has important implications for the public perception of refugees, one's willingness to reflect and act on this highly politicized issue, and, most importantly, for the experiences of the people fleeing. In an intriguing study of a private photography collection made by Estonian refugees fleeing the Red Army via Sweden, Mannik (2012) juxtaposes the intimate and the private in the visual capture of refugeehood made by people fleeing with de-individualized, de-historicized, and public mainstream portrayals. Whereas the private photography accounts for 'personal expression and political perspectives, as well as myriad other human attributes' (p. 263), the public depictions leave us with de-faced masses of bodies shot from distance, emphasizing the positionality of 'us' here gazing in safety and 'them' out there in precarity.

Relatedly, Johnson (2011) argues that since the Cold War the refugee has been racialized, feminized and victimized. The dominant depiction has changed from that of white-European refugees to those of refugees racialized as non-white and localized as South from Europe; from the strong political figure – a man being politically prosecuted, to that of a depoliticized victim – often co-opted in the imagery of women holding children. The victimization frame is found to work better in eliciting empathy, since negative emotions such as sadness or despair elicit more compassion (Small and Verocci, 2009). As Zhang and Hellmueller (2017, p. 502) note, these frames are 'more effective to generate viewers' sympathy and thus emotionally engage viewers in the distant suffering.' However, I argue that the issue at stake is more complex than this and I align with Susan Sontag and her thoughts about compassion fatigue – the idea that the more exposed we are to the images of indignity and suffering, the more normalized it becomes until we cannot feel anything anymore. Therefore, images have the power to 'anesthetize' (Sontag, 2008).

In the context of the visual construction of refugeeness, Johnson argues that 'Victimisation removes political agency from the figure of the refugee establishing a condition of political voicelessness' (2011, p. 1028). Portrait photography and depictions of smaller groups of people are frequently used to attain the above-mentioned victimization frame, especially in the iconic shots of the so-called 'Madonna and Child', whereby women and children are the most common visual depiction of refugees as victims (Wright, 2002; Johnson, 2011). On the other hand, recent research findings show that, across different geographical contexts, people fleeing are overall most commonly constructed as medium to large groups of de-faced and de-named bodies threatening to destabilize the nation state (Mannik, 2012; Bleiker et al., 2013; Zhang and Hellmueller, 2017; Jovičić, 2018). Hence, the visual construction of refugeeness has historically been changing (Wright, 2002; Johnson, 2011). Despite the complex histories and current intersectional struggles of refugees in Europe, very specific imageries, such as those of either voiceless victims or threats to national security, seem to persist into the present.

Additionally, the abundance of visual portrayals of people fleeing is a process that can have serious implications for lives of refugees. For example, Slovic et al. (2017) argue that the iconic image of Alan Kurdi's lifeless body (see also chapter 4) had an impact in terms of the relative popularity of search terms such as 'refugees' or 'Syria', as well as the spike in terms of donations to the Swedish Red Cross campaign supporting Syrian refugees in Sweden. However, the major finding of their study is that this impact was short-lived or, as they write: 'Our search data show that the world was basically asleep as the body count in Syria rose steadily into the hundreds of thousands' (p. 641). In addition to the finding of the short-livedness of empathetic reactions to tragic images of lifeless refugee bodies, what persists is the violence, and not only in the sense of depicting the current condition of flight but in visually reproducing the power divisions imposed by deadly border regimes in Europe. Whereas the images of refugee suffering in precariousness present and document the subjective violence that is lived through (and mediated for the rest of the world), this visual mass mediation simultaneously normalizes this violence (Sontag, 2003). In her work *Regarding the Pain of Others*, Sontag (p. 72) writes:

> The exhibition in photographs of cruelties inflicted on those with darker complexions in exotic countries continues this offering, oblivious to the considerations that deter such displays of our own victims of violence; for the other, even when not an enemy, is regarded only as someone to be seen, not someone (like us) who also sees.

In the shadow of mass visualizations of direct, bodily violence lies hidden the symbolic violence (Bourdieu, 1991; Žižek, 2009) embedded in the images of the refugee crisis that construct boundaries between 'us' and 'them' (Richardson, 2015). Images depicting the crisis can further (re) produce harm for people fleeing if they do not intend to challenge the symbolic and systemic violence inherent in the current border regimes. With this in mind I move to elaborate on the method and findings of the current study.

**Critical visual analysis**

For this chapter, I collected and analysed front-page photography from two of the largest national newspapers in Sweden – *Dagens Nyheter* and *Svenska Dagbladet* – with an average daily circulation around 260,000 and 170,000 copies in 2015–2016, respectively (Statista, 2019). Only front-page photographs were selected for analysis, since the most pressing socio-political topics commonly find their way there. Final selection criteria were gathering images relating to national or international topics concerning asylum seekers and refugees. Photographs were gathered from the digitized media archive located in the National Library of Sweden in Stockholm. The archive offers access to digitized versions of most Swedish newspapers. All daily issues starting 1 April 2015 to 30 April 2016 were manually browsed. The sample

# Images of crisis and the crisis of images

consists of all identified images: there were 70 in *Dagens Nyheter* and 83 in *Svenska Dagbladet* – a total of 153 images. The period April 2015 to April 2016 was chosen because it marks the height of the refugee crisis – most asylum applications were received between August and December 2015 (Migrationsverket, 2016). Additionally, most front-page images covering the crisis were recorded in the period August 2015–February 2016. This selection of images is not exhaustive in either of the newspapers; other images were present as a part of the full newspaper content. Moreover, this is not a direct or comprehensive comparison of the two outlets – it should rather be seen as a critical visual analysis of the refugee crisis in two dailies available to a sizeable proportion of Swedish readers.

In this chapter, I have translated and considered the immediate headlines and captions accompanying the front-page newspaper photography. Focus here, however, is on the analysis of photography; therefore the visual is taken as the main point of analysis, and coding and reflections are derived from the image itself. I make use of a more deductive approach to content analysis – I first coded the images freely, made descriptive notes along the way, double checked if any two codes were referring to a similar visual cue and whether they could be merged into one broader code. Moreover, I counted the frequency of all the codes, marked and selected the most common ones while keeping in mind the overarching research question and the theoretical and empirical framework (Rose, 2016, p. 96) within which I work. Finally, the most frequent codes were closely examined and then grouped under four visual frames – these being the victimization, securitization, reception and humanization frames. A total of 111 images comprise the four frames identified here. This was a challenging task, as visual frames tend to overlap (Bleiker et al., 2013). For example, victimization and securitization frames can be found in the same photograph at times. These difficulties are acknowledged and further discussed in the findings section. Given the critical approach that I follow in my analysis, and since the premise of my approach is that the images on hand are part of a process whereby refugees experience violence and exclusion, I make the deliberate choice of not reproducing them in my analysis. These images are published in mainstream newspapers and are digitally archived, which makes them readily available for those interested in further analysis or who merely wish to satisfy their curiosity.

## The visual construction of flight

In this section, I present the findings with the aim of quantifying the dominant depictions as well as qualitatively illustrating the complexities of the visual construction of flight in Swedish dailies. The visual analysis resulted in four dominant visual frames: securitization – refugee bodies amassed and posing threats to destabilize sovereignty of the 'nation state' (see also chapter 3); victimization – refugee bodies as voiceless victims caught in suffering; humanization – private portraits of people fleeing depicted as complex individuals and active political subjects; and reception – images of refugees being welcomed and living in Sweden. These frames were established in a deductive manner – they arose from the images studied, yet they are partly in line with other research on the framing of the refugee crisis and constructing refugeeness in newspaper media (Bleiker et al., 2013; Parker, 2015; Greussing and Boomgaarden, 2017; Zheng and Hallmueller, 2017; Abdelhady, 2019).

The visual content analysis of the photographs supports previous research in that refugee bodies are the main motive of the visual construction of flight, and the representation is dominantly that of the refugee as a victim (in 43.2 per cent of the images), or as a security threat to the nation state (in 25.3 per cent of the images). The victimhood frame mainly captures children, or parents holding children in distress, often just after arriving to the European shores. The depictions of refugees as a security threat comes through images of large groups of unidentifiable people – the mass exodus (mostly men) and that of the pairing of refugee bodies with those of police and confinement symbols. The reception frame accounts for 18.9 per cent of depictions, whereas the humanization frame accounts for 12.6 per cent of the images (see Table 1).

In terms of locating images in relation to the Swedish nation state, there is a pattern of difference in depiction of events inside and outside of Sweden's national borders. A total of 47 per cent of images depict events taking place outside of the Swedish national borders, whereas 53 per cent depict people and events relating to the refugee crisis positioned inside Sweden. Moreover, the victimization and criminalization frames are mainly positioned outside the Swedish nation state whereas reception and humanization frames are most commonly situated inside Sweden. Beyond the sheer numbers, it is important to examine the visual composition of newspaper photographs and the kinds of knowledge they construct and reproduce. I

Table 1 Overview of the distribution of images across four visual frames

|  | Victimization | Securitization | Reception | Humanization |
| --- | --- | --- | --- | --- |
| *Dagens Nyheter* | 24 | 23 | 6 | 4 |
| *Svenska Dagbladet* | 24 | 15 | 15 | 10 |
| Total | 48 | 28 | 21 | 14 |
| Per cent | 43.2 | 25.3 | 18.9 | 12.6 |

proceed with examples of newspaper photography to illustrate ways in which flight and people fleeing were constructed in Swedish dailies.

Victimization frame

The victimization frame counts over 40 per cent of photographic depictions of refugees in Swedish newspapers. Images belonging to this frame usually capture individuals and small groups of people. Importantly, children are the overall most common depiction in the visual representation of a refugee crisis – they appear in a total of 33 per cent or fifty images. They are the common denominator of victimhood, since the visual compositions of mothers holding children, or the Madonna and Child, are regarded as iconic representations of refugees as victims (Wright, 2002; Johnson, 2011). Terence Wright writes about the Christian iconographic symbolism behind these compositions, as well as the imagery behind children holding food, or lack thereof, as a way to portray poverty and victimhood (Wright, 2002, pp. 57–58). In line with this is Image 1 (DN), dating back to 11 September 2015, in which a woman is placed at the centre of the image while holding a toddler who is grabbing a bread bun tightly while eating it. The mother looks ahead, away from the camera, and so does the child. In the background to the left we see another toddler holding food. These findings are also in line with research on victimization and feminization of refugees (Johnson, 2011), and present a complex issue whereby the depiction of refugees has been linked to stereotypical understandings of women and children as weak and in need of protection. Sixteen per cent of the victimization frame, however, accounts for the depiction of what I call the Male Madonna – men holding children (Palczewski, 2005; Jovičić, 2018). Image 2 (SvD), a photograph from 23 August 2015, depicts a man crying while holding his daughter on his right and embracing his son on his left. He stands strong, dominating the centre of the image as he protects them. The girl is in visible distress, crying, her small arm wrapped around his neck, and she is holding the top of her dad's life-vest. Her other arm lies on top of her yellow life-vest, close to her heart. The boy is captured from the side, his face barely visible. This image was taken just as they reached the shore on Lesvos by boat coming from the Turkish coast. These depictions still aim to elicit compassion through victimhood, yet there is a gendering aspect to them. The composition of men holding children is more readily linked to an active state – holding children high up in sign of celebration for reaching European shores, boarding children onto trains, outdoors walking, whereas women are more commonly captured holding children while sitting, hugging, kissing or playing with them. Therefore, the iconic meaning imbedded in the picture of Madonna and the child and its male counterpart reproduce stereotypical gendered portrayals of female refugees as passive, weak and voiceless, and of male refugees as active, strong and protective. On the other hand, it could also be argued that the Male Madonna, who shows emotions and protects his children, resists victimization, or at least complicates the stereotype of (male) refugees as posing danger, as I describe later.

One of the most striking constructions of refugees as victims in the Swedish public eye is therefore reduced to that of a helpless child in need of protection. In line with Johnson's (2011) work on how the refugee has been feminized and made into a passive victim in need of protection, in the Swedish case we also see an infantilization of the refugee. Sweden is understood as a country that takes the rights of children seriously and in 2015 a large number, exactly 35,369, of unaccompanied migrant children were registered by the Migration Agency in Sweden. This is the highest reception number across the EU in relation to the country's population. The recurrence of images of children is therefore understandable, but it also has important consequences for public understandings of the refugee.

Furthermore, a common depiction of refugees in the Swedish press is that of refugees queuing, living precariously such as sleeping rough, waiting in queues or crowds for food and transport, being rescued at sea, and reaching European shores terrified and exhausted. Take an example of Image 3 (DN), dating from 9 August 2015, where three women fleeing were photographed during a boat recue. This is an unusual front-page for Swedish newspapers; there is very little text and most of the page is covered by the photograph of a sea rescue where refugee bodies are stacked up on a small boat, only their faces sticking out of their life-vests. Three women are visible at the front centre of the image, their faces blank in shock, their bodies exposed to the dangers of the open sea. Behind them a large boat on which it is written 'Migrant Offshore Aid Station', the title accompanying the photograph reads 'SAVED'. Another related visual symbol of victimhood is that of ragged or no clothes covering bodies of people fleeing, as is the linking of refugee bodies with that of outdoors, public spaces – walking along train tracks and fields, waiting at the border (Wright, 2002; Jovičić, 2018). These images are of great concern when considering individual's right to privacy and dignified representation.

Securitization frame

A total of thirty-three images (25 per cent) count towards the securitization frame of representation. With this in mind, I approach the issue of securitization on two levels, by looking at the pairing of refugee bodies with those of the police and other confinement symbols, and by commenting on the de-historicized and de-individualized depictions of masses of people threatening the nation state. Just as with the victimization frame, the securitization of the refugee bodies is most commonly done by capturing images of people fleeing outdoors in the fields and in public spaces such as train

# Images of crisis and the crisis of images

stations and ports. Most images belonging to this frame were shot outside of Sweden, especially during 2015, whereas after the closure of the Swedish-Danish border and the asylum policy restrictions that followed (see also chapters 5 and 12 in this volume), securitization became the dominant frame inside Swedish national borders too. The difference to the victimization frame is that the refugees are now amassed, de-individualized and de-historicised (Mannik, 2012).

Depictions of medium and large groups of people, as well as the stereotypical portrayal of the mass exodus of people, dominate this frame (Wright, 2002). The mass exodus of people is a frame which captures refugees as stacked up, endless, de-individualized bodies, usually outdoors (Wrights, 2002). Mass exodus is a gendered and racialized portrayal of refugees since it is most commonly embodied by black and brown bodies of men. Larger groups of men dominate the photographs, especially in *Dagens Nyheter* – their bodies are often coupled with police cordons and border officials. Such is Image 4 (SvD), dated 27 February 2016, depicting a long queue of people, visible as dark silhouettes of men standing against the sunset with their faces unidentifiable. The caption reads 'Ninety per cent of refugees that came to the EU in 2015 are believed to have been in contact with criminals on their way', whereas the title under the image reads 'Smuggling – a growing industry'. This visual pairing of refugee bodies with captions on criminality are in line with previous research showing that refugees are illegalized at the border and visually constructed as a threat to sovereignty and security of the nation state. This visual portrayal, therefore, hardly challenges the reasons *why* smuggling of refugees is a growing business or exists in the first place (see also chapters 1 and 2).

Moreover, refugees are often depicted at border crossing sites, surrounded by symbols of confinement such as cordons of police and barbed wire. This is in line with previous research on the securitization of flight. Bleiker et al. (2013, p. 408) write that 'images that show small groups of asylum seekers next to barbed wired fences or flanked by uniformed border control personnel already promote different and potentially less empathy-generating themes: those linked to illegality, invasion and potential guilt.' Image 5 (DN), dating back to 25 October 2015, depicts a large group of refugees at the Slovenian border stacked up behind a plastic tape which reads 'STOP POLICE' (*Stop Policija*). At the front right of the image is a police officer shown from the back, with special protective equipment. He overlooks the group of people fleeing in front of him, their bodies countless, stretching across the rest of the image. In the very back we see smoke rising up above their bodies to the sky, most probably from the tear gas launched at them. In the centre of the image a man holding a toddler up in the air visibly crying while the mother reaches out to help and comfort; a young child next to them squats on the ground, looking directly into the camera. The title reads 'Thousands takes new road north'.

This photograph is an example of the impossibility for every single image to be assigned to only one category or frame. Here we have the victimization frame depicting families with children exposed to police violence, while at the same time we can understand this picture as the end of the victimization frame altogether and criminalization of all refugee bodies, including children and families. These dynamics in turn link to what De Genova (2013, p. 1181) calls the 'Border Spectacle' – 'a spectacle of enforcement at "the" border, whereby the spectre of migrant "illegality" is rendered spectacularly visible.' De Genova cites Debord in saying that the spectacle is much more than the moment in which the image is captured in that 'The spectacle is not a collection of images; rather, it is a social relationship between people that is mediated by images' (Debord 1995, p. 12 in De Genova 2013). Thus, the refugee body captured against police cordons, barbed wire and other symbols of confinement is being criminalized, securitized and positioned mostly outside of the Swedish nation state in the newspaper photography in the period from August to the end of October 2015.

By mid-November 2015, the securitization frame crosses the border to Sweden when images begin to depict police and train security officers checking IDs and setting up metal fences inside the train stations. These images therefore follow the political U-turn in Sweden from looking at refugees as a humanitarian issue and responsibility (through victimization *and* humanization) to that of refugee bodies as illegalized masses posing a threat to the law and order of the Swedish nation state (Bleiker et al., 2013). The shift, from the intimate portrayals of people suffering, close up and identifiable, to that of 'potential criminals' is a stark one, since it brings the crisis inside the Swedish public eye by creating a security panic through the intense visual presence of police and policing in action. This is the same period in which the Swedish government, led by the Social Democrats/Green alliance, called for breathing space, *andrum* in Swedish (see also chapters 3 and 7 in this volume), and limited taking in refugees to that of the EU minimum (Sager and Öberg, 2017, p. 3). In line with Susan Sontag (2008), the evidence here shows that images do not create but rather support the dominant moral position – photography follows the naming of the event.

Furthermore, Bhambra (2017) urges us to reconsider the positionality of the crisis. In contrast to the securitization and criminalization discourses served by politicians and the media in Europe urging us that a crisis is 'facing Europe', it is the people fleeing who are actually facing crisis, given the violence and devastation of their current condition (p. 395). These arguments can be linked to the fact that, as seen in this Swedish newspaper photography, the majority of images portraying amassed groups of people fleeing, coupled with police and border officials, can be located at the physical edges of the EU – such as the Greek Islands, Lampedusa and the Spanish enclaves of Ceuta and Melilla, or at the physical borders of the nation state: in the case of Sweden most images are from Öresund Bridge, connecting mainland Denmark with that of Sweden, where the contested border closure happened (Barker, 2018). The securitization visual frame is therefore constructed against the boundaries of the Swedish nation state.

Reception frame

The reception frame counts twenty-one images (18.9 per cent): it is best illustrated though images of welcome culture and refugees being integrated in Sweden (see also chapter 9) and the construction of whiteness against the refugees' bodies. In particular, Swedish whiteness as part of the construction of the crisis stands out through the depictions of Swedes as welcoming, such as in Image 6 from SvD, dated 7 September 2015. The image reads 'Gathering for the refugees'. In the photograph, a smaller group of white, blond Swedes at *Medborgarplatsen* in central Stockholm gather at a large public gathering for welcoming refugees to Sweden. At the centre of the image is a young girl – eight years old – identified by her name and holding a sign that reads 'Everybody is Welcome' (*Alla är välkomna*). The sign is written in child-like writing and has a heart drawn on it. Left from her is a woman in a red raincoat whose gaze follows the girl holding the banner – she smiles at her in a proud, parent-like way. On the one hand, this image evokes warm feelings about friendly and welcoming Swedes, who stand in solidarity with refugees. In relation to the other numerous depictions of children as vulnerable victims exposed to indignity, the Swedish child is depicted as a strong and active member of society. Thus, photography capturing the reception of refugees constructs Swedes as helpful, welcoming, friendly and as majority white.

In line with Johnson (2011), people fleeing are commonly racialized as non-white, and this is often done in depicting their bodies against those of volunteers and other locals (Swedes), police and border patrols and teachers – who, in this sample of images, are predominantly racialized as white. The refugee crisis, it is argued, commences with the 'unsightly accumulation of dead black and brown bodies' after the tragic event of the 19 April 2015 in the Mediterranean Sea, when about 850 people lost their lives trying to reach Europe (De Genova, 2018, p. 1). The first images from the period studied are the photographs depicting the Lampedusa tragedy, which visually marked the onset of the refugee crisis in the Swedish dailies. Visual representations of this tragic event and the period immediately after are dominated by images of boats, sea and black bodies exposed to indignity (see also De Genova, 2017). Consequently, De Genova (2017, p. 2) puts forward the term 'racial crisis' when arguing that, in the wake of the European outer borders becoming mass graves for predominantly black and brown bodies, the 'racial fact of this deadly European border regime is seldom acknowledged, because it immediately confronts us with the cruel (post)coloniality of the "new" Europe'. Given that the majority of the people who are visualized as central subjects of the crisis are brown and black bodies publicly exposed, and that refugees account for the majority of these depictions, when talking about the racial crisis we need to address and deconstruct whiteness as a visual imagery in Swedish newspapers.

As an example, I refer to Image 7, dated 22 January 2016 (SvD), and Image 8 from 14 February 2016 (SvD). Both photographs capture introductory classes – in this case Swedish for Immigrants (SFI) and sex education (*samlevnadsundervisning*). The titles read 'Newcomers Receive Sex Education' and 'Swedish for Newcomers Attracts More Teachers'. Both photographs have similar compositions – they capture the white body of the Swedish teacher standing in front of the whiteboard and pointing at it. Whereas the teachers are visibly identifiable, their bodies are also constructed against the bodies of refugee-students, in this case black and brown bodies captured from behind, unidentifiable. The teachers are portrayed as active agents – physically they are the tallest point in the images, captured while working, whereas the refugees are depicted as passive and anonymous recipients of knowledge, being integrated.

There is a kind of fixation in research, just as there is in the media, to gaze at and research the refugee body as the central place of knowledge extraction on the matter. In this process, we tend to leave behind a sizeable amount of critical knowledge when we fail to talk about whiteness. As Werner et al. (2014, p. 43) writes, 'whiteness is rendered invisible, all while attention is focused on non-whiteness.' Whereas intensifying violence and death has been inflicted on the bodies of refugees, it is those same bodies that are being criminalized and held responsible for the refugee crisis that has come upon Europe (Bhambra, 2017). What De Genova calls the racial crisis might seldom be written about, yet it is directly co-opted in the newspaper photography in question: black and brown bodies suffer and threaten the nation state while white bodies educate and defend the nation state. As seen here, even some visual attempts to humanize and welcome refugees end up reproducing whiteness and the discourses of refugee bodies posing a threat to the nation state.

Humanization frame

The smallest share – fourteen images or about 23 per cent – counts towards the humanization frame. Inside Sweden, the newspaper photography rarely, and only late during the sample period, depicts refugees as large masses of de-individualized people. Rather, within this frame, refugees are depicted as individuals or small groups set in private spaces such as rooms inside accommodation centres or public spaces such as cafes, classrooms or nurseries. This finding can be illustrated by pointing to the portrait photography depictions. As an example, let us take Image 9 (SvD), an intimate family portrait dated 25 April 2015, which shows a mother to the left, father to the right and their daughter embraced by both of them in the middle, caught in the moment of playing. The adults are looking at the camera, calmly with a glimpse of a smile, no extreme emotions on either end. Their full names are mentioned, the title reads 'Flight Over the Sea of Death' and emphasizes the violence of the border regimes that is inflicted on refugees trying to reach safety, yet without the sensational imagery of indignity and suffering.

Another depiction of humanization is through hetero-normative portraits of family and the home building in Sweden. These portrayals can also be understood as attempts to reimagine Swedishness through that of the newcomer Other. Image 10 (SvD), dated 12 September 2015, captures a father and two children standing in front of a typical Swedish yellow cabin house, a welcome sign hanging on the wall behind them. They are all smiling directly into the camera. The title reads 'Sweden Was the Goal'. Another image, from 19 September 2015, depicts the playful tickling of a boy by his mother inside an accommodation centre. In the background are stacked up IKEA-like metal beds and mattresses with one matress placed on the ground just behind them. These visual representations of refugees through the symbolism of home and homecoming – and protection and care – are in line with what has been written on the construction of Swedish exceptionalism, especially in the context of the Swedish welfare state (Barker, 2012; Barker, 2018). The idea of a Swedish state-promised sense of social security and belonging (*trygghet*) is co-opted in images of refugees, yet this finding cannot be traced in the political and social reality of the refugee condition in Sweden at this time. Other than the initial generosity concerning the number of people that the Swedish state took in, the period from November 2015 has been dominated by restrictions and deterrence, as well as an increased number of detentions and expulsions of asylum seekers (Sager and Öberg, 2017). We can therefore conclude that the humanization frame did not reflect the political reality concerning asylum protection in Sweden. One could argue that the humanizing images of refugees in Sweden attempt to balance the harsh reality of a mass scale securitization of refugee bodies during the refugee crisis, especially since the border closure with Denmark and the increased policing of the borders.

## Conclusion

In this chapter, I have used visual content analysis to critically examine the portrayal of flight and people fleeing, as found in the Swedish daily newspapers. Firstly, the empirical evidence gathered points to the prevalence of four visual frames: victimization, securitization, reception and humanization of refugees. In line with previous research on representation of flight in newspapers, refugees are most commonly visually depicted either as vulnerable victims or as posing security threats to the Swedish nation state (Malkki, 1995; Wright, 2002; Mannik, 2012; Bleiker et al., 2013; Jovičić, 2018). Additionally, there was a solid attempt to humanize refugees through visual compositions such as portrait photography of named individuals and small groups, hetero-normative families and home-building. This finding demonstrates the process through which whiteness disappears or renders itself invisible in most other visual frames, and instead becomes more visible in the instances of positive engagement such as welcoming culture, teaching language and integrating the Other into Sweden.

Secondly, this study shows a specific pattern of representation, whereby a symbolic visual boundary is constructed in relation to the refugee crisis inside and outside Sweden. The crisis is mainly represented through victimization and securitization frames outside Sweden and at the Swedish borders, whereas reception and humanizing the refugees is constructed as dominantly taking place inside Sweden. From the images, we learn that the destabilizing chaos of the crisis, as well as the indignity and suffering of refugees, is constructed as mainly outside of the Swedish nation state, whereas reception and attempts to humanize the refugee bodies happen from within.

Finally, in terms of the timeline of the crisis, visual frames are found to be shifting and different representations are re-actualized at different points in time (Greussing and Boomgaarden, 2017, p. 1759). This is in line with recent research findings in which newspaper framing of the refugee crisis provided for a rather diffused representation, meaning that the identified frames would come and go throughout the time period studied (Abdelhady, 2019). When looking at the collection of photographs as a whole, one starts to understand that contradiction and ambivalence are the building blocks of the visual construction of the crisis (Abdelhady, 2019). In the case of Swedish newspaper photography, this is evident in the way visual frames are structured over time – starting with that of the victimization in the first months of the crisis, moving on to the securitization in the months of November 2015 and January 2016, with the gradual return of the victimization frame in the months in between. The humanization frame, on the other hand, is dispersed throughout the time studied but is most frequently present alongside securitization framing.

In conclusion, deconstructing visually fabricated realities is important, since images are not neutral or unfiltered reflections of specific events. As shown in this chapter, on the one hand, they follow the dominant political discourses and the naming of the events, whereas on the other hand they have the power to resist, disrupt and construct new realities through knowledge dissemination on a mass scale.

## References

Abdelhady, D. (2019). 'Framing the Syrian Refugee: Divergent Discourses in Three National Contexts', in Menjivar, C., Ruiz, M. and Ness, E. (eds.) *The Oxford Handbook of Migration Crises*, Oxford: Oxford University Press, pp. 635–656.

Barker, V. (2012). Nordic Exceptionalism Revisited: Explaining the Paradox of a Janus Faced Penal Regime. *Theoretical Criminology*, 17(1), pp. 5–25.

Barker, V. (2018). *Nordic Nationalism and Penal Order: Walling the Welfare State*. London and New York: Routledge.

Bhabha, H. K. (1983). The Other Question ... *Screen*, 24(6), pp. 18–36.

Bhambra, G. K. (2017). The Current Crisis of Europe: Refugees, Colonialism, and the Limits of Cosmopolitanism. *European Law Journal*, 23(5), pp. 395–405.

Bleiker, R., Campbell, D., Hutchison, E., and Nicholson, X. (2013). The Visual Dehumanisation of Refugees. *Australian Journal of Political Science*, 48(4), pp. 398–416.

Bourdieu, P. (1991). *Language and Symbolic Power*. Cambridge: Polity Press.

Debord, G. (1995) *The Society of the Spectacle*. New York: Zone, in De Genova, N. (2013).

De Genova, N. (2013). Spectacles of Migrant 'Illegality': The Scene of Exclusion, the Obscene of Inclusion. *Ethnic and Racial Studies*, 36(7), pp. 1180–1198.

De Genova, N. (ed.) (2017). *The Borders of 'Europe': Autonomy of Migration, Tactics of Bordering*. Durham: Duke University Press.

De Genova, N. (2018). The 'Migrant Crisis' as Racial Crisis: Do Black Lives Matter in Europe? *Ethnic and Racial Studies*, 41(10), pp. 1765–1782.

Greussing, E., and Boomgaarden, H. G. (2017). Shifting the Refugee Narrative? An Automated Frame Analysis of Europe's 2015 Refugee Crisis. *Journal of Ethnic and Migration Studies*, 43(11), pp. 1749–1774.

Jovičić, J. (2018) 'Visual Constructions of "Refugeeness" and Portrayal of Flight in German Newspapers', in Hamburger, A., Hancheva, C., Özcürümez, S., Scher, C. Stankovic, B. and Tutnjevic, S. (eds.) *Forced Migration and Social Trauma: Interdisciplinary Perspectives from Psychoanalysis, Psychology, Sociology and Politics*, New York: Routledge.

Johnson, H. L. (2011). Click to Donate: Visual Images, Constructing Victims and Imagining the Female Refugee. *Third World Quarterly*, 32(6), pp. 1015–1037.

Malkki, L. H. (1995). Refugees and Exile: From 'Refugee Studies' to the National Order of Things. *Annual Review of Anthropology*, 24, pp. 495–523.

Mannik, L. (2012). Public and Private Photographs of Refugees: The Problem of Representation. *Visual Studies*, 27(3), pp. 262–276.

Migrationsverket (2016). Statistics reports on asylum. Link: www.migrationsverket.se/English/About-the-Migration Agency/Statistics/Asylum.html. Last accessed 5 December 2019.

Palczewski, C. H. (2005). The Male Madonna and the Feminine Uncle Sam: Visual Argument, Icons, and Ideographs in 1909 Anti-Woman Suffrage Postcards. *Quarterly Journal of Speech*, 91(4), 365–394.

Parker, S. (2015). 'Unwanted Invaders': The Representation of Refugees and Asylum Seekers in the UK and Australian Print Media. *Myth and Nation*, 23, pp. 1–21.

Richardson, C. (2015). '"On Devrait Tout Détruire": Photography, Habitus, and Symbolic Violence in Clichy-sous-Bois and Regent Park', in Mannik, L. and McGarry, K. (eds.), *Reclaiming Canadian Bodies: Visual Media and Representation*, Waterloo: Wilfrid Laurier University Press.

Rose, G. (2016). *Visual Methodologies: An Introduction to Researching with Visual Materials* (4th ed.). London: SAGE.

Sager, M. and Öberg, K. (2017). 'Articulations of Deportability: Changing Migration Policies in Sweden 2015–2016', *Refugee Review*, 3, pp. 2–14.

Slovic, P., Västfjäll, D., Erlandsson, A., and Gregory, R. (2017). Iconic Photographs and the Ebb and Flow of Empathic Response to Humanitarian Disasters. *Proceedings of the National Academy of Sciences of the United States of America*, 14(4) pp. 640–644.

Small, D. A. and N. M. Verrochi (2009). The Face of Need: Facial Emotion Expression on Charity Advertisements, *Journal of Marketing Research*, 46(6), pp. 777–787.

Sontag, S. (2003). *Regarding the Pain of Others*. New York: Picador.

Sontag, S. (2008) *On Photography*. London: Penguin.

Statista (2019). Newspaper Circulation in Sweden. Link: www.statista.com/statistics/764274/ranking-of-local-newspaper-companiesin-sweden-by-circulation/. Last accessed 5 December 2019.

Werner, J., Arvidsson, K., Werner, J., and Björk, T. (2014). *Blond och blåögd: Vithet, svenskhet och visuell kultur* (Blond and Blue-Eyed: Whiteness, Swedishness, and Visual Culture). Gothenburg: Göteborgs Konstmuseum.

Wright, T. (2002). Moving Images: The Media Representation of Refugees. *Visual Studies*, 17(1), pp. 53–66.

Zhang, X., and Hellmueller, L. (2017). Visual Framing of the European Refugee Crisis in *Der Spiegel* and *CNN International*: Global Journalism in News Photographs. *International Communication Gazette*, 79(5), pp. 483–510.

Žižek, S. (2009). *Violence: Six Sideways Reflections*. London: Profile Books.

### Offline media

Image 1 *Dagens Nyheter*, Issue from 11 September 2015. Free Access at: Media Archive of the National Library of Sweden, Stockholm.

Image 2 *Svenska Dagbladet*, Issue from 23 August 2015. Free Access at: Media Archive of the National Library of Sweden, Stockholm.

Image 3 *Dagens Nyheter*, Issue from 9 August 2015. Free Access at: Media Archive of the National Library of Sweden, Stockholm.

Image 4 *Svenska Dagbladet*, Issue from 27 February 2016. Free Access at: Media Archive of the National Library of Sweden, Stockholm.

Image 5 *Dagens Nyheter*, Issue from 25 October. 2015 Free Access at: Media Archive of the National Library of Sweden, Stockholm.

Image 6 *Svenska Dagbladet*, Issue from 7 September 2015 Free Access at: Media Archive of the National Library of Sweden, Stockholm.

Image 7 *Svenska Dagbladet*, Issue from 22 2016 January Free Access at: Media Archive of the National Library of Sweden, Stockholm.

Images of crisis and the crisis of images 121

Image 8 *Svenska Dagbladet*, Issue from 14 February 2016. Free Access at: Media Archive of the National Library of Sweden, Stockholm.

Image 9 *Svenska Dagbladet*, Issue from 25 of April 2015. Free Access at: Media Archive of the National Library of Sweden, Stockholm.

Image 10 *Svenska Dagbladet*, Issue from 12 September 2015. Free Access at: Media Archive of the National Library of Sweden, Stockholm.

# 7  Dalia Abdelhady

# Media constructions of the refugee crisis in Sweden: institutions and the challenges of refugee governance

In an article entitled 'The Death of the Most Generous Nation on Earth', American journalist James Traub (2016) claims that 'The vast migration of desperate souls from Syria, Iraq, and elsewhere has posed a moral test the likes of which Europe has not faced since the Nazis forced millions from their homes in search of refuge. Europe has failed that test.' Sweden stands out as an exception in Traub's analysis due to the country's generous refugee reception policies. These policies, however, are bound to fail, and Traub argues that Sweden has to pay 'for its unshared idealism'.

That Sweden had a generous refugee policy (see also chapter 5) is a component of Swedish identity, both as viewed by most Swedes themselves and as viewed by others, despite the variety of academic arguments challenging that image.[1] To name a few examples: researchers have documented the negative experiences of asylum seekers awaiting a decision (Brekke, 2004); the inhumane conditions at detention centres (Khosravi, 2009); the process of credibility assessment that assumes fraudulence on part of asylum seekers (Noll, 2005); the institutionalised power imbalance between asylum claimants and the authorities that challenge these claims in the legal process (Joormann, 2019; see also chapter 2); and the inhumane views of the Other that shape different levels of the migration bureaucracy (Barker, 2012; Schoultz, 2013; see also chapter 9). It is, therefore, logical to wonder how Sweden's image as generous, humane and righteous has persisted despite such evidence. Additionally, given the drastic shifts in refugee policies following the summer of 2015 (see chapter 3), and if we accept Traub's characterisation of 'unshared idealism' as the basis for such shifts, tracing the transformation of such an idealism helps our understanding of Swedish cultural and political climate and the position of refugees within it. Importantly, and to use the arguments put forth in this book, if we understand the policy changes as a form of bureaucratic violence, how has this form of violence been formulated, communicated and consolidated in society?

While it is beyond the aims of this chapter to address the cultural construction of refugees in Swedish society at large (see e.g. Eastmond, 2011), the chapter focuses on one significant snapshot. Focusing on 2015 as the year that brought a drastic shift in Swedish asylum policies, this chapter traces media representations of the inflow of large numbers of refugees which was later coined the refugee crisis. The analysis of mainstream newspapers that is provided here tackles the self-understanding of Sweden's image and the cultural justification of restrictive asylum policies. As such, this chapter has two goals: first, it provides an overview of the ways the refugee crisis was constructed in the media and discusses the specific forms of representation associated with it. Second, it focuses on one of several frames discussed – institutional responsibility – which is the most frequent frame in the selection of newspaper articles (on the visual representation of similar frames in Swedish media, see chapter 6). The analysis then proceeds to show that the refugee crisis was mostly discussed in terms of a challenge to the regular functions of bureaucratic institutions and approached in terms of management and containment. By staying away from moralistic arguments, mainstream media and political discourses of a refugee crisis were left largely uncontested and used to justify restrictive asylum policies. Such a strategy can be taken for granted in a society where emphasis on organisational efficiency and pragmatic approaches to problems are held in high regard (Graham, 2003).[2] Representing the inflow of refugees as an institutional crisis, however, led to a drastic shift in asylum policies, which were tacitly accepted on pragmatic grounds.

The chapter starts with a brief discussion of media coverage of immigrants and refugees. This section also brings attention to the Swedish context and presents an overview of research on Swedish media with a specific focus on the representation of immigrants. The second section includes a description of the research methodology. The chapter then presents an overview of newspaper coverage of the inflow of refugees in 2015 and highlights the strong focus on institutional arrangements and crisis. The last section shows that emphasis on an institutional crisis opened space for a previously unthinkable critique of Swedish institutions and for extreme rightist voices. As contending voices do not question the institutional logic of the crisis, the form of bureaucratic violence that proceeded was also left unchallenged.

**Media and refugees**

Mass media 'provide the guiding myths which shape our conception of the world' (Cohen and Young, 1973, p. 9). With regards to immigration in particular, research documents media's role in shaping public attitudes. While some authors emphasise that negative media portrayals of migrants and asylum seekers can foster anti-immigrant attitudes (Crawley, 2005; Innes, 2010; Rasinger, 2010; Balch and Balabanova, 2014), others emphasise that news coverage can create sites of contestation (Chavez, 2001; Clare and Abdelhady, 2016) where multiple articulations can be given space. Yet newspapers, especially those in high circulation, reflect general attitudes and popular ideas in society, and dominant discourses can be discerned in the major dailies and weeklies in a given context (Clare and Abdelhady, 2016). Circulation among large audiences amplifies the power of these discourses in shaping the construction of a given reality (Mautner, 2008). As such, the lens through which a reader receives mainstream news stories 'is not neutral but evinces the power and point of view of the political and economic elites who operate and focus it' (Gamson et al., 1992, p. 374). An analysis of media content, therefore, is important to understand social constructions of a specific phenomenon independent of the audience's engagement and interpretation of media messages.

Similar to studies of migration and media elsewhere, othering is considered an important theoretical concept for understanding media representations of immigrants in Sweden (see Brune, 2000; Nohrstedt, 2006; Burns et al., 2007; Hultén, 2007; Tigervall, 2007; see also Gale, 2004; Nolan et al., 2011; Arlt et al., 2019 for other contexts). Brune (2000) observes that Swedish media does not discuss the particulars of immigrants' backgrounds or everyday life but makes them exclusively visible in connection to events that she describes as conflict-filled. For example, Brune (2000; 2004) shows that immigrants and refugees are repeatedly represented in stories on deportation, mass migration and crime. This sort of coverage, again as the studies cited above show, is connected to who media rely on as the source of the story and whose perspective gets to be represented. For Brune, the perspective of governmental and official institutions tends to be central in media representation, in terms of who defines the issues and proposes solutions. Consequently, refugees and migrants end up being represented in the form of an invading mass, which triggers anxiety and frustration instead of sympathy and support (Brune, 2000). Specifically, refugees tend to be 'described as objects of various control measures, while representatives of the Swedish government, who are the focus of interest, emerge as a brave-but-tired everyone's salvation army' (Brune, 2000, p. 11; see also Hultén, 2007). Both Brune and Hultén stress the ways media homogenise the refugee/immigrant populations while separating them from the Swedish host. Additionally, faith is put in the Swedish model of cooperation and the welfare state to solve the problems of adaptation and incorporation into Swedish society. I find these strategies to be common in news coverage in 2015, albeit with stronger emphasis on control and management as is shown in the analysis. Additionally, newspapers' constructions of the refugee crisis in 2015 open up space for questioning norms and institutions in ways that may have been previously unthinkable.

## Methodology

In the age of digital media, paid circulation of newspapers does not reflect a newspaper's actual readership but can still be taken as a proxy for the general level of readership the newspapers attract. For the analysis offered here, I chose to include the two largest daily national newspapers, *Dagens Nyheter* (DN) and *Svenska Dagbladet* (SvD), and one tabloid, *Aftonbladet* (AB), as it has the largest circulation of all newspapers in Sweden.[3] Using the Retriever search-engine, three independent searches for each of the newspapers (print version) were conducted, using the search words refugee/immigrant, Middle East and Sweden (respectively, *flykting\**, *invandrare*, *mellanöstern* and *Sverige*). Search words are limited in their utility for research and, in this case, the results included large numbers of newspaper articles that were later read and coded or discarded based on their content.[4] For example, a large number of articles made no reference to Sweden and were, therefore, discarded, given the interest in relating the construction of the refugee crisis to Sweden's self-image and the rationalisation of Swedish policy changes. A total of 370 articles are included in the analysis from 2015.

The way news media presents, selects, emphasises or downplays certain aspects of social processes, events and issues in news coverage, sometimes at the expense of others, is theoretically understood as framing (Tuchman, 1978; Gitlin, 1980; Benson, 2013). Frames are 'interpretative packages' that give meaning to an issue (Gamson and Modigliani, 1989), and refer to 'the ability of a text – or a media presentation – to define a situation, to define the issues, and to set the terms of a debate' (Tankard, 2001, p. 96). Frames are also considered interpretive frameworks that represent 'windows on the world' through which people have the opportunity to learn about themselves and others (Tuchman, 1978). Research into media frames demonstrates that news coverage relies on a variety of specific frames to communicate the news to audiences, and that different frames can influence readers' or viewers' perceptions of public issues (for reviews see McCombs et al., 1997; Scheufele, 1999; McCombs and Ghanem, 2001). Semetko and Valkenburg (2000) assert that media reports (on diverse topics) tend to fall within five specific frames: conflict, human interest, economic consequences, morality and responsibility. In analysing the articles collected for this chapter, these frames were found to be of great relevance and were distributed according to Table 2. In this distribution, however, morality was merged with human interest or institutional responsibility.[5] The analysis that follows focuses on the selection of articles falling within the institutional responsibility frame. As Table 2 shows, this selection is two-thirds of all the articles found in the study and is taken to be the most significant in understanding the construction of the sense of crisis in Sweden. Referred to as the responsibility frame by some authors, this frame presents the issues

Table 2 Frame distribution of news articles in Swedish newspapers in 2015

|  | Conflict | Human interest | Economic consequence | Institutional responsibility | Total |
|---|---|---|---|---|---|
| *Aftonbladet* | 13 | 21 | 4 | 68 | 106 |
| *Dagens Nyheter* | 23 | 25 | 1 | 90 | 139 |
| *Svenska Dagbladet* | 19 | 21 | 9 | 76 | 125 |
| *Total* | 55 | 67 | 14 | 234 | 370 |

'in such a way that the responsibility for causing or solving a problem lies with the government, an individual or group' (d'Haenens and de Lange, 2001, p. 850). The significance of this frame can be elucidated after a brief discussion of the other three frames. This discussion draws upon and is further detailed in Abdelhady (2019).

Conflict as a frame speaks the most to the sense of a 'crisis', as it emphasises tensions between individuals, groups or institutions while reducing complex social and political problems to simple conflicts (d'Haenens and de Lange, 2001). Research on immigrants in Western media confirms the overwhelming focus on conflict-filled (or hostility-themed) stories (Leudar et al., 2008, p. 188) where immigrants and immigration are presented foremost as a threat (van Dijk, 2000; Benson, 2013). The threat frame portrays immigrants threatening wage systems or taking jobs from domestic workers, bringing diseases, draining the welfare system and depleting national resources (Greenberg and Hier, 2001; Leudar et al., 2008; Benson, 2013). Often it includes some sort of security frame, which relates immigration (and especially refugees) with criminality (Greenberg and Hier, 2001; Leudar et al., 2008; Steimel, 2009; Threadgold, 2009; Bradimore and Bauder, 2011). While my data shows that conflict is not the largest frame used for portraying Syrian refugees in the wake of the declared refugee crisis, many of the narratives within this frame parallel findings of previous research on the portrayal of immigrants and refugees. Given the relative infrequency in which this frame is used, it cannot be taken as an entry into understanding the construction of the refugee crisis.

Neuman et al. (1992) find the human-interest frame to be, next to conflict, the second most common frame across a variety of news content. Valkenburg et al. (1999, p. 551) argue that the human-interest media frame 'brings an individual's story or an emotional angle to the presentation of an event, issue or problem'. By doing so, a human-interest frame describes the news in terms that personalise, dramatise and emotionalise the news. D'Haenens and de Lange (2001) find the human-interest frame to be the frame most commonly used in their analysis of refugee coverage in Dutch

# Media constructions of the refugee crisis in Sweden

newspapers. In Swedish mainstream newspapers, however, the human-interest frame is the second largest used.

In discussing the framing of economic consequences, d'Haenens and de Lange (2001) explain that this frame is often used to clarify the economic consequences of an issue to the public and as a result involve the public more closely with the issue. As Table 2 above demonstrates, this frame is negligible in the Swedish context. Moreover, the discussion within this frame relates to institutional reform, as it often highlights the need for the labour market integration of refugees in order to offset the cost of welfare expenditures, turning the argument to institutional responsibility. This further highlights the importance of the institutional frame in the Swedish context, which is detailed in the following section.

## Institutional framing of the refugee crisis

The importance of efficiency in Swedish society has been remarked upon by numerous commentators (e.g. Milner, 1989; Lane, 1991; Graham, 2003). Describing the scene at the Migration Agency in Malmö, Traub (2016) narrates:

> When I arrived at the migration office a little past noon, 50-odd people stood on a line that snaked outside the building in order to be interviewed, while another 200–300 asylum-seekers stood or sat inside, waiting to be assigned a bed for the night. Some recent arrivals had to wait a day or two – but no longer – to be processed. Refugees in Germany have rioted at food lines, while conditions at the refugee camp in Calais, France, known as 'The Jungle' are notoriously dismal. The atmosphere in Malmö, by contrast, was remarkably calm and quiet. Nobody shouted; I don't recall hearing a child cry. *The Swedes were efficient* and extraordinarily protective of their charges ... *The interview line moved smartly. Officials had abandoned an earlier effort to gain background information about applicants; now interviewers simply asked their name, date of birth, and home country, and took a photograph and a set of fingerprints.* (emphasis added)

This narration points to the omnipresence of order and efficiency even when the narrator is not interested in making that point (recall Traub's interest in making a moral argument). Despite the appearance of order and efficiency to the outside observer, the refugee situation was constructed as a crisis as a result of institutions' inability to fulfil their mandates efficiently. The specific axes along which the refugee crisis was narrated in Swedish mainstream newspapers are: the lack of preparations; new challenges (transit migrants, see also chapter 4), which meant the inability to work according to established rules; and the need to discipline asylum seekers (and refugees). I discuss each of these themes individually before I turn to the discussion of foreseeable solutions.

### The need for (and failure of) a Swedish plan

As early as 28 February 2015, the need for a refugee strategy and concrete plan was called for when dealing with the increasing arrivals of individuals seeking asylum in Sweden. An article published in DN focuses mainly on the need for a strategy to help Syria and Iraq but also includes the need for a home strategy for dealing with asylum seekers (Malm, 2015). The latter point is elucidated in an SvD article on 23 May 2015:

> We need to take a national approach, possibly adding more resources and taking action. We look at the process to see if we do the right things, if we overhaul certain pieces and if we can make the process easier, says Ljepoja, operations expert at the Operational Management and Coordination Unit at the Swedish Migration Agency. (Delling, 2015)

The plan, according to the author of the article, would bring about faster refugee management. The pressure produced by the continuous increase in the number of people seeking asylum is approached pragmatically. For example, referring to Malmö as the municipality that receives the highest number of new arrivals, the added work pressure is simply discussed as: 'This should be facilitated by the director to plan long term' (Assarsson and Svanberg, 2015). The process of coming up with a plan still reflects dominant Swedish cultural norms such as coordination, cooperation and consensus. For example, one article is simply titled 'Coordinator saves the world' (Gudmundson, 2015a). An article in DN, published on 4 October under the title 'When We Cooperate We Accomplish a Lot', argues that an organised reception plan can proceed as 'the government has invited authorities, organizations, companies, unions and voluntary associations, to a national assembly for the improvement of the establishment of the newcomers' (Eriksson, 2015).

The inadequacy of the Swedish plan was a conclusion that was quickly drawn by the autumn of 2015. As one article describes that conclusion: 'Several authorities, municipalities and NGOs are involved in refugee reception, but as the inflow of refugees has escalated, the lack of coordination has become increasingly evident' (Treijs, 2015). Another article, which focuses on the perspective of county-level administration, claims that 'the counties describe the situation as critical for foundational social functions such as schools and social services if the wave of refugees continues to the same extent as today' (Kärrman and Olsson, 2015). A third example discusses the responsibility of labour unions. The article was published in DN on 12 October and does not miss the opportunity to critique the Prime Minister, Stefan Löfven, saying that 'his plan is incomplete and inadequate' (Dagens Nyheter, 2015a, p. 4). Finally, when ID checks were introduced on the border with Denmark, the discussion concluded that it was necessary to regain control and revise the plans. For example, an article in AB published on 12 November uses a quote from a refugee as its title 'We Are Already

Too Many' (Nygren, 2015). The story presented in the article claims that newly arrived refugees welcome the strengthened border controls that were introduced on that day: 'Hanni Abdel Fattah, 21 years old, said: "close the border. We who have come are absolutely too many. *They cannot take care of all of us*"' (emphasis added). The article continues to say that the staff of the Migration Agency are too stressed, that people are sleeping on the floors in the corridors of the building, and that families have to wait for twelve hours before getting a room. Another male asylum seeker is quoted: 'Amer Anaout from Syria, 37 years old, said "I am surprised how it is in Sweden. If they cannot take care of us *in an orderly manner*, so they should not take in so many"' (emphasis added). Having found asylum seekers who are best representatives of the firm attitude needed and later taken by the Swedish government, the journalist turns to softening the story by describing the situation of the children: 'many children have thin clothes and place their hands on bus lamps to stay warm.' Looking back at 2015, an article published in December argues that the failure witnessed in receiving refugees is due to a lack of planning or, as the title of the article describes, 'Sweden's preparedness did not hold when the crisis came' (Dagens Nyheter, 2015e, p. 8).

Thus far, I have highlighted the prominence of institutional arguments within Swedish mainstream press in the construction of a refugee crisis in 2015. The need for an adequate plan, and the ultimate failure to deliver one, are presented as the foundation of Swedish failure to meet the demands of the increased flow of people seeking asylum. The various problems that were posed as challenging to the Swedish government or administrative systems are namely: transit, integration and discipline. These three problems relate to the need for the management and control of individuals showing up at the Swedish border, which further supports my claim that the refugee crisis was constructed around issues of governance rather than morality (see also chapter 3). In the next paragraphs I illustrate the three problems and then move to a discussion of the tensions within these constructions.

### Sweden as a transit country

Swedish reception of asylum seekers is based on the assumption that people are seeking asylum in Sweden. In other words, there are no policies or mechanisms to address the needs of those transiting through Sweden. One article from AB explains:

> But at the same time, we are facing a new situation. Many of those who come to Sweden are not at all interested in seeking asylum here. It may be contrary to our self-image as the most perfect and best little country in the world, but a significant part of those who get off the trains at Malmö Central want to move on. They see their future in Finland or Norway. *Our system is not*

*equipped for these so-called transit refugees.* (Karlsson, 2015, p. 6, emphasis added)

Transit migrants were almost exclusively helped by volunteers, playing a significant role in mobilising volunteer efforts to begin with. For example, another article from DN quotes a volunteer with Stockholm's City Mission, Marika Markovits, who explains: 'What we did not expect was that there would be so many who did not want to seek asylum in Sweden. *These are outside the system and have no one to help them*, it is for them that we must mobilise non-profit forces' (Ahlstrand, 2015, p. 33, emphasis added).

Sustainable integration

As discussed earlier, the lack of a clear plan that rendered Sweden ready to receive refugees was the basis of the media construction of crisis in 2015. The perception of inadequate planning was similarly brought about when discussing the absence of plans to integrate refugees. As early as March and April, there were references to problems related to integration. Two examples from SvD are worth mentioning. First, an article published on 28 March argued that (proposed) policy changes would not result in a decrease in the numbers of Syrians seeking asylum in Sweden. Instead, the article critiqued the policies for their potential to worsen the conditions under which Syrian refugees would be expected to 'integrate' to Sweden (Ruist, 2015). A second article also critiqued the government, but for its inability to plan for the integration of the increasing numbers of low-educated refugees (Jansson, et al., 2015).

Following the long summer of migration, debates on integration continued. One article from DN stressed the importance of societal-level coordination between the different actors, and not only government and immigrants (Dagens Nyheter, 2015b). Equally important, an article from the same newspaper posed the question as to whether welfare policies facilitate integration. The article, published on 3 November under the title 'Politicians Must Create a Sustainable Integration', listed housing problems, school deficits and police lack of resources as obstacles to integration. These problems are all institutional and relate to the governance of the daily activities of refugees and immigrants in general (Frykman, 2015, p. 25).

Disciplining bodies

The inability of various organisations to maintain order over the inflow of asylum seekers is best understood as the portrayal of a lack of control over refugee bodies. Institutions such as housing, healthcare and education, which all perform important disciplining roles in society as per Foucault's (1979; see also Hewitt, 1983) analysis, were recurrently highlighted as facing serious challenges following the long summer of migration. Concerns for finding accommodation for asylum seekers featured in almost every description of the institutional crisis facing Sweden. Accommodation was needed for unaccompanied minors:

> The situation is pressured. Many municipalities say that they find it difficult to receive more refugees, regardless of age, and that they do not have enough accommodation for more single children. (Lifvendahl, 2015, p. 4)

> Recently, heavy overcrowding in municipal housing has occurred. It affects both the children and the staff. … Today, the Swedish Migration Agency is unable to register the children at the rate they come in, which means that the system is being violated. (Jammeh, 2015, p. 6)

> The municipality must fight every day to find sleeping places for the children. Several of them are sick with MRSA, TB and scabies. (Dagens Nyheter, 2015e, p. 8)

Accommodation was also needed for those who found internships and were on their way to settle:

> So our concern is to find accommodation for those who have jobs or internships so that they can continue … says Emilia Ciokota, team leader at the accommodation in Västberga. (By, 2015a, p. 4)

Warning signs that the capacity to accommodate asylum seekers had been reached were repeated in October and the beginning of November. The lack of planning to deal with the situation was derided in one article from AB that explained: 'Stefan Löfven expects that over 150,000 will have applied for asylum if the flow continues at the same pace. There are places to live in the schools, gyms, but when they are filled, tents might be the only last solution' (Holmqvist and Wågenberg, 2015, p. 14). Just a few days before instating ID checks at the border with Denmark, one article in DN declared that 'there is no roof over the head' of asylum seekers (Larsson and Kärrman, 2015). While referring to 50,000 new beds in converted sports halls, which were offered by the Migration Agency, the article quoted the Minister for Migration stating that Sweden had reached its limit and run out of sleeping spaces. The Minister for Migration, Morgan Johansson continues:

> Until this week we have managed to give all [those in need] food for the day and a roof over the head. But if this continues for another week or fourteen days, we will end up in a position where we must deliver such a message to asylum seekers that they cannot secure a roof over their heads. (Larsson and Kärrman, 2015, p. 9)

The narrative of running out of space was further strengthened the day after border controls were instated when an article, describing the problems faced by the city of Malmö, refered to camps of tents having become a reality:

'There is no longer space for everyone that arrives to sleep somewhere, some had to sleep outside the Migration Agency' (Lindberg, 2015, p. 2).

The strong emphasis on housing and the need to provide accommodation for asylum seekers stems from the general need to organise society in a particular fashion. Asylum seekers must be registered before they can be provided accommodation. Importantly, once within the provided housing, an asylum seeker is monitored and controlled. While asylum seekers narrate their sense of being controlled in these facilities (see e.g. chapter 12), newspaper coverage verbalises the process in much simpler terms. For example, when referring to an asylum seeker who was suspected of being involved in planning a terrorist attack, an article from SvD offered the following to deny the accusations: 'Living in an asylum centre means that you are being watched and everyone knows your whereabouts, so there is no possibility that the man was involved in planning anything in Stockholm' (Gummesson, 2015, p. 9).

The importance of the disciplinary power of the state is further exemplified when reading news articles that emphasise the role of schools and health care facilities in maintaining the social order. These institutions do not have the ability to control asylum seekers and their children the same way as housing does, but they play multiple roles of educating asylum seekers and their children, monitoring them, and controlling them to make them fit for integration into Swedish society and culture. For example, schools 'survey refugee children' (By, 2015b), and provide 'the key to life as a Swede' (Kadhammar, 2015) even if the child sits in a room that is not designated for teaching. Similarly, free health care has the dual role 'to explain the system, and control the spread of disease' (Gustafsson, 2015, p. 4), and 'increases the possibility for work and strengthens parenting' (Fried and Ekblad, 2015, p. 8).

**Resolving the crisis: institutions versus morality**

In this section, I analyse news articles that debate specific proposals or approaches to dealing with the constructed refugee crisis in Sweden. While differences between the three newspapers were not significant in understanding the construction of the crisis, discernible differences can be found in the debates over how to deal with it. The most significant differences are between SvD and AB, which are located, at least initially, at opposite ends of the political spectrum.

SvD comes close to what Wodak (2019) terms a post-shame discourse. In the post-shame era, 'refugees and migrants serve as *the* scapegoat and simplistic explanation for all woes' (Wodak, 2019, p. 2, emphasis in the original) alongside 'the normalisation of far-right ideologies in both content and form' (Wodak, 2019, p. 2). In a post-shame discourse, agreed-upon norms and values are ignored and what was previously unsayable and unacceptable becomes normalised. In the constructions of a refugee crisis in 2015, SvD provides room for the previously unsayable as the following examples indicate.

Institutional framing of the refugee crisis inevitably included the questioning of the Swedish welfare model, which is considered one of the most sacred institutions in Swedish national culture. The Swedish welfare model depicts a society without any significant class barriers, where everyone, regardless of their background, has a chance at an education and a career. In one example, the authors of an article published on 4 February 2015 declared that 'opening our hearts is not enough ... the consequences [of refugee migration] are seen as regards to dependency, housing, segregation and child poverty' (Sonesson and Westerlund, 2015, p. 5). The article proceeded to mention that 'the Swedish social model is not adapted for extensive refugee migration of low-skilled people' and urged political actors to 'assess the capacity and limitations of Swedish society to receive and integrate people fleeing to our country' (Sonesson and Westerlund, 2015, p. 5). A second example posed the question of 'Where is the Limit to Welfare?' In this editorial, the author argued that 'the conflict between the welfare state and free movement has been known for a long time. Nevertheless, Sweden seems to respond by continuously expanding welfare commitments. In the long run, something has to go, either mobility or welfare, maybe both' (Gudmundson, 2015b, p. 4). These two articles question Swedish welfare policies, and specifically the principle of 'The People's Home' (*folkhemmet*, see e.g. Lawler, 2003). This vision of universal welfare, coined by Social Democrat leader Per Albin Hansson in 1927, has – at least from the early 1930s until the late 1980s – been considered sacred in Swedish public culture.

Additionally, the post-shame discourse is exemplified in providing space for politicians from the ultranationalist and extreme rightist Sweden Democrats (SD) to present their views on refugee policies and thus normalising the role played by such a party in Swedish political discourse. At the height of the long summer of migration, an article authored by three SD politicians referred to the restrictive policies initiated by Denmark and explained that 'the efficient policies of our Nordic neighbours are entirely in accordance with the [Geneva] convention and nothing prevents us from following their example' (Bieler et al., 2015, p. 6).[6] It is important to note that the post-shame discourse takes on a specific Swedish flavour as it continues to emphasise the importance of international institutions and legal frameworks, their capacities and limitations, and even their directives, as demonstrated by the reference to the Geneva Convention by SD politicians.

At the other end of the political spectrum, AB contradicts the post-shame discourse by arguing that 'immigration is an asset for Sweden, as well as a moral question' (Pettersson, 2015, p. 2), and that temporary residence permits are expensive, lead to worse integration (Rehbinder, 2015) and increase the institutional pressures on the Migration Agency, since refugees have to re-apply every three years (Dahlin et al., 2015). The leftist politics that historically marked the debates within AB can still be observed in the coverage of refugee policies and reception. In one example, an editorial poses the question: 'Which System is Collapsing?' and goes on to explain that 'Swedes are getting richer. The OECD predicts positive Swedish growth and a decrease in the unemployment rate. At the same time, Swedes will buy Christmas gifts for sixteen billion crowns this year' (Aftonbladet, 2015, p. 2). In these examples, despite the occasional reference to asylum being a moral question, the argument does not shift away from the institutional framework: immigration is an economic asset, temporary permits are an institutional hurdle, and Swedish economic institutions are performing positively.

DN is positioned in the middle of the political spectrum, and news articles oscillating between the two ends are observable along its coverage of the refugee crisis. On the conservative side of the debate, a number of articles stress the lack of institutional capacity to welcome more asylum seekers and draw on some of the expressions that were made popular and most associated with the construction of the crisis. In one example, an article interviews the Minister of Foreign Affairs, Margot Wallström, who refers to the much-discussed notion of 'system collapse' in Swedish debate and explains that:

> most people know that we cannot maintain a system where there maybe 190,000 people arriving every year, in the long run our systems will collapse … We want it to offer a worthy reception of those who come here … We believe that a good society to live in is a society that is generous, but it's also a society that is functional. (Stenberg, 2015, p. 8)

An editorial published on 6 November 2015 explained that 'to say that the Migration Agency and the municipalities are overworked is no malicious, calculated exaggeration – it is a painful reality' (Dagens Nyheter, 2015d, p. 4). The next day, an article continued the narrative of this 'painful reality' and stated that, 'it is clear, however, that if Sweden fails with the integration of new arrivals, tension in society can be large. At the moment we do not even have tent places for everyone, and the housing issue is at least a challenge' (Dagens Nyheter, 2015c, p. 4). In this line of narration, notions of collapse, challenges, tensions and responsibility come together to explain the institutional problems associated with refugees and asylum seekers. Implicitly understood is that these challenges are temporary, and hence the need for temporary recourse to extreme measures. It is noteworthy that, at times, a reference to morality and values is made in order to deny possible misunderstandings that the author supports the closure of the border based on value judgements. Even the SD politicians referred to above would not engage in a moral argument in mainstream news media, which affirms that a moral argument is not a conceivable avenue to support policy restrictions.

At the other end of the debate, there are a number of articles published by DN that offer a different view on the institutional crisis. While many articles refer to the unequal distribution of asylum seekers within Europe and call for the need to share the burden, one example takes the argument further by emphasizing the collective European responsibility:

> The EU crisis has absolutely nothing to do with the inability to receive sixty million refugees – a situation that does not exist at all. It is about the Union as a whole not having a common answer on how to help six hundred thousand asylum seekers – this year perhaps up to one million – in an area with five-hundred million inhabitants.
>
> People do not have to suffocate in trucks on European highways. People do not have to be overrun by high-speed trains on the English Channel. People must not drown in the Mediterranean. That it has become so is our own inability to bring about political solutions at the European level, solutions that safeguard the rights of those in need of help. This is our real crisis. And it's homemade. (Wolodarski, 2015, p. 5)

While not specifically questioning the morality of Swedish society, the author of the article highlights the political failure in resolving the plight of refugees. Another example denounces the changes in asylum policies that were introduced in November 2015 and uses the discourse of risk society (see the Introduction to this volume) in order to mobilise support:

> It is also time to distinguish between costs and investments in the economic debate. It is a cost to establish border controls that prevent refugees from claiming their right to asylum, but it is an investment to give asylum-seekers a good reception and rapid integration. We can lend to investments because it will pay our pensions in the future. (Westin, 2015, p. 35)

Again, the author does not question the morality of Swedish society but brings attention to the political failure. While the author points out that politicians failed as they did not act in a moralistic manner and build a better world, the focus is kept on the rationality of offering help to refugees by rendering it productive and profitable (as also discussed in the Introduction above). One final example, on Christmas Eve a number of church leaders expressed their concerns:

> We have respect for the courage of our politicians in the difficult decisions made. Municipalities and county councils are faced with major stresses in terms of housing, care and school. At the same time, we are worried about the new decisions on the country's asylum rules ... *Temporary residence permits make life insecure, complicate integration and increase administration for our authorities.* (Dagens Nyheter, 2015f, p. 8, emphasis added)

These last examples are important attempts to redefine the notion of crisis and to draw attention to the failure of political institutions in coming up with morally sound and institutionally effective policies, which would aid the refugees and strengthen the welfare state's ability to fulfil its goals of supporting the people. As the examples provided from DN and AB show, views that challenged the specific ways the refugee crisis was constructed and used to justify policy shifts do not contest the institutional logic that informed the very construction of the crisis.

**Conclusion**

In this chapter, I have traced the construction of a refugee crisis in 2015 in Swedish mainstream newspapers. Focusing on the most dominant frame, institutional responsibility, I demonstrate that a sense of panic emerged when increasing numbers of people were seeking asylum in and through Sweden. This panic transpired when old rules and regulations were found inadequate to promptly address the needs of the asylum seekers. The inability to categorise and order people (transit migrants for example) rendered these people illegible for the welfare state, increasing the sense of heightened risk and the additional needs for management. An ongoing desire to discipline refugees' bodies through mechanisms of control in housing, schooling and healthcare services added to the pressures on the welfare state institutions to act and manage the risks associated with refugees. Institutional failure to manage refugees and asylum seekers gave rise to a sense of crisis. Thus, the emphasis on institutional crises and the failure to manage and mitigate risks associated with refugees and asylum seekers was drawn by mainstream media to signify the refugee crisis. Political institutional failure, rather than the inadequacy of moral ideals, justified extreme policy measures. These were left largely uncontested in mainstream media, given the cultural context of faith in pragmatism, bureaucratic efficiency and widespread support for Swedish institutions. When constructed as an institutional need, policy restrictions can proceed without challenging the dominant Swedish self-image of being generous, ethical and efficient. This strategy opens up space for a post-shame discourse where (previously) unthinkable and unsayable arguments can be presented. A few contending voices remind us of the moral responsibility towards refugees, but they do not challenge the institutional logic predominant in the debates. As a consequence, violent measures are implemented and self-perceptions of a society that is benevolent and efficient are left unchallenged.

**Notes**

1 It is not my intention to refute Sweden's generosity. An objective argument that is often taken up to support such a view is that, in 2015, Sweden received the

largest number of refugees per capita compared to other countries in the Global North (UNHCR 2017). The contention here, rather, is the ways that perception of generosity was not challenged by reversing refugee reception policies.
2 Anthropologist Mark Graham (2003) argues that in the Scandinavian context in general, and the Swedish case in particular, there is an emotional continuity between bureaucracies and the people they serve, which facilitates service and ensures popular support. This emotional continuity helps reproduce the ideology of the welfare state.
3 A few studies on Swedish media argue that, historically, there has existed a partisan structure of the national dailies that has kept them closely affiliated with political parties in their content, ownership and readership (Hadenius, 1983). *Aftonbladet* has been a left-leaning newspaper and is currently described as an independent socially-democratic newspaper. *Dagens Nyheter* is described as liberal, while *Svenska Dagbladet* is characterised as moderate. Over the last few decades, however, political affiliations have reduced and there has been a change towards more market-driven journalism, which focuses on newsworthiness rather than political affiliation (Asp, 2006; Pettersson et al., 2006; Strömbäck and Nord, 2008). Strömbäck and Nord (2008) refer to this change as part of the mediatisation process, which is characterised by professional journalistic values and the adoption of a media logic (what is news-worthy) as opposed to a political logic in news coverage (see also Nord 2001).
4 I am grateful for the research assistance provided by Sara Lundgren, Gina Fristedt Malmberg, Pernilla Nilsson and Serena Nilsson in compiling and coding the newspaper articles. They also provided an important sounding board for sharing insights about Swedish media analysis. All translations provided here were carried out by the author.
5 d'Haenens and de Lange (2001, p. 850) explain that 'the morality frame adds a religious or moral charge to an event, problem or subject'. The religious charge was seldom observed in the articles referred to in this analysis. The moral charge, whenever strong, was often used in human-interest stories or discussions of institutional responsibility, as is shown in the analysis.
6 It should be mentioned here that Denmark has been criticised for not fulfilling international conventions with regards to family reunifications (http://denstoredanske.dk/Samfund,_jura_og_politik/Jura/Enkelte_navngivne_retssager/Tamilsagen) and stateless people (www.dr.dk/nyheder/politik/forstaa-statsloese-sagen-paa-5-minutter) (Accessed 13 March 2020).

## References

Abdelhady, D. (2019). 'Framing the Syrian Refugee: Divergent Discourses in Three National Contexts', in Menjivar, C., Ruiz, M. and Ness, E. (eds.) *The Oxford Handbook of Migration Crises*. Oxford: Oxford University Press, pp. 635–656.

Aftonbladet. (2015). Panikslagna politiker som sprider paranoia (Politicians Struck by Panic Are Spreading Paranoia), *Aftonbladet*, 14 November, p. 2.

Ahlstrand, L. (2015). Stadsmissionen. 'Vår styrka är vår uthållighet. Vi kommer att hjälpa till' (City Mission: 'Our Strength is Our Endurance: We Will help'), *Dagens Nyheter*, 13 November, p. 33.

Arlt, D., Dalmus, C. and Metag, J. (2019). 'Direct and Indirect Effects of Involvement on Hostile Media Perceptions in the Context of the Refugee Crisis in Germany and Switzerland', *Mass Communication and Society* 22(2), pp. 171–195.

Asp, K. 2006. Rättvisa nyhetsmedier. Partiskheten under 2006 års valrörelse (Fair News Media. Partisanship During the 2006 Election Campaign). Gothenburg: Gothenburg University.

Assarsson, S. and Svanberg, N. (2015). Arbete under ständig press (Work Under Continuous Pressure), *Svenska Dagbladet*, 20 August, p. 9.

Balch, A. and Balabanova, E. (2014). 'Ethics, Politics and Migration: Public Debates on the Free Movement of Romanians and Bulgarians in the UK, 2006–2013', *Politics* 36(1), pp. 19–35.

Barker, V. (2012). 'Global Mobility and Penal Order: Criminalizing Migration, A View from Europe', *Sociology Compass* 6(2), pp. 113–121.

Benson, R. (2013). *Shaping Immigration News: A French American Comparison*. New York: Cambridge University Press.

Bieler, P., Ekeroth, K. and Wiechel, M. (2015). Sverige kan inte hysa alla som flyr (Sweden Cannot Accommodate All Who Flee), *Svenska Dagbladet*, 6 August, p. 6.

Bradimore, A. and Bauder, H. (2011). 'Mystery Ships and Risky Boat People: Tamil Refugee Migration in the Newsprint Media', *Canadian Journal of Communication* 36(4), pp. 637–661.

Brekke, J.-P. (2004). *While We are Waiting: Uncertainty and Empowerment Among Asylum-Seekers in Sweden*. Oslo: Institutt for Sam-funnsforskning.

Brune, Y. (2000). *Stereotyper i förvandling svensk nyhetsjournalistik om invandrare och flyktingar* (Stereotypes in Transforming Swedish News Journalism About Immigrants and Refugees). Stockholm: Norstedts Tryckeri.

Brune, Y. (2004). *Nyheter från gränsen. Tre studier i journalistik och 'invandrare', flyktingar och rasistiskt våld* (News from the Border: Three Studies in Journalism and 'Immigrants', Refugees and Racist Violence). PhD, Gothenburg University.

Burns, T. R., Machado, N., Hellgren, Z. and Brodin, G. R. (2007). 'Avslutande reflektioner (Concluding Remarks)', in Burns, T. R., Machado, N., Hellgren, Z. and Brodin, G. r. (eds.) *Makt, kultur och kontroll över invandrares livsvillkor. Multidimensionella perspektiv på strukturell diskriminering i Sverige* (Power, Culture and Control Over Immigrants' Living Conditions: Multidimensional Perspectives on Structural Discrimination in Sweden). Uppsala: Acta Universitatis Upsaliensis, pp. 535–543.

By, U. (2015a). Studiecirklar ska ge avbrott i väntan (Study Circles Will be Interrupted in Waiting), *Dagens Nyheter*, 31 August, p. 4.

By, U. (2015b). Här kartläggs flyktingbarn inför skolstarten (Here Refugee Children Are Surveyed Before Starting School), *Dagens Nyheter*, 10 October, p. 4.

Chavez, L. (2001). *Covering Immigration: Popular Images and the Politics of the Nation*. Berkeley: University of California Press.

Clare, M. and Abdelhady, D. (2016). 'No Longer a Waltz Between Red Wine and Mint Tea: The Portrayal of the Children of Immigrants in French Newspapers (2003–2013)', *International Journal of Intercultural Relations* 50(1), pp. 13–28.

Cohen, S. and Young, J. (1973). 'Introduction', in Cohen, S. and Young, J. (eds.) *The Manufacture of News: Social Problems, Deviance and the Mass Media*. London: Constable and Co., pp. 9–11.

Crawley, H. 2005. Evidence on Attitudes to Asylum and Immigration: What We Know, Don't Know and Need to Know. *Centre on Migration, Policy and Society Working Paper Series*. Oxford: University of Oxford.
d'Haenens, L. and de Lange, M. (2001). 'Framing of Asylum Seekers in Dutch Regional Newspapers', *Media, Culture and Society* 23(6), pp. 847–860.
Dagens Nyheter (2015a). Facket har också ansvar (The Labour Unions also have a Responsibility), *Dagens Nyheter*, 12 October, p. 4.
Dagens Nyheter (2015b). Gränser handlar om annat än nationstillhörighet (Borders Are About Something Other Than National Belonging), *Dagens Nyheter*, 11 September.
Dagens Nyheter (2015c). LO Står i vägen för jobben (LO Stands in the Way of Work), *Dagens Nyheter*, 7 November, p. 4.
Dagens Nyheter (2015d). Tydligare signaler (Clearer Signs), *Dagens Nyheter*, 6 November, p. 4.
Dagens Nyheter (2015e). Svenska beredskapen höll inte när krisen kom (Sweden's Preparedness Did Not Hold When the Crisis Came), *Dagens Nyheter*, 18 December, p. 8.
Dagens Nyheter (2015f). Hårdare praxis om migration riskerar vår medmänsklighet (Tougher Practices on Migration Risk Our Humanity), *Dagens Nyheter*, 24 December, p. 8.
Dahlin, E., Banke, V., Dane, L. and Ratcovich, M. (2015). Signalpolitik hejdar ingen flyktingström (Signal Politics Does Not Stop the Stream of Refugees), *Aftonbladet*, 16 October, p. 6.
Delling, H. (2015). Akutplan ska ge snabbare asylhantering (An Emergency Plan Will Bring About Faster Refugee Management), *Svenska Dagbladet*, 23 May, p. 10.
Eastmond, M. (2011). 'Egalitarian Ambitions, Constructions of Difference: The Paradoxes of Refugee Integration in Sweden', *Journal of Ethnic and Migration Studies* 37(2), pp. 277–295.
Eriksson, K. (2015). När vi hjälps åt klarar vi mycket (When We Cooperate We Accomplish a Lot), *Dagens Nyheter*, 4 October, p. 8.
Foucault, M. (1979). *Discipline and Punish: The Birth of the Prison*. Harmondsworth: Penguin.
Fried, H. and Ekblad, S. (2015). Det förflutnas tragedier går igen idag (The Tragedies of the Past Are Haunting Us Today), *Dagens Nyheter*, 9 September, p. 8.
Frykman, O. (2015). Politikerna måste skapa en hållbar integration (Politicians Must Create a Sustainable Integration), *Dagens Nyheter*, 3 November, p. 25.
Gale, P. (2004). 'The Refugee Crisis and Fear: Populist Politics and Media Discourse', *Journal of Sociology* 40(4), pp. 321–340.
Gamson, W. A. and Modigliani, A. (1989). 'Media Discourse and Public Opinion on Nuclear Power: A Constructionist Approach', *American Journal of Sociology* 95(1), pp. 1–37.
Gamson, W. A., Croteau, D., Hoynes, W. and Sasson, T. (1992). 'Media Images and the Social Construction of Reality', *Annual Review of Sociology* 18, pp. 373–393.
Gitlin, T. (1980). *The Whole World is Watching: Mass Media in the Making and Unmaking of the New Left*. Berkeley: University of California Press.

Graham, M. (2003). 'Emotional Bureaucracies: Emotions, Civil Servants, and Immigrants in the Swedish Welfare State', *Ethos* 30(3), pp. 199–226.

Greenberg, J. and Hier, S. (2001). 'Crisis, Mobilization and Collective Problematization: "Illegal" Chinese Migrants and the Canadian News Media', *Journalism Studies* 2(4), pp. 563–583.

Gudmundson, P. (2015a). Samordnare räddar världen (Coordinator Saves the World), *Svenska Dagbladet*, 16 September, p. 4.

Gudmundson, P. (2015b). Var går välfärdens gräns? (Where is the Limit of Welfare?), *Svenska Dagbladet*, 29 July, p. 4.

Gummesson, J. (2015). Säpo klarade inte att hålla huvudet kallt (Säpo Failed to Keep Its Head Cold), *Svenska Dagbladet*, 23 November, p. 9.

Gustafsson, A. (2015). Ökat tryck skapar kö i flyktingvården (Increased Pressure Creates a Queue in Refugee Healthcare), *Dagens Nyheter*, 10 December, p. 4.

Hadenius, S. (1983). 'The Rise and Possible Fall of the Swedish Party Press', *Communication Research* 10(3), pp. 287–310.

Hewitt, M. (1983). 'Bio-Politics and Social Policy: Foucault's Account of Welfare', *Theory, Culture & Society* 2(1), pp. 67–84.

Holmqvist, A. and Wågenberg, J. (2015). Krisplanen. De får bo i tältläger (The Crisis Plan: They Will Have to Live in Tent Camps), *Aftonbladet*, 10 October, p. 14.

Hultén, G. (2007). Främlingar i nationens spegel (Foreigners in the Mirror of the Nation), in Burns, T. R., Machado, N., Hellgren, Z. and Brodin, G. (eds.) *Makt, kultur och kontroll över invandrares livsvillkor. Multidimensionella perspektiv på strukturell diskriminering i Sverige* (Power, Culture and Control over Immigrants' Living Conditions: Multidimensional Perspectives on Structural Discrimination in Sweden). Uppsala: Acta Universitatis Upsaliensis, pp. 23–53.

Innes, A. (2010). 'When the Threatened Become the Threat: The Construction of Asylum-Seekers in British Media Narratives', *International Relations* 24(4), pp. 456–477.

Jammeh, K. S. (2015). Orimlig situation för Malmö (Unreasonable Situation for Malmö), *Svenska Dagbladet*, 20 August, p. 6.

Jansson, L., Voltaire, F. and Lindberg, U. (2015). Skolplikt väg till försörjning (Compulsory Schooling Route to Livelihood), *Svenska Dagbladet*, 20 April, p. 8.

Joormann, M. (2019). *Legitimized Refugees: A Critical Investigation of Legitimacy Claims Within the Precedents of Swedish Asylum Law*. PhD, Lund University.

Kadhammar, P. (2015). Här får Sara 11, nyckeln till ett liv som svensk (Here, Eleven-Year-Old Sara Gets the Key to a Life as a Swede), *Aftonbladet*, 5 November, p. 16.

Karlsson, N. (2015). Vi kan inte hjälpa transitflyktingarna (We Cannot Help Transit Refugees), *Aftonbladet*, 29 September, p. 6.

Kärrman, J. and Olsson, H. (2015). Länsstyrelserna. Vår situation är kritisk (County Administration: Our Situation is Critical), *Dagens Nyheter*, 10 October, p. 10.

Khosravi, S. (2009). 'Sweden: Detention and Deportation of Asylum Seekers', *Race & Class* 50(4), pp. 38–56.

Lane, J.-E. (ed.) (1991). *Understanding the Swedish Model*. London: Frank Cass.

Larsson, M. and Kärrman, J. (2015). Det finns inte tak över huvudet (There is No Roof Over the Head), *Dagens Nyheter*, 6 November, p. 9.

Lawler, P. (2003). 'Loyalty to the Folkhem?' in Waller, M. and Linklater, A. (eds.) *Political Loyalty and the Nation-State*. London: Routledge, pp. 154–170.

Leudar, I., Hayes, J., Nekvapi, J. and Baker, J. T. (2008). 'Hostility Themes in Media, Community and Refugee Narratives', *Discourse & Society* 19(2), pp. 187–221.

Lifvendahl, T. (2015). Vi måste tänka annorlunda (We Must Think Differently), *Svenska Dagbladet*, 19 July, p. 4.

Lindberg, A. (2015). Malmö har blivit vårt skyltfönster (Malmö Has Become Our Display Storefront), *Aftonbladet*, 13 November, p. 2.

Malm, F. (2015). Sex insatser som kan hjälpa Syrien och Irak på lång sikt (Six Strategies that Can Help Syria and Iraq in the Long Term), *Dagens Nyheter*, 28 February, p. 6.

Mautner, G. (2008). 'Analyzing Newspapers, Magazine and Other Print Media', in Wodak, R. and Krzyzanowski, M. (eds.) *Qualitative Discourse Analysis in the Social Sciences*. New York: Palgrave Macmillan, pp. 30–53.

McCombs, M. and Ghanem, S. (2001). 'The Convergence of Agenda Setting and Framing', in Reese, S. D., Oscar H. Gandy, J. and Grant, A. E. (eds.) *Framing Public Life: Perspectives on Media and Our Understanding of the Social World*. London: Lawrence Erlbaum Associates, pp. 67–82.

McCombs, M. E., Shaw, D. L. and Weaver, D. H. (eds.) (1997). *Communication and Democracy: Exploring the Intellectual Frontiers in Agenda-Setting Theory*. New York: Routledge.

Milner, H. (1989). *Sweden: Social Democracy in Practice*. Oxford: Oxford University Press.

Neuman, W. R., Just, M. R. and Crigler, A. N. (1992). *Common Knowledge: News and the Construction of Political Meaning*. Chicago: University of Chicago Press.

Nohrstedt, S. A. (2006). 'Krigsjournalistiken och den strukturella diskrimineringen' (War Journalism and Structural Discrimination), in Camauër, L. and Nohrstedt, S. A. (eds.) *Mediernas vi och dom. Mediernas betydelse för den strukturella diskrimineringen* (The Media's Us and Them: The Meaning of the Media for Structural Discrimination). Stockholm: Fritzes, pp. 257–308.

Nolan, D., Farquharson, K., Politoff, V. and Marjoribanks, T. (2011). 'Mediated Multiculturalism: Newspaper Representations of Sudanese Migrants in Australia', *Journal of Intercultural Studies* 32(6), pp. 655–671.

Noll, G. (2005). 'Salvation by the Grace of State? Explaining Credibility Assessment in the Asylum Procedure', in Noll, G. (ed.) *Proof, Evidentiary Assessment and Credibility in Asylum Procedures*. Leiden: Martinus Nijhoff, pp. 197–214.

Nord, L. W. (2001). *Vår tids ledare. En studie av den svenska dagspressens politiska opinionsbildning* (The Contemporary Editorial: A Study of Political Opinion Making in the Swedish Press). PhD, Stockholm University.

Nygren, S. (2015). Vi är redan för manga (We are Already Too Many), *Aftonbladet*, 12 November, p. 10.

Pettersson, O., Djerf-Pierre, M., Holmberg, S., Strömbäck, J. and Weibull, L. 2006. Report from the Democratic Audit of Sweden 2006: Media and Elections in Sweden. Stockholm: SNS-Centre for Business and Policy Studies.

Pettersson, K. (2015). Billiga poäng ger inte bra integration (Cheap Points Do Not Yield Good Integration), *Aftonbladet*, 3 February, p. 2.

Rasinger, S. (2010). '"Lithuanian Migrants Send Crime Rocketing": Representation of "New" Migrants in Regional Print Media', *Media Culture & Society* 32(6), pp. 1021–1030.

Rehbinder, C. (2015). Trygga människor integreras lättare (Safe People Integrate Easier), *Aftonbladet*, 20 February, p. 6.

Ruist, J. (2015). Därför flyr syrier just till Sverige (Therefore Syrians Flee to Sweden), *Svenska Dagbladet*, 28 March, p. 6.

Scheufele, D. A. (1999). 'Framing as a Theory of Media Effect', *The Journal of Communication* 49(1), pp. 103–122.

Schoultz, I. (2013). 'Seeking Asylum and Residence Permits in Sweden: Denial, Acknowledgement, and Bureaucratic Legitimacy', *Critical Criminology* 22, pp. 219–235.

Semetko, H. A. and Valkenburg, P. M. (2000). 'Framing European Politics: A Content Analysis of Press and Television News', *The Journal of Communication* 50, pp. 93–109.

Sonesson, J. and Westerlund, U. (2015). Antalet måste få diskuteras (It Must Be Possible to Discuss the Numbers), *Svenska Dagbladet*, 4 February, p. 5.

Steimel, S. (2009). 'Refugees in the News: A Representative Anecdote of Identification/Division in Refugee Media Coverage', *Kentucky Journal of Communication* 28(1), pp. 55–75.

Stenberg, E. (2015). Margot Wallström om bränderna. SD har ett ansvar (Margot Wallström on the Fires: SD Holds a Responsibility), *Dagens Nyheter*, 30 October, p. 8.

Strömbäck, J. and Nord, L. W. (2008). 'Still a Second-Order Election: Comparing Swedish Media Coverage of the 2004 European Parliamentary Election and the 2002 National Election', in Kaid, L. L. (ed.) *The EU Expansion: Communicating Shared Sovereignty in the Parliamentary Elections*. Oxford: Peter Lang, pp. 137–152.

Tankard, J. W. (2001). 'The Empirical Approach to the Study of Media Framing', in Reese, S. D., Gandy, O. H. and Grant, A. E. (eds.) *Framing Public Life: Perspectives on Media and Our Understanding of the Social World*. New York: Routledge, pp. 111–121.

Threadgold, T. 2009. The Media and Migration in the United Kingdom, 1999 to 2009. Washington: Migration Policy Institute.

Tigervall, C. (2007). 'Svenska invandringsfilmer'. Antirasistiska motbilder i samtidsdebatten? (Swedish Immigration Films: Anti-Racist Counterparts in Contemporary Debate?' in Burns, T. R., Machado, N., Hellgren, Z. and Brodin, G. (eds.) *Makt, kultur och kontroll över invandrares livsvillkor. Multidimensionella perspektiv på strukturell diskriminering i Sverige* (Power, Culture and Control over Immigrants' Living Conditions: Multidimensional Perspectives on Structural Discrimination in Sweden). Uppsala: Acta Universitatis Upsaliensis, pp. 55–70.

Traub, J. 2016. The Death of the Most Generous Nation on Earth. *Foreign Policy*. Available at: https://foreignpolicy.com/2016/02/10/the-death-of-the-most-generous-nation-on-earth-sweden-syria-refugee-europe/ (Accessed 5 December 2019).

Treijs, E. (2015). Flyktingboendet i Nacka stängs (Asylum Accommodation in Nacka Closes), *Svenska Dagbladet*, 3 October, p. 28.
Tuchman, G. (1978). *Making News: A Study in the Construction of Reality*. New York: Free Press.
UNHCR 2017. *Global Trends: Forced Displacement in 2016*. Available at: http://file://uwfpcluster01.uw.lu.se/socl-mtj$/Desktop/DISS/UNHCR%20Global-Trends-2016.pdf (Accessed 30 November 2017).
Valkenburg, P. M., Semetko, H. A. and De Vreese, C. H. (1999). 'The Effects of News Frames on Readers' Thoughts and Recall', *Communication Research* 26(5), pp. 550–569.
van Dijk, T. A. (2000). '(New)s Racism: A Discourse Analytical Approach', in Cottle, S. (ed.) *Ethnic Minorities and the Media*. Maindenhead: Open University Press, pp. 33–49.
Westin, M. (2015). Stäng inte dörren. Lyft blicken i stället (Do Not Close the Door: Look Up Instead), *Dagens Nyheter*, 26 November, p. 35.
Wodak, R. (2019). 'Entering the "Post-Shame Era": The Rise of Illiberal Democracy, Populism and Neo-Authoritarianism in Europe', *Global Discourse: An Interdisciplinary Journal of Current Affairs*, 9(1), pp. 195–213.
Wolodarski, P. (2015). Flyktingspöket går åter genom debatten (The Refugee Ghost Under Debate Again), *Dagens Nyheter*, 30 August, p. 5.

# 8 Marie Sundström and Hedvig Obenius

# (De-)legitimation of migration: a critical study of social media discourses

'She is old and sick and will not live for many more years, you have to be humane by letting her stay and not be so damn bureaucratic (two angry smileys)'.[1] The quote comes from a comment adding to a discussion on Facebook about the case of Sahar, a 106-year-old woman whom the Swedish Migration Agency denied a permit to remain in Sweden.[2] The Agency argued that despite Sahar's old age and poor health, there was no reason for her not to return to the province of Kunduz in Afghanistan, which used to be her home. According to the Agency, this province was safe for Sahar to return to. That she was blind, partly paralysed, unable to speak, and had no one who could look after her in Afghanistan did not make her a 'particularly vulnerable person'[3] in need of refugee protection on humanitarian grounds, in the eyes of the Agency. The decision of the Agency was later overturned by the Migration Court, who argued it would be objectionable from precisely a humanitarian perspective to deport Sahar and that the deportation would amount to an inhumane and degradable treatment in violation of Article 3 (the right to life) of the European Convention on Human Rights. Instead, the court granted Sahar a temporary permit to remain in Sweden for 13 months. As this chapter reveals, the case of Sahar and the court's decision came to be much debated by the public in Sweden, especially on social media.

The chapter provides a critical analysis of the debate about this particular asylum case, using Van Leeuwen's analytical tool for analysing discursive (de-)legitimation, which is inspired by Habermas' understanding of public discourse and legitimacy. The aim of the analysis is to explore how social media users (de-)legitimised the decision of the court while they were discussing it on the Swedish evening paper *Expressen*'s Facebook page. The collection of data followed recommendations on collecting data online by Sveningsson et al. (2003). Firstly, a broad search was conducted, followed by a progressive limitation of the material. The keywords used when searching on Facebook were the Swedish word for 'Migration Court' (*Migrationsdomstol*) and 'Migration Court of Appeal' (*Migrationsöverdomstolen*).

# (De-)legitimation of migration 145

The search results were then filtered by choosing posts from some of the most recognised and largest newspapers in Sweden within the time frame 2015–2017. When searching for Migration Court cases that are discussed on social media, the case of Sahar had considerably more comments than similar cases discussed on established newspapers' commentary fields. The article about Sahar was posted by *Expressen* on 4 October 2017 and the comments were posted 4–7 October 2017. At the last date of data collection (18 December 2017), the article had 84 comments (74 of relevance for this study, 10 off topic), 21 shares and 1022 reactions.

As our study is set in Sweden at a time when it is increasingly difficult to be granted asylum, and many unsuccessful applicants are deported to unsafe situations and places (see chapter 5), the findings of our analysis are addressed while taking into account the inclusion/exclusion dichotomy that nation state borders imply (Fauser et al., 2019). This means that the discourses analysed correspond to either the inclusion or exclusion of asylum seekers like Sahar. In the analysis, we interpret the dichotomy of inclusion/exclusion through the conceptual lens of discursive violence; that is, when 'groups or persons' (in this case asylum seekers), through discourse, 'are cast into subaltern positions' (Jones et al., 1997, p. 394). Much like how borders are always violent (Jones, 2017), discourses on the (unwanted) crossing of state borders inevitably contain forms of violence (see also chapter 2). By adding the notion of discursive violence to the analysis, it becomes more relevant to both critical migration research and socio-legal studies. The application of discursive violence as the guiding concept illuminates how discourses subordinate and dehumanise migrants, making it legitimate to exclude them from the nation state.

While scholars have devoted considerable attention to the discursive legitimacy and political discussion generated by the authorities with top-down approaches (see e.g. Joormann, 2019), as well as to how traditional media (Strömbäck, 2009; Callaghan and Schnell, 2011) and courts affect the public discourse (e.g. Ura, 2014; Clark et al., 2018), they have paid relatively little attention to bottom-up discourses on legitimacy in civil society, particularly on social media. The growing importance of social media in the political landscape, however, makes it an important area to study (Bruns and Highfield, 2015). By focusing on one particular case at the micro-level, that is by going into the specificities in the discourses on the case of Sahar, we gain a novel insight into some of the processes that dehumanise asylum seekers and refugees.

According to Habermas, the 'deliberative legitimation process' (2006, p. 415) encompasses political discourses on three levels, affecting each other top down and bottom up: institutionalised discourses, mass media discourses and civil society discourses. Although this study focuses on the level of civil society, these levels are not isolated from each other, with the discourses in civil society being affected by the discourses on the other levels and vice versa. By adding a contemporary layer to the Habermasian understanding of public discourse, inasmuch as it takes place in social media, we argue that social media is potentially more inclusive when it comes to discussing and ultimately (de-)legitimising migration law and policy. In this sense, the chapter fills a gap in the literature of socio-legal research on discourses about legitimacy and legality in contemporary (civil) society.

### Public discourse as grounds for law's legitimacy

Habermas, having published extensively on the rule of law and its roots in the process of democratic will formation in Western liberal law contexts (Habermas, 1996), views the concept of public discourse as a fundamental part of legitimacy, rather than understanding the law's legitimacy in terms of legal correctness (Alexy, 2000, p. 138f.) To Habermas, it is the consensus achieved through a reflective public discourse that establishes what is considered as fair and good (Habermas, 1997). Thus, in order to understand legitimacy, one needs to turn to the discourses that emerge in the public sphere. It is here that critical discussions on law are to be found (Habermas, 1996, p. 42). Consequently, like in the case of Sahar, many discussions among citizens in the public sphere serve to legitimise law (Jacobsson, 1997). Moreover, it is not just the discourses that occur in the incipient stages of the law-making process that legitimise law. Habermas argues that 'Deliberative politics acquires its legitimating force from the discursive structure of an opinion- and will-formation that can fulfil its socially integrative function only because citizens expect its results to have a reasonable quality' (Habermas, 1996, p. 304). The implementation of law, and the outcome of such, is critically reviewed in the public discursive formation of opinion (Habermas, 2006). Public opinion in the singular 'only refers to the prevailing one among several public opinions' (Habermas, 2006, p. 417). Habermas suggests that both media and everyday conversation form such opinions in this phase of the legitimation process (Habermas, 2006).

In our analysis, this means that it is equally important to analyse the discourse about the court's decision as part of the discourse on migration policy and legislation (such as the regulations of the Swedish Migration Agency or the national Alien's Act 2005: 716). In the context of migration research, a strictly Habermasian understanding of gaining legitimacy through public discourse is problematic, however, since the participants within such discourse are, first and foremost, full or 'native' citizens (Fraser, 2007). The people that are most directly affected by immigration policies – asylum seekers, in the context of this study – are normally excluded from critical discussions about the legitimacy of these policies. Nonetheless, when public discourse takes place on social media, anyone with a stable internet connection, a registered user account for the respective social media

# (De-)legitimation of migration

platform, and sufficient command of the language in which the discussion happens can partake. Arguably, this makes social media a more inclusive platform than those of traditional public debates. Yet this inclusion is not unproblematic. Whilst it enables potentially anyone, including asylum seekers themselves, to have a say, social media today also hosts an important share of far right and racist discourse.

## The case of Sahar

Our analysis of the discourse in the case of Sahar is carried out by using Van Leeuwen's analytical tool, which is comprised of four discursive categories (e.g. Van Leeuwen and Wodak, 1999; Van Leeuwen, 2007). These categories can be used separately or combined. Thus, several categories can be identified in the same comment. This is also evident in our analysis, where some categories overlap at times. The four categories are: authorisation, moral evaluation, rationalisation and mythopoesis. The latter category only figures briefly in the analysis and involves (de-)legitimation through narrative, with cautionary tales being one subcategory (Van Leeuwen, 2008, pp. 117–118).

Our analytical work started with organising the comments into those who legitimised and those who de-legitimised the court's decision. Although there are many more legitimising comments than de-legitimising ones (forty-six legitimising, twenty-six de-legitimising and two indifferent), there is no consensus. After organising the comments into these two categories we identified Van Leeuwen's discursive categories in the comments before interpreting the discursive dichotomy of inclusion/exclusion through the concept of discursive violence. Introduced above, the concept of discursive violence is defined as processes and practices through which statements are made, recorded and legitimised through linguistic and other means of circulation.

> Discursive violence, then, involves using these processes and practices to script groups or persons *in* places, and in ways that counter how they would define themselves. In the process, discursive violence obscures the socio-spatial relations through which a group is subordinated. The end effect is that groups or persons are cast into subaltern positions. (Jones et al., 1997, p. 394, italics in original).

## Authorisation

The category of authorisation contains several subcategories: the authority of conformity, authority of tradition, expert authority, personal authority, role model authority and impersonal authority (for an example of laws and courts, see Van Leeuwen, 2008, p. 106). When de-legitimising the court's decision, references to the Migration Agency and (their interpretation of) migration regulations are made, for instance in this quote:

> She is registered and documented as a refugee in Croatia. Therefore, the Migration Agency made a correct decision, as the rules say that you should stay in the first safe country ... The authority must comply with the rules, then it is up to the Court if they want to break or follow them. If it becomes custom to break them due to high age being ground for asylum, it will be tough on the municipalities.[4]

This comment refers to impersonal authority when de-legitimising the court's decision whilst at the same time legitimising the Agency's decision. Furthermore, the last sentence can be seen as an example of mythopoesis and its subcategory of cautionary tales: The author claims that the court, a part of the Swedish state bureaucracy, is acting illegitimately. This comment refers to the Migration Agency's decision to legitimise Sahar's expulsion, thus excluding her because she is a non-citizen, because it is, as the commentator states, in accordance with the law. Thus, the commentator refers to the bureaucratic implementation of Swedish migration law to legitimise exclusion: 'Invoking the power of the Law legitimises the means by which inclusion and exclusion takes place' (Lynn and Lea, 2003, p. 427).

**Moral evaluation**

Van Leeuwen's category of moral evaluation concerns discourses connected to moral values. Such moral values are contextual and dependent on cultural values of 'common sense'. The values can be more or less explicit, or implied by using adjectives such as 'bad' or 'good'. The category of moral evaluation is also divided into two subcategories: abstractions and analogies. (De-)legitimation through evaluation links adjectives describing how a practice, action or phenomenon occurs, to a quality, which the discussants either praise or criticise. Abstractions refer to practices connected to moral qualities or values (Van Leeuwen, 2008, pp. 109–112). The subcategory of analogies refers to comparisons between actions, or events, which relate to certain moral values. The comments that are identified as belonging to the category of moral evaluation almost exclusively legitimise the court's decision. This corresponds to Van Leeuwen and Wodak's (1999, p. 111) conclusion that 'legal systems must ultimately always be grounded in moral systems'. Only two of the comments that de-legitimise the decision fall into the subcategory of abstractions. These comments question Sahar's age and her sincerity in claiming that she is 106 years old. By doing so, they refer to the practice of lying, which is generally considered immoral. Since she is perceived to be lying, she does not deserve a residence permit. Interdiscursively,[5] these comments can be seen as similar to certain streams of the

# (De-)legitimation of migration 149

discourse about unaccompanied refugee children in Sweden. In such discourse, people argue that the children are lying about their age, claiming to be younger than eigtheen (Stretmo, 2014, pp. 41, 151–153). This is also seen in several of the comments analysed, where one commentator writes: 'Funny that she knows her age when there are grown men who do not know if they are 16 or 40 (laughing smiley).'[6] Asylum seekers are also accused of lying about other things, such as their sexuality (Parker, 2015) or their religious beliefs (Lillian, 2006). This adds up to a violent discursive construction of asylum seekers as liars. By linking asylum seekers to an immoral practice these discourses ascribe refugees with negative attributes, which serve to other them (van Dijk, 1999).

Although the most commonly found subcategory in the legitimising comments is that of evaluation, there are also several legitimising comments that use abstractions. These comments are often short and contain words such as 'humanity', 'unethical', 'charitable', 'inhumane', 'humanistic', 'shameful' and 'humane'.[7] Their shared feature is that they include some kind of adjective regarding a quality that encompasses a moral value. In addition to de-legitimising the Migration Agency's decision, these comments also de-legitimise the comments that oppose the court's decision in favour of Sahar's asylum application, and in doing so they legitimise the court's position.

One longer comment of moral abstractions also contains theoretical rationalisation and evaluation by referring explicitly to bureaucratisation: 'She is old and sick and will not live for many more years, you have to be humane by letting her stay and not be so damn bureaucratic (two angry smileys)'. This commentator uses 'humane' as a moral value, putting it in contrast to bureaucracy and its practices. A similar comment states that: 'It shouldn't have been any hassle from the start. What kinds of robots are working with this? Happy for her sake.'[8] This comment uses the metaphor of 'robots' making decisions at the Migration Agency – and robots cannot be humane. Correspondingly, the following comment indicates that bureaucracies tend to interpret rules in a rigid way, with no room for values and humanity: 'I understand that there are regulations et cetera, but to throw out a 106-year-old??!! Thank God that someone used their brain and [showed] some humanity'.[9] Furthermore, the comment can be seen as referring to theoretical rationalisation (which is legitimation by referring to truth claims, as discussed later in this chapter) in stating that Sahar is old and sick, since it is known that this will result in her passing away in the somewhat near future – thus, she does not risk becoming a burden on the welfare state and its taxpayers. This refers to a common fear of the risk of migration (see the Introduction to this volume) and of a lack of (economic) integration of newcomers.

There are a few comments that can be placed into the subcategory of analogies. For example, one commentator writes that one should: 'Show solidarity with those who are vulnerable in the world. However, I get very sad when those who are wanted due to links to terrorist groups are not expelled at once! They should not be here for one second longer!'[10] Constructing asylum seekers as potential terrorists, and thus a potential threat to the host society, is a common phenomenon when asylum seekers and refugees are represented in public discourse (for example, see Goodman and Speer, 2007; Innes, 2010; Abdelhady and Malmberg, 2018). Other comments in the thread contain slander about migrants in general (including asylum seekers as well as refugees), such as the claim that they commit crimes and are engaged in raping, killing and shooting. This construction is also manifest in other studies on discourses about migrants (see e.g. Masocha, 2015; Devlin and Grant 2017; Moore et al., 2018). It forms a part of the discourse that constructs asylum seekers as a threat. When claiming that some are involved in criminal (read: immoral) practices, so posing a threat to the citizens of the nation, the above comments also serve to position certain groups (for example retired native Swedes versus asylum seekers, refugees and migrants in general) against each other.

The discursive construction of the asylum seeker as a threat is related to the discursive construction of 'genuine' and 'bogus' asylum seekers. The 'bogus asylum seeker' is portrayed as the problem (Lynn and Lea, 2003, p. 433). It is claimed that these are people who are not in sincere need of protection, whilst 'genuine' asylum seekers have a real need for refuge. 'Genuine asylum-seekers appear to earn their claim to citizenship rights' (Lynn and Lea, 2003, p. 434), while the 'bogus' asylum seeker does not. 'Bogus' asylum seekers are presented as being a threat to, and sabotage for, the 'genuine' ones (Lynn and Lea, 2003). This construction has generated a perception that many asylum seekers are bogus, which in turn questions 'the legitimacy of all asylum seekers' (Goodman et al., 2017, p. 106). This construction is also used as a rhetorical strategy by politicians to legitimise a restrictive immigration policy (van Dijk, 1993). Along with other studies, for example the one provided by Lynn and Lea (2003), this chapter shows that the discursive construction of bogus asylum seekers has become so established in Sweden and many other countries that it is no longer questioned.

The quote above also shows how the discursive construction of genuine and bogus asylum seekers is used as a rhetorical disclaimer against accusations of racism (see Hewitt and Stokes, 1975). By stating, 'Show solidarity with those who are vulnerable in the world', the commentator alleviates criticism of being a racist in the forthcoming argument that some asylum seekers and migrants are terrorists: 'However, I get very sad when those who are wanted due to links to terrorist groups are not expelled at once! They should not be here for one second longer!' The main moral aspect of the legal decision on the case of Sahar (that is, should an elderly and sick woman be granted refugee status?) is often illuminated in the media (Jenkins, 2009) and tends to engage the public (Eriksen and Weigård, 2000). Even

# (De-)legitimation of migration

if there is no consensus within the legitimation process in Sahar's case on social media as we analysed, the dominant position legitimises the decision by appealing to morality. Habermas argues that moral norms transcend diversity and plurality in a modern society, but it is not only moral norms that are important and visible in legal discourse (Habermas, 1996, pp. 106–111). Collective goals, social problems and material conflicts are also significant (Eriksen and Weigård, 2000, p. 175). This becomes evident in the comments below that refer to cost, taxes and other problems that should be prioritised. Such comments claim to be concerned about the welfare of 'our own' Swedish pensioners, which we discuss in the next section.

## Rationalisation

The category of rationalisation describes the legitimation strategy by reference to rationality (though it can also contain traces of morality). Following Van Leeuwen's model, there are two subcategories of rationalisation: instrumental rationalisation and theoretical rationalisation. The first subcategory is applicable when discussants (de-)legitimise a practice by referring to goals, purposes, uses and effects together with an element of moralisation (Van Leeuwen, 2008, pp. 113–117). Theoretical rationalisation is (de-)legitimation through 'truth claims', such as a discussant claiming to describe 'the way things are' (Van Leeuwen, 2008, p. 116).

A few comments suggest that giving Sahar a residence permit poses a threat to Swedish welfare. Several commentators question who is paying for her living costs (health care, accommodation, dental care, etc.), and argue, for example, that: 'She has not contributed a penny to the pension system. Nor paid taxes. [But only] takes from Swedish pensioners!'[11] This comment, along with similar comments that de-legitimise the court's decision to let Sahar stay, refers to instrumental rationalisation inasmuch as it claims that it is an immoral practice to use someone else's money (which Sahar does not deserve, as the argument continues). The principle idea of this argument is that those who pay taxes are those who are eligible to benefit from the welfare system in Sweden (see also Introduction in this volume). Such discourse shifts the focus from asylum seekers' need of protection (Lynn and Lea, 2003) to constructing asylum seekers as scroungers (Anderson, 2013).

It also implies a rhetoric of 'us versus them', in which the refugees are 'them' in their deviancy. In the case of Sahar, the 'us' is akin to Swedish citizens (or possibly even white native Swedes), with an emphasis on Swedish pensioners. Meanwhile, Sahar is categorised as 'them'. The 'us' are those who should be the primary beneficiaries of the Swedish welfare system, whereas 'their' claims to such rights are highly disputed. By presenting a group, in this case Swedish pensioners, as vulnerable, such comments try to seize the 'opportunity to maximize the sense of injustice, and heighten the feelings of animosity generated' (Lynn and Lea, 2003, pp. 437).

There are several similar arguments where asylum seekers and refugees are considered to pose a threat to the Swedish economy. One commentator writes: 'We cannot take care of all foreigners over 100. Contrary to what some think, we do not have unlimited resources. She should have never come here!'[12] Conclusively, Sahar is considered a threat to the Swedish welfare state because she needs welfare provisions, and so is seen as taking from Swedish citizens who are legitimate welfare recipients. A similar inter-discursive argument is evident in a study by Joormann (2019, p. 125) on asylum cases decided by the Swedish Migration Court of Appeal. In 'the legal discourse of MIG 2007:25 [one of the court's decisions] ... one important argument for the final decision is the "threat" of every sick child in the world coming to Sweden for healthcare.' Many such descriptions are also found in the wake of the refugee crisis of 2015. This has been defined as 'the *economisation frame* [which] perpetuates the image of asylum seekers and refugees as economic burdens and threat to the host country's economic prosperity and welfare by referring to large quantities of money' (Greussing and Boomgaarden, 2017, p. 1756, italics in original). When asylum seekers and refugees are constructed as an economic threat to the host state and its welfare system, they are, at the same time, being de-legitimised as eligible recipients of Swedish welfare resources. Swedish citizens are, in such discourses (as represented in the quote above), perceived as legitimate inhabitants of the nation state, hence eligible to the state's welfare resources. By constructing refugees as a threat to the Swedish welfare system, the 'walling' of the welfare state through restrictive migration laws and policies (Barker, 2018) appears to be the rational response in the Nordic context (see also chapters 6 and 7).

Some of the legitimising comments also refer to instrumental rationalisation. Several of them state that they do not mind if their taxes go to Sahar, or individuals in her situation. This can be seen as creating a counter discourse to the one trying to safeguard native Swedes' welfare. One commentator, for instance, writes: 'Don't be afraid, I can cover all the costs, if the Migration Agency accepts it (heart emoji)'.[13] This comment entails the (moralised) purpose of letting Sahar stay, and the means to achieve that goal is the commentator's money. This is a more humanitarian approach visible in the discourse on refugees in the aftermath of the perceived refugee crisis. It opposes the economisation frame, addressing humanitarianism (see Greussing and Boomgaarden, 2017). As seen above, this humanitarian approach is also evident when legitimising the court's decision due to moral evaluation.

Another comment from this counter discourse states that: 'She will get about 3,800–4,300 Swedish crowns a month, so do not worry, your tax money will probably not go to her.'[14] This comment contains elements of theoretical rationalisation as the commentator argues that Sahar will get a very low pension, as if this was the truth and 'the way things are' (Van Leeuwen, 2008, p. 116). On the other hand, other comments containing truth claims de-legitimise the court's decision by referring to theoretical rationalisation: 'Afghanistan is safe almost everywhere'[15] and 'You do not have to flee from Croatia!'[16] They are stated as short sentences and as truth claims, with no need for the commentator to provide further arguments.

## Discursive violence and inclusion/exclusion

In the comments on social media about the case of Sahar, discursive violence is manifest through the exclusionary discourses that ascribe migrants and asylum seekers with inferior attributes. These discourses define who is legitimately excluded from, or included within, the borders of the state. For example, when a commentator claims that Sahar does not have valid reasons for seeking asylum, the discourse constructs her as a liar, which undermines her credibility. This is an example of discursive violence inasmuch as someone is described in a degrading way. The process of discursive violence may have material effects when the discourse serves to legitimate a decision that will deny Sahar asylum.

Imperative to the inclusion/exclusion dichotomy of the borders of the nation state is the construction of the legal identity of being an asylum seeker or refugee. To belong to this identity is not built upon anything like a common origin, ethnicity or culture. It is rather the experience of being 'a victimised object of bureaucratic intervention' (Fernando, 2016, p. 395). To be recognised as an asylum seeker or refugee makes a person hyper-visible, such as in public discourses like the case of Sahar.

Many of the comments that legitimise the decision refer to morality, where the consensus is that it is wrong of the Swedish migration bureaucracy to expel Sahar. By doing so, they argue that what would be morally legitimate is to let her stay and to include her in Swedish welfare provisions. Reasons for being inclusionary in this case are frequently illuminated in the comments that 'we' should take care of Sahar, being sick, elderly and female. The understanding and framing of the comments are that Sahar is a victim in need of protection (i.e. inclusion), where health status, age and gender are of great significance. These attributes match the construction of the female asylum seeker as being vulnerable and helpless (Malkki, 1996; Fernando, 2016; Lugones, 2016). Accordingly, she is perceived by the authors of these comments as a 'legitimate refugee', meaning that she 'deserves' the inclusion within the Swedish state through a residence permit. An inclusionary discourse is also evident in comments referring to instrumental rationalisation on economic resources; for instance, where one commentator argues that they are willing to pay for her.

This inclusive discourse is countered by an exclusionary one, based on who is considered as an illegitimate recipient of the Swedish state's welfare resources. Such comments claim that Sahar has not paid any taxes and therefore should be excluded from Swedish welfare provisions such as health care and pensions. This exclusionary discourse is based on a rhetoric of 'us versus them', in which Swedish pensioners are the core of the 'us', and Sahar and other asylum seekers are not only constructed as 'them' but even claimed to be a threat to, for instance, Swedish pensioners and welfare resources more generally. In this discourse, Swedish citizens are already included in the welfare system. They have paid taxes and are, therefore, to be considered legitimate recipients of welfare resources.

Another example of an inclusionary discourse is that Sahar is asserted to be a 'genuine' asylum seeker by some commentators. Nonetheless, when expressing solidarity and inclusion towards Sahar, there is also a construction of the 'bogus' asylum seeker embedded in their argument. The construction of the 'bogus' asylum seekers, who pose a threat towards the welfare state, is mainly built on the argument that it is the perceived mass of migrants that is problematic (Lynn and Lea, 2003). By referring to masses of bogus asylum seekers there is a legitimate case for excluding all asylum seekers. This discourse legitimises the exclusionary practice of re-bordering through restrictive migration laws and border controls, in order to protect the welfare state against such risks (see also the Introduction to this volume).

## Conclusion

The chapter contributes to the understanding of the discursive underpinnings of contemporary discourses about asylum seekers and migrants. In critically analysing how discourses on social media (de-)legitimise the court's decision on the case of Sahar through an inclusionary/exclusionary perspective, we have also identified discursive violence against asylum seekers, refugees and migrants in general. There are nearly twice as many Facebook comments that legitimise the court's decision to grant Sahar a thirteen-month residence permit compared to those that de-legitimise it. The analysed material also includes, however, discursive violence against asylum seekers, refugees and migrants through the use of binaries such as Us and Them on the one hand and 'genuine and bogus' asylum seekers on the other. Discursive violence is also illustrated in the comments that ascribe asylum seekers with inferior attributes and supposedly immoral behaviour, such as lying. Asylum seekers are constructed as a threat to the welfare state through an economic framing where the monetary costs are attached to the de-legitimatisation of claims for asylum like Sahar's.

This study adds a contemporary layer to socio-legal studies of migration by focusing on social media discourses. Adopting a contemporary

# (De-)legitimation of migration

Habermasian perspective on law's legitimacy as something attained through public discourses on social media, we have illustrated how these discourses not only (de-)legitimise the court's decision in the case of Sahar, but also how the recently adopted restrictive migration laws and policies in Sweden can be legitimised. According to Habermas, it is crucial to study the discursive 'deliberative legitimation process' (Habermas, 2006, p. 415) on three levels, one of them being that of civil society. Thus, in order to understand the complexities of the legitimation processes of the current re-bordering of the Swedish state, we argue that it is important to study the discourses in civil society by using a bottom-up approach. Our analysis of social media comments on the case of Sahar exemplifies this approach. This analysis does not only contribute to an understanding of the normative and discursive dimensions of the legitimation process in civil society, but also constitutes a novel addition to critical migration research in Sweden. At the same time as we learn a lot about Sahar, which arguably serves to humanise her, both the discourses that legitimise and de-legitimise the court's decision also contribute to the dehumanisation of Sahar in the sense of othering her. That is, by debating and scrutinising Sahar and her story on social media she is made into an object. The refugee. The Other.

## Notes

1 'Hon är gammal och sjuklig och kommer inte leva så många år till då måste man va human och låta henne stanna och inte va så jävla byråkratisk (två arga smileys)'.
2 The Swedish Migration Agency makes the initial decision on applications for visa, residence permit, Swedish citizenship or asylum. In the event of a rejection, the applicant can appeal the decision to the Migration Agency. If the Agency does not change its decision, the appeal is brought to the Migration Court (The Swedish Courts, 2018; see also chapter 2 above).
3 Chapter 5 paragraph 6 of the Aliens Act SFS 2005:716.
4 Hon är registrerad och dokumenterad flykting i Kroatien. Då beslutade migrationsverket rätt då reglerna är sådana att man ska stanna i första säkra land.. Myndigheten ska följa reglerna sen får domstolen välja om de skall bryta mot dem eller inte. Blir det praxis att bryta mot dem med hög ålder som asylskäl blir det tufft för kommunerna.
5 Interdiscursivity is the link between different discourses (Vaara and Tienari, 2010, p. 245).
6 'Roligt att hon vet sin ålder när det finns vuxna män som inte vet om de är 16 eller 40 (skrattande smiley).'
7 'mänsklighet', 'oetiskt', 'välvilligt', 'omänskligt', 'humanistiskt', 'skamligt' and 'humant'.
8 'Skulle inte varit strul från början. Vad är det för robotar som jobbar med detta? Glad för hennes skull.'

9   'Jag förstår att det finns regelverk osv men att slänga ut en 106-åring??!! Tack och lov att nån använde hjärnan och använde lite medmänsklighet'.
10  'Visa solidaritet med de utsatta i världen. Däremot blir jag väldigt ledsen när de som är efterlysta för kopplingar till terrorgrupper inte blir utvisade med det samma! De ska inte vistas här en enda sekund!'
11  'Hon har inte tillfört pensionssystemet ett öre. Inte betalat skatt. Alltså tar hon från Svenska pensionärer!'
12  'Vi kan itnte ta hand om alla utlänningar över 100. Till skillnad från vad somliga tror har vi inte gränslösa resurser. Hon skulle aldrig kommit hit!'
13  'Va inte rädda jag kan stå för alla kostnader om migrationsverket accepterar <3'.
14  'Hon kommer få ca 3800–4300 I månaden så va inte orolig din skatt går förmodligen inte till henne.'
15  'Afghanistan är säkert nästan överallt.'
16  'Man behöver inte fly från Kroatien!'


**References**

Abdelhady, D. and Malmberg, G. Fristedt (2018). 'Media Representation of the Refugee Crisis: Islam, Securitization and Self-Reflection', in O'Donnell, E. (ed.) *Anti-Judaism, Islamophobia, and Interreligious Hermeneutics: How Conflicts in the Middle East and Beyond Shape the Way We See the Religious Other*. Leiden: Brill Publishers, pp. 108–136.

Alexy, R. (2000). 'On the Thesis of a Necessary Connection between Law and Morality: Bulygin's Critique', *Ratio Juris* 13(2), pp. 138–147.

Anderson, B. L. (2013) *Us and Them? The Dangerous Politics of Immigration Control*. Oxford: Oxford University Press.

Barker, V. (2018). *Nordic Nationalism and Penal Order: Walling the Welfare State*. Abingdon: Routledge.

Bruns, A. and Highfield, T. (2015). 'Is Habermas on Twitter? Social Media and the Public Sphere', in Bruns, A. Enli, G., Skogerbo, E., Larsson, A. O. and Christensen, C. (eds.) *The Routledge Companion to Social Media and Politics*. London: Routledge, pp. 56–73.

Callaghan, K. and Schnell, F. (2011). 'Assessing the Democratic Debate: How the News Media Frame Elite Policy Discourse', *Political Communication* 18(2), pp. 183–213.

Clark, T. S., Staton, J. K., Wang, Y. and Agichtein, E. (2018). 'Using Twitter to Study Public Discourse in the Wake of Judicial Decisions: Public Reactions to the Supreme Court's Same-Sex Marriage Cases', *Journal of Law and Courts* 6(1), pp. 93–126.

Devlin, A. M., and Grant, C. (2017). 'The Sexually Frustrated, the Dumb and the Libtard Traitors: A Typology of Insults Used in the Positioning of Multiple Others in Irish Online Discourse Relating to Refugees, Asylum Seekers, Immigrants and Migrants', *European Journal of Communication* 32(6), pp. 598–613.

Eriksen, E. O. and Weigård, J. (2000). *Habermas politiska teori* (Habermas' Political Theory). Lund: Studentlitteratur.

Fauser, M., Friedrichs, A. and Harders, L. (2019). 'Migrations and Borders: Practices and Politics of Inclusion and Exclusion in Europe from the Nineteenth to the Twenty-First Century', *Journal of Borderlands Studies* 34(4), pp. 483–488.

Fernando, N. (2016). 'The Discursive Violence of Postcolonial Asylum in the Irish Republic', *Postcolonial Studies* 19(4), pp. 393–408.

Fraser, N. (2007). 'Special Section: Transnational Public Sphere: Transnationalizing the Public Sphere: On the Legitimacy and Efficacy of Public Opinion in a Post-Westphalian World', *Theory, Culture & Society* 24(4), pp. 7–30.

Goodman, S., and Speer, S. A. (2007). 'Category Use in the Construction of Asylum Seekers', *Critical Discourse Studies* 4(2), pp. 165–185.

Goodman, S., Sirriyeh, A. and McMahon, S. (2017). 'The Evolving (Re)Categorisations of Refugees Throughout the "Refugee/Migrant Crisis"', *Journal of Community & Applied Social Psychology* 27(2), pp. 105–114.

Greussing, E. and Boomgaarden, H. G. (2017). 'Shifting the Refugee Narrative? An Automated Frame Analysis of Europe's 2015 Refugee Crisis', *Journal of Ethnic and Migration Studies* 43(11), pp. 1749–1774.

Habermas, J. (1996). *Between Facts and Norms: Contributions to a Discourse Theory of Law and Democracy*. London: Polity.

Habermas, J. (1997). *Diskurs, rätt och demokrati* (Discourse, Right and Democracy). Gothenburg: Daidalos.

Habermas, J. (2006). 'Political Communication in Media Society: Does Democracy Still Enjoy an Epistemic Dimension? The Impact of Normative Theory on Empirical Research', *Communication Theory* 16(4), pp. 411–426.

Hewitt, J. and Stokes, R. (1975). 'Disclaimers', *American Sociological Review* 40(1), pp. 1–11.

Innes, A. J. (2010). 'When the Threatened Become the Threat: The Construction of Asylum Seekers in British Media Narratives', *International Relations* 24(4), pp. 456–477.

Jacobsson, K. (1997). 'Discursive Will Formation and the Question of Legitimacy in European Politics', *Scandinavian Political Studies* 20(1), pp. 69–90.

Jenkins, P. (2009). 'Failure To Launch: Why Do Some Social Issues Fail to Detonate Moral Panics?' *The British Journal of Criminology* 49(1), pp. 35–47.

Jones, J. P., Nast, H. J. and Roberts, S. M. (eds.) (1997). *Thresholds in Feminist Geography: Difference, Methodology, Representation*. Lanham: Rowman & Littlefield.

Jones, R. (2017). *Violent Borders: Refugees and the Right to Move*. London: Verso Books.

Joormann, M. (2019). *Legitimized Refugees: A Critical Investigation of Legitimacy Claims within the Precedents of Swedish Asylum Law*. PhD, Lund University.

Lillian, D. L. (2006). 'Neo-Conservative Racist Discourse: A Canadian Case Study', *Word* 57(1), pp. 71–95.

Lugones M. (2016). 'The Coloniality of Gender', in Harcourt W. (ed.) *The Palgrave Handbook of Gender and Development*. London: Palgrave Macmillan, pp. 13–33.

Lynn, N., and Lea, S. (2003). 'A Phantom Menace and the New Apartheid: The Social Construction of Asylum-Seekers in the United Kingdom', *Discourse & Society* 14(4), pp. 425–452.

Malkki, L. (1996). 'Speechless Emissaries: Refugees, Humanitarianism, and Dehistoricization', *Cultural Anthropology* 11(3), pp. 377–404.

Masocha, S. (2015). *Asylum Seekers, Social Work and Racism.* London: Palgrave Macmillan.

Moore, K., Berry, M. and Garcia-Blanco, I. (2018). 'Saving Refugees or Policing the Seas? How the National Press of Five EU Member States Framed News Coverage of the Migration Crisis', *Justice, Power and Resistance* 2(1), pp. 66–95.

Parker, S. (2015). '"Unwanted Invaders": The Representation of Refugees and Asylum Seekers in the UK and Australian Print Media', *Myth and Nation* 23(1), pp. 1–21.

Stretmo, L. (2014). *Governing the Unaccompanied Child: Media, Policy and Practice.* PhD, Gothenburg University.

Strömbäck, J. (2009). *Makt, medier och samhälle. En introduktion till politisk kommunikation* (Power, Media and Society: An Introduction to Political Communication), Stockholm: SNS förlag.

Sveningsson Elm, M., Lövheim, M. and Bergquist, M. (2003). *Att fånga nätet. Kvalitativa metoder för internetforskning* (To Capture the Internet: Qualitative Methods for Internet Research). Lund: Studentlitteratur.

Swedish Courts (2018). Available at: www.domstol.se/Funktioner/English/The-Swedish-courts/County-administrative-courts/Migration-Courts (Accessed 10 February 2018).

Ura, J. D. (2014). 'Backlash and Legitimation: Macro Political Responses to Supreme Court Decisions', *American Journal of Political Science* 58(1), pp. 110–126.

Vaara, E. and Tienari, J. (2010). 'Critical Discourse Analysis', in Mills, A. J., Durepos, G. and Wiebe, E. (eds.) *Encyclopedia of Case Study Research.* Thousand Oaks: SAGE, pp. 245–247.

van Dijk, T. A. (1993). *Elite Discourse and Racism.* Beverly Hills: SAGE.

van Dijk, T. A. (1999). Discourse and Racism. *Discourse & Society* 10(2), pp. 145–159.

Van Leeuwen, T. (2007). 'Legitimation in Discourse and Communication', *Discourse & Communication* 1(1), pp. 91–112.

Van Leeuwen, T. (2008). *Discourse and Practice: New Tools for Critical Analysis.* Oxford: Oxford University Press.

Van Leeuwen, T and Wodak, R. (1999). 'Legitimizing Immigration Control: A Discourse-Historical Analysis', *Discourse Studies*, 1(1), pp. 83–118.

# PART III

# The meaning of refugeeness

# 9 Nina Gren

# Living bureaucratisation: young Palestinian men encountering a Swedish introductory programme for refugees

> My dream is to study at the university. But when you go to [the caseworkers], they do not listen to your ambitions and dreams. They make you believe that you can tell them what you want. In the end they will write in their plans what *they* want. You want to study? Okay, you are going to study. They write 'Amir wants to continue his education. Amir wants to study Swedish. Amir is going to take the social integration course. And this basically means that according to this [action] plan, you should show us that you have attended [language] school.' (Amir)

This chapter discusses the experiences of young Palestinian men in an introductory programme for refugees in Sweden. The programme was designed to support people who had been accepted for asylum in learning Swedish and introducing them to the labour market (Larsson, 2015; Ennerberg, 2017). Despite the good intentions of policy-makers, my interlocutors, like Amir who is quoted above, often feel that it is a waste of time to follow the programme. The programme is not adjusted to their individual aspirations, and they have few possibilities of deciding what to do with their own lives while being enrolled in it. In this chapter, I argue that their frustrations can be understood primarily as reactions to a bureaucratisation of daily life and to the institutional requirements that limit their sense of agency. Bureaucratisation in this case leads to resistance but also to hopelessness and readjustments of personal ambitions.

Many migrants from war-torn and poor countries are well prepared for multiple losses in life and for enduring hardships (Jackson, 2008). Among Palestinians, there is even a frequently used term, *sumud*, for patience or endurance, which means to keep going despite all (Peteet, 2005, pp. 148ff.). However, migrants are seldom prepared for the bureaucratisation of everyday life that is set in motion in Northern European welfare states when dealing with different institutions and authorities as asylum-seekers or refugees (see also chapter 10).[1] The Swedish street-level bureaucrats are, in general, described as friendly and caring by my interlocutors; still, their practices are, as we will learn, experienced as constraining and excluding.

In addition, I claim that the bureaucratic labelling of my interlocutors as 'refugees' (Zetter, 1991), whose reason for migrating was fleeing persecution and violent conflict, conceals their aspirations to attain or continue higher education. This co-existence (or sometimes blending) of different motivations for mobility, and its connection to imagining a better life in faraway places after migration, is well-known within anthropology (Salazar, 2011), even though this particular mixing of political reasons for fleeing, on the one hand, and aspirations for social mobility through education, on the other, has received little attention. Appadurai (1996) emphasises that the practice of imagining (for example distant places, upward social mobility, safety) is a driving force behind increased migration globally. Imagination seems vital when deciding to migrate: either one does so in a context of war and violence or unemployment and poverty, or both. Appadurai (2013, pp. 286ff.) sees the capacities to imagine and to aspire as grounded within local systems of value, meaning, interaction, and opposition, even though recognisably universal. The frustrations my interlocutors experienced while being in the introductory programme highlight that wishes to find 'safety' often mingle with imagination of what a good life constitutes for many Palestinian refugees. The need to flee does not automatically diminish other needs or wishes in life. For migration agencies, introductory programmes and other parts of national bureaucracies, such co-existence seems difficult or even impossible to handle. As a result, my ethnographic material shows that from the perspective of some refugees, introductory programmes that do not take educational ambitions into account may seem meaningless, and refugees may, either deliberately or not, ignore bureaucratic requirements in an attempt to break out of conditions that are experienced as immobilising.

After a section on methodology and a theoretical framework, I briefly discuss Palestinian migration to Sweden, Palestinian desires for education, and Swedish introductory programmes for refugees in general. Then, I discuss my material in two ethnographic sections. First, I examine the procedures within the introductory programme, and the feeling of being stuck that my interlocutors experience. Second, I outline the tactics they use to juggle institutional requirements while maintaining their aspirations for higher education. The final section includes a summary of my findings and more general conclusions about my interlocutors' future in Sweden. My analysis points out that a focus on institutional requirements within introductory programmes for refugees may create hopelessness and frustration among participants to an extent that they give up on their aspirations for higher education and instead focus on getting employed in a low-status job or, possibly, migrating onwards. Ironically, the introductory programme, which aims at the socio-economic integration of refugees, makes some of them give up on ever becoming part of Swedish society.

## Methodology

This chapter builds on ethnographic material collected since 2011 among Swedish-Palestinians. The bulk of fieldwork was carried out in relation to an introductory programme for refugees in a city in southern Sweden during 2014–2015. The Swedish Public Employment Service (SPES, *Arbetsförmedlingen*) coordinates the introductory programme; my fieldwork included participant observation, qualitative interviews and informal conversations with staff at a local branch of the authority, and with refugees enrolled at the programme. I also attended information meetings for new refugees and held meetings about preliminary findings with personnel to get additional perspectives from a wider range of staff.

In this chapter, I concentrate on the accounts of four young Palestinian men with whom I established more long-term relationships. They were between twenty-five and thirty-three years of age and had waited for asylum for six to nine months before starting the introductory programme. I did not intend to focus on males but since Palestinian migration is dominated by young men this is how my snowballing turned out. The four men come from different parts of the Middle East: one grew up in Gaza, two are from the West Bank and one is from Syria. They have different socioeconomic backgrounds and have grown up in Palestinian refugee camps run by United Nations Relief and Work Agency for Palestine Refugees in the Middle East (UNRWA).[2]

Being a Swede and thus a native in the receiving society was initially a disadvantage, since some refugees, out of courtesy, hesitated to be critical of the introductory programme in front of me. When I got to know them better such politeness disappeared. In this chapter, all names are pseudonyms and some personal details have been changed so to ensure the anonymity of individuals interviewed and the confidentiality of the local office of the SPES where I conducted fieldwork.

## Bureaucratisation in welfare states

Weber's work (2013 [1922]) is the point of departure for most contemporary research about bureaucracy. He saw the convenience of a well-managed bureaucracy, which can promote trust and smooth interactions between citizens and representatives of the state, even though he also feared the expansion of bureaucracy, which he saw as an inevitable and self-reproducing aspect of capitalist production. Weber famously termed the entrapments of modern societies building on bureaucratic over-rationalisation rather than tradition and higher values as 'an iron cage' (Bauman, 1989; Cochrane, 2018). When people meet and interact with bureaucracy, they thus risk being turned into cases and divested of their individuality.

For Eisenstadt (1959, p. 312), bureaucratisation implies that bureaucratic activities and power expand to many different areas of social life and that bureaucratic service goals tend to become less important in relation to the interests of bureaucracy itself and/or the society's elite. In this chapter, bureaucratisation is primarily about the extension of bureaucracy and less about the underlying power interests, even though the displacement or dwindling significance of service goals can be taken as signs of power and control. This also implies that the tentacles of bureaucratisation have reached areas of social life that many hoped would be free from bureaucratic regulations.

Scandinavian welfare programmes have intervened in people's private lives to a larger extent than in many other places (Olwig, 2011, p. 180). There are, however, differences between categories of citizens and residents and their relation to the state (Lister, 2007; Lundberg and Strange, 2017). Healthy and employed citizens are left at peace, while those who are directly economically dependent on the state, such as citizens on sick leave or newly arrived refugees on state allocation (that is, with asylum and residency but not yet taxpayers or citizens) tend to face more interventions. The latter's everyday lives are bureaucratised and controlled to a larger extent than those who can provide for themselves. There are strong ideals of reciprocity in the social contract between welfare systems and citizens within Scandinavia; a 'good' citizen does not remain dependent on the welfare state, but rather works and pays taxes so as to continue to receive benefits and reciprocates all the benefits that the citizen has received since birth (Olwig, 2011). In a comparable way, the introductory programme under scrutiny expects the inscribed refugees to reciprocate benefits (such as allocations and free courses) by following institutional procedures, for instance, by attending language classes as agreed, and thus showing that they are becoming 'good', responsible and self-supporting citizens.

**Refugee labels**

The people who are allowed to follow the programme discussed in this chapter have been accepted for asylum and are thus legally defined refugees. Since a ground-breaking article with examples from the Greek-Cypriot refugee situation by Zetter (1991), many scholars have argued that the bureaucratic labelling of refugees is a complex and dynamic process occurring inter-relationally between people who have fled and the international and national institutions that attempt to assist them (e.g. Peteet, 2005; Ludwig, 2013; Janmyr and Mourad, 2018). Implicit values guide refugee assistance, and the labelling of target groups is not neutral (Zetter, 1991, p. 45). Through labelling, a process of stereotyping occurs. Refugees become conflated with certain characteristics and needs depending on the context they are in, and on the degree and nature of control and opportunities provided by institutions within host countries and aid organisations (Zetter, 1991, p. 41).

As Zetter (2007) notes, the international refugee regime has changed significantly since the early 1990s. Today, it is often governments in the Global North, rather than NGOs and humanitarian organisations in the South, that form and transform the refugee label. In the case of Sweden, it is primarily the Migration Agency that forms the refugee label by interpreting the Aliens Act, accepting some individuals and groups as refugees or in need of protection and granting them asylum, and refusing others. However, it is in everyday practices of many different authorities, among those the SPES, that refugees are labelled and stereotypes are acted upon.

Refugees tend to experience 'speechlessness' (Malkki, 1996), since the production of authoritative narratives about refugees is frequently done by refugee relief and policy-making rather than by refugees themselves. In the case discussed here, the problem seems to be an unwillingness or inability within bureaucratic practices to make use of the capacities and wants of refugees, even when policy documents clearly state that interventions should be focused on individual needs and resources (Regeringens proposition, 2009).

Refugees do not always remain docile to their helpers or to bureaucratic procedures, however. Zetter (1991, p. 49) notes that the primary concern of refugees within, for instance, rehabilitation is often to reconstruct pre-existing identities. Such wishes seem key to understanding my interlocutors' frustrations with the introductory programme. By looking at what the label implies and refugees' experiences of institutional practices, we can understand that irritations among the refugees grow because the programme did not address their main aspiration. My Palestinian interlocutors have problems finding meaning in the introductory programme since it does not help them to pursue their dream of upward social mobility through reassuming or starting their higher education. In my research material, it is apparent that refugees with political reasons to move also have ambitions for higher education. However, the refugee label – often coloured by victimhood, passivity and emergency (Malkki, 1996; Janmyr and Mourad, 2018) – does not connote long-term migratory aspirations and future hopes other than safety.

**Palestinian migration to Sweden and desire for education**

Palestinian migration to Sweden started in the 1960s and rocketed in the 1980s during the Lebanese civil war (Lindholm with Hammer, 2003; Christou, 2017). But, as many Palestinians live without citizenship in unstable countries in the Middle East, their migration continues and at times intensifies, recently due to the Syrian war. It is unclear how many individuals of

Palestinian origin reside in Sweden, since they have often been registered as 'stateless' or 'of unknown citizenship', but estimates suggest that there are at least 70,000 individuals (Gren, 2015). Palestinians are, however, a minor part of the refugee migration to Sweden, which amounts to half a million refugees 1980–2014 (excluding family members) (Migrationsverket, n.d.).

Although most Palestinians in Sweden arrive due to violent conflicts, some come for educational purposes (Lindholm with Hammer, 2003). In the Palestinian territories, it is common to migrate for higher education to the neighbouring Arab countries (Rosenfeld, 2004, p. 123f.) and many are educated in Eastern European countries, such as Belarus and Ukraine, thanks to comparably low university fees. During the Cold War era, there were also various scholarships that Palestinians could apply for via various Leftist political parties with links to Eastern Europe (Rosenfeld, 2004, p. 125).

There is a wish for education among Palestinians that is related to the war and the following losses in 1948 when the state of Israel was established and the hope for Palestinian independence was put on hold. About 750,000 Palestinians fled during the same war (Pappe, 2004, p. 139), and the majority of those who ended up in camps had limited schooling (Peteet, 2005). During the 1950s, the UN built schools in Palestinian refugee camps in neighbouring countries, making schooling available to everyone. Palestinian refugees used education as a way to recover from displacement and loss of resources, for instance by employment in the Gulf economies during the 1960s and 1970s (Peteet, 2005, p. 64). Importantly, higher education has often been a family project rather than an individual trajectory to upward social mobility (Rosenfeld, 2004). Nowadays in Gaza and the West Bank, increasing numbers of people study at local colleges or universities (Gren, 2017).

Higher education has also been considered crucial for the Palestinian national project. Since Israel is overwhelmingly powerful militarily and economically, a way for Palestinians to fight back is supposedly by becoming educated. In the long run, this strategy reflects their desire to change the rules of the game and gain international support for their cause (Akesson, 2014, pp. 197ff.).[3] My interlocutors were, of course, affected by the importance most Palestinians put on higher education. If they do not succeed in continuing their higher education in Sweden, their feelings of failure are compounded given the need to explain to their families and friends why they have failed to get educated in a country where you get student aid and do not pay any university fees. Failure is further accentuated because many of their peers in the occupied territories are finishing up their education.

### Swedish introductory programmes for refugees

Swedish official discourse has underlined the necessity for refugees to become self-supporting (Borevi, 2014), although there is recognition of the need to assist those refugees who are unable to provide for themselves (Byström, 2015).[4] The requirements of the Swedish labour market have influenced both rhetoric about refugees and the different introductory programmes that have been in place since the 1980s (Graham, 2003; Eastmond, 2011). Employment is not only an economic issue but is seen as both producing and proving integration (Valenta and Bunar, 2010; Larsson, 2015).

Employment rates among refugees used to be high until the 1980s (Schierup et al., 2006, p. 207). However, since an economic crisis in the early 1990s, ethnic divisions in the Swedish labour market have become striking; immigrants, either work migrants or refugees, have typically entered the labour market through low-income, low-status jobs and many have remained in such jobs (Larsson, 2015 p. 36). In particular, those who are foreign-born and/or assumed to be 'culturally different' have problems getting access to employment (Lundborg, 2013, p. 219). Although actual employment rates among groups of immigrants vary between nationalities and legal statuses, as well as change over time (Belevander and Pendakur, 2012), the perception in society is that large groups of foreign-born depend on social welfare or unemployment compensation. Public debates reflect concerns that it takes too many years for immigrants, and especially for refugees, to become employed (Larsson, 2015, p. 44). Today, this is increasingly seen as a societal problem and/or a waste of human resources.[5]

Due to the widespread concern about unemployment among refugees, the responsibility of refugee introduction was moved from municipalities to the SPES in 2010 (Regeringens proposition, 2009/10:60). The SPES is a governmental agency with many local offices, and one purpose of the reform was to make the accommodation of refugees equal and fair, independent of local and regional policies. In the new regime, the SPES functions as a coordinator, collaborating with many other institutions, such as municipalities, social services, the Migration Agency and language schools. The introductory programme is called *Etableringen* in Swedish (literally the Establishment, referring to gaining a foothold in the labour market) and goes on for about two years (Arbetsförmedlingen, 2013; Larsson, 2015; OECD, 2016; Ennerberg, 2017).

There are strong norms about the necessity of speaking Swedish to be formally employed in Sweden, even for rather simple jobs (Eastmond, 2011). Thus, the programme places much emphasis on language training. It is not an exaggeration to say that language proficiency has become a sign of national integration. The programme also includes courses on Swedish society, culture and the political system; Swedish language for specific professions; validations of previous work experience and foreign degrees; internship opportunities; and government-subsidised employment. Through 'active participation' in the programme, a refugee is entitled to a modest sum of money to cover living expenses, distributed by the Swedish Social Insurance Agency. This allocation is about SEK 1,504 per week (about EUR 150).[6] Participation in the programme is voluntary, but in practice only those refugees who are economically independent can afford to not follow the programme, since attendance is bound up with the distribution of allocations.

The main goal of the introductory programme is not that refugees should become educated, but that they should become employed or at least employable. Eastmond (2011, p. 283) concludes that, since 1998, *Arbetslinjen*, a policy prioritising employment of all citizens and residents, reflects increasing worries about people remaining jobless and consequently eternal welfare recipients (see also Larsson, 2015; Ennerberg, 2017). For the Swedish state, education of refugees thus seems important when it leads to quick employment. Basically, refugees without advanced degrees are only included in the Swedish labour market if they accept blue-collar jobs. They are seldom seen as equals who have their own hopes and dreams of a good life.[7]

'Integration' is an unclear concept that is used in multiple ways in daily life and for diverse political and scientific purposes (Diedrich and Hellgren, 2018; Rytter, 2018). Although the introductory programme is mostly focused on economic integration, a number of cultural and social agreements are part of the practices and settings of the programme. Similar to Norwegian integration measures, 'a compulsory re-socialisation' based on cultural conventions about how to properly behave in society are promoted and expected to be followed (Engebrigtsen, 2007 p. 733). Hence, it seems that a collective self-perception of Swedes as punctual, active, hard-working and willing to follow agreed-upon plans also influences how the introductory programme is carried out in practice.

**Stuck within the introductory programme**

In a dull office building close to the city centre, a big room is filling up with people. The people who enter are gathering around three different persons – the interpreters between Swedish and Arabic or Dari or Somali. A middle-aged, blond woman from the SPES introduces herself as Fredrika Lundgren and distributes brochures, congratulating everyone for having been granted asylum. Then some general information follows about the SPES and its introductory programme. It is underlined that the programme is individualised and that each refugee should talk to their caseworker so as to adjust the programme according to one's health, previous experiences and wishes. Fredrika explains about the compulsory and individual action plan, a document where caseworker and refugee collaboratively schedule a programme for the refugee's participation. Specific courses, language training, internships and other events should be chosen 'according to your thoughts about the future', Fredrika adds. Moreover, she explains that the action plan should be similar to a 'normal job', which is why eight hours per day should be scheduled Monday to Friday. The aim is that the refugees should 'become

# Living bureaucratisation

part of society' in Fredrika's words. On her power-point, Fredrika shows the local addresses of two authorities that the refugees need to visit as soon as possible as to get their allocations: the Swedish Tax Agency and the Social Insurance Agency. She explains that the Tax Agency manages the civil registration and that everyone needs to have a local postal address to register. By registering, everyone will get a personal identity number. Several people nod, seemingly aware of the importance of having a personal identity number in Sweden. Fredrika continues to explain that with a personal identity number, each one will also be able to apply for a Swedish ID card. Furthermore, to be able to receive their allocations without further ado, Fredrika recommends a certain procedure:

> First, you visit the Tax Agency to get your personal identity number and then your ID card. Second, you visit a bank of your choice. You bring your ID card and you open a bank account. The third step is to visit the Social Insurance Agency – bringing your ID card with your personal identity number and the number of your bank account. Then you will start to receive allocations.

As she touches the computer's keyboard to show the next slide on her power-point, Fredrika tries to joke: 'If you haven't noticed that yet, we like papers in Sweden, especially at authorities.' Nobody laughs while she goes on to explain the four valid reasons for being absent during the programme.

An action plan for each individual refugee is a significant document within the introductory programme. The action plan should be filled with assignments such as language training and internships, during 40 hours per week, which equals the working hours at an ordinary full-time job in the Swedish labour market (see also Larsson, 2015, p. 49). The idea is that in this way the refugees will learn about working life in Sweden. In contrast to most employees, people who follow the introductory programme do not have the right to vacation during the two years of the programme. In practice, there are often gaps in the implementation of the action plans, however, which means that people may, for instance, have to wait for a course to start, and some of the activities are not as 'demanding' in reality as on paper.

The second significant document is what staff and refugees call the school card, that is, the attendance form, which not only proves attendance at language school but at all assignments scheduled in action plans. Once a month, refugee clients stand in line, waiting to hand in their cards to the staff who send them onwards in the system so the refugees receive money from the Social Insurance Agency. This is a monthly procedure, which is debated among the employees. In fact, all unemployed people registered with the SPES need to fill in attendance forms but, unlike the refugees, others can fill in their activities online and thus avoid the tedious queuing. Some of the employees feel that the queuing is disgraceful and makes the refugees unnecessarily uncomfortable. Others argue that this is something 'normal that one has to do at any job.' Attendance proved by the school card is the basic institutional requirement for cash distribution.

Except from the hassle when starting the programme, my interlocutors' daily routines quickly fill with Swedish lessons, meetings with mentors, queues to hand in attendance forms, occasional meetings with their caseworkers, evaluations of previous educational degrees, the writing of CVs, and the search for internships and jobs. But they also often find themselves waiting: waiting for the exam papers to be returned from the authorities, waiting for a rewritten action plan, waiting for a new course on the Swedish political system to start or a caseworker to agree on a specific internship. Waiting is an exercise of power, especially when delaying but not totally destroying hope, argues Bourdieu (2000). For my interlocutors, experiences of waiting add to the dampening effect on the excitement of coming to a new country and fulfilling their dreams (see e.g. Khosravi, 2014; see also chapter 11).

To my interlocutors, the programme and its bureaucracy, as well as individual bureaucrats, hinder rather than support their future aspirations. One case in point is Yousef's story. After a series of arrests, which included beatings by the Israeli security forces, Yousef managed to get out of the West Bank and travel to Sweden. After eight months of waiting, he was granted political asylum. He has some work experience at a Palestinian municipality and a bachelors' degree in social work from a local university. His caseworker promised to send in his exam papers to the Swedish Council for Higher Education, which is in charge of evaluating foreign degrees and exams but, unfortunately, she forgot. When he discovered this after months of waiting, he was furious and sent his papers himself, but all this meant that the evaluation was delayed by several months. His degree was eventually recognised in Sweden. Meanwhile, Yousef studied Swedish and finished his language exam quickly and was thus given a financial 'award' from the authorities. The only problem is that now there is not much for him to do within the introductory programme. His caseworker advised him to take the *same* Swedish course he had just finished one more time. Frustrated, Yousef tells me: 'The [Swedish] system makes you sleep and eat and smoke. For two months, I have been waiting for a new course, I have nothing to do.' He wants to study academic English to be able to follow an international MA programme at a Swedish university, but instead he ends up doing an internship at an Arab friend's falafel kiosk 'to practise Swedish', as it was framed by his caseworker.

Part of my interlocutors' frustration is that the introductory programme is not flexible enough to meet their needs. As discussed earlier, neither bureaucracy nor refugee labelling leaves room for individualisation (due to educational background, work experience, health issues and so on), but, on the contrary, emphasises standardisation. However, at the local office where I conducted interviews and participant observation, as well as in the policy documents of the programme, individualisation is repeatedly underlined as a necessity for successful matching between refugee and labour market (see also Ennerberg, 2017, p. 192f.). Bureaucratic practices and limited resources limit individualisation. In the end, standardisation and procedure become the rule.

Rarely can individualisation occur, and only after long negotiations, often including a number of medical certificates. For instance, Rashid, a Palestinian from Syria, has finally succeeded in getting his action plan adjusted to his own needs. Since his arrival in Sweden, he has been suffering from depression and other psychological issues. The little energy he has is mostly spent on his work in a Syrian activist network, for instance by going to conferences on the Syrian war in other Swedish cities. Attending such conferences sometimes leads to his absence from language school, which his first caseworker did not accept or, as Rashid phrases it: 'she did not understand that those events are also important to me, otherwise I'd get more depressed.' He tried to gain his caseworker's trust by showing her documentation of his participation but, despite this, she threatened to lower his allocation due to his absence. In his own words, his encounter with this first caseworker was a total collision with Swedish bureaucracy. He felt that she cared about his mental health but at the same time she neither understood what he was going through nor shared his priorities. Her caring for his health stayed within the confines of medicalised understandings that did not necessarily extend to seeing the need for Rashid to pursue activities that are meaningful to him but may contradict the action plan. Rashid explains this lack of understanding in ethnic terms: this caseworker is an ethnic Swede without any migrant background, while the two successive ones both come from families with their own stories of flight. In his third caseworker, Rashid meets an employee who acknowledges his problems:

> It was my third caseworker who [finally] tackled my case as an individual and who saw potential in me. ... She found a particular law to help me. Since then, I do three days of work because of my depression and I'm allowed to follow SFI [Swedish for immigrants] in a flexible way. I was crushed when I came to her. She pushed me to get medical certificates from my doctor and from a psychologist.

Even though he feels that bureaucracy in Syria is worse than in Sweden, since it has often been used as 'a political tool to humiliate some people' as he says, there are rules that can be ignored. In Sweden, on the other hand, everything is supposedly about laws, especially when his caseworker wants him to do something in particular. Yet, to Rashid, the law is used in an arbitrary way in Sweden. The law, as he phrases it, seems to be focused on the refugees living up to the institutional requirements of the programme: being active 40 hours a week, keeping to the action plan by following the schedule or having pre-approved reasons not to. The system has problems dealing with refugees who are not well, who are traumatised or who just intend to do something different than what has been entered in the action plan. In this context, being able to integrate seems to mean following the programme and its institutional requirements, not necessarily being or becoming employable or part of society more generally speaking.

This does not mean that the caseworkers I interviewed within the introductory programme are unaware of the heterogeneity among their refugee clients. On the contrary, they underline the differences they note among refugees, for instance, depending on national background, education, age and gender. They are acutely aware that, for instance, lack of housing, worries about family members abroad and experiences of torture or other kinds of extensive violence often influence their clients' ability to follow the programme. It seems clear that neither politicians nor bureaucrats have intended to standardise the programme. However, there are a limited number of courses and activities that can be part of an action plan. Those bureaucrats also have limited time with each of their clients in addition to budget restrictions.

As Yousef notes, the caseworkers have mixed educational and professional backgrounds. Few have a degree in social work as Yousef does himself and he concludes: 'There should be social workers at the SPES who could help us. My mentor doesn't know anything about society. It is just that her Swedish is good. Knowing the language is like having a PhD in this country.' To Yousef, the support that is given within the programme is not of the right kind. Nobody is able to advise him on university studies, for instance.

## Juggling institutional requirements and aspirations for the future

My interlocutors navigate the Swedish politics of integration while trying to keep up hope and pursuit of a good future on their own terms. While the young Palestinians I interviewed were granted asylum on political grounds, their migration is associated with aspirations they have for their own lives that go beyond escaping political persecution and war. For many of them, migration and integration involve pursuing the life trajectories that they were on before fleeing. In other words, they attempt to conform to the demands of the introductory programme while simultaneously aspiring for and imagining a better life.

As mentioned, higher education is one of the common forms of aspirations for my interlocutors. For instance, Rashid, who belongs to a highly educated Palestinian family in Syria, sought to restart his university studies as soon as possible:

> I have a job that the SPES pays for.[8] But I plan to go back to university. ... I didn't graduate from university in Syria. It was because of the 'normalisation'

of the abuses. There was a detention centre at the university, so I boycotted the exams. ... I want to study for a BA at a Swedish University. But our grades [those of the Syrian and Swedish grading systems] are not comparable so it's hard to get accepted. I have also been outside academia for a while and I'm psychologically affected [by the war and by fleeing].

Syria, where Rashid grew up, used to be the host country in the Middle East that gave most rights to Palestinian refugees prior to the on-going war, including the right to attend higher education for free (Gabiam, 2016). Thus, many of the Palestinians who flee the war in Syria already have higher education or had expected to get a university degree without obstacles.

My interlocutors' aspirations for higher education tend to clash with the caseworkers' prioritisation of the programme's institutional requirements and the rules for the allocation. Amir explains to me that he has two goals with his migration: first, getting away from Gaza and the threats of both Hamas and Israel, and second, starting a university education. For the Swedish Migration Agency, he emphasised the first to obtain asylum, and for the SPES, he underlines the second. However, when he prioritised his aspirations to be accepted at a university through taking a Test of English as a Foreign Language (TOEFL), he failed to fulfil the requirements of the introductory programme.

> I told [my caseworker] that I don't have English B [that is an English course required for university studies in Sweden] so I have to do an exam instead. And I can't pay for this. It costs like 3,500 Swedish crowns. But [the SPES] rejected. ... I needed to study English but at the same time I had to go to SFI. I said that I didn't want to go to SFI, I want to do the English test. I had even borrowed money for this exam and I registered for it. I studied and studied. I didn't go to SFI and they rejected my application for money because I hadn't been at SFI. 'But I told you in my action plan that I want to continue my education so I need to do this exam.' So I went [for the exam] anyway. I was so stressed. I couldn't sleep very well and then I did the exam and I failed.

The requirement of the course English B to apply to university studies in Sweden can be fulfilled by taking an evening class or a TOEFL. In Amir's case, it is clear that taking a TOEFL was not the course of action that is expected from him during the introductory programme; he was not following the expected procedure. Quite the contrary, according to the logic of the programme, he should continue to study Swedish and only later, after finishing the programme, would he be advised to take an English course or perhaps a TOEFL. In my interviews with the caseworkers, dreams of higher education are often taken rather lightly as long as the refugee in question is not already highly educated within a shortage occupation, such as medicine. If discussed at all, higher education is referred to the time after the introductory programme. Besides, there are no funds that are earmarked for expenses such as the TOEFL in the budget of the SPES. According to

Amir, he has been financially punished by the system for not having followed the action plan as he was engaging in a trajectory that he hopes will bring him closer to his aspiration for higher education. Additionally, the Swedish my interlocutors learn during the introductory programme is not enough for following an academic programme in Swedish; hence, the desperate attempts to improve their English. In relation to this, another of my interlocutors, Hassan from the West Bank, notes that Swedish language instruction seems less efficient than in other countries. For instance, he knows Palestinian students in Ukraine who only spend a year on language training; thereafter, they are able to continue their university studies in Ukrainian.

Within the SPES, enrolling in the introductory programme means being 'ready to follow the programme as agreed', neither suffering too much nor being too agentive, too independent or too ambitious. Some individual initiatives, such as actively looking for internships or job opportunities, are praised, but only within limits. According to my interlocutors, some enterprises, such as Amir's skipping Swedish classes for some weeks to study for an English language exam, are definitely not acceptable and even punished by holding back cash distributions. Other acts, like Yousef finishing his Swedish exam too quickly, become difficult to handle bureaucratically, even though on paper he does what he is supposed to. Neither should people be too traumatised – they should basically be governable according to the action plan. Such bureaucratic demands have a dampening effect on my informants' ambitions and plans.

Being aware of their limited options and living with experiences suppressing their dreams, the young Palestinians re-formulate their ideas about the future after the introductory programme. Hassan, who was mentioned above, has given up on a university course in academic English that he started. He is unemployed and dreams of going back to the Gulf state where he partly grew up due to his father's work. Such dreams are at least attempts to indirectly ward off the risk of remaining uneducated and unemployed in Sweden. Amir has already tried leaving. He still hopes to start a university education or at least get a job according to his work experiences from international NGOs in Gaza, but it seems impossible in Sweden. He has visited the UK, Denmark, Spain and Germany trying to find a 'suitable' job. Sometimes he was successful, but then the authorities in those countries stopped him, since he is not a Swedish citizen and thus needs work permits to work in another EU country. Now he is back in Sweden and delivers newspapers in the early morning hours. Amir has adjusted his immediate plans so they are more in line with Swedish society's expectations of him to hold a low-paid, low-status job.

My two other informants experience different levels of success. Rashid is one of four who is back to university studies after the two years at the introductory programme. His achievement is probably related to the fact that his parents had advanced university degrees from Syria, which is not the case with the parents of the other three. Yousef wants to study for an MA in social work in English, but is, for the time being, pleased to have found a job. He had a temporary post at a home for unaccompanied minors – a job that fits his education in social work – but he now works in a more profitable unskilled job. This job is more desirable than the alternative unemployment, which would also mean continuous interaction with the SPES.

## Conclusion

My interlocutors' frustrations and disobedience within the Swedish introductory programme should be read as responses to a bureaucratisation of their daily lives that leaves little room for individual agency. In addition, they are pushed to focus on the immediate institutional requirements rather than their own long-term goals of higher education and upward social mobility. To the refugees, the programme and its content often seem meaningless since their dreams for the future are seldom prioritised. On the contrary, some of their initiatives that focus on higher education are, at times, punished because they are not scheduled in the programme. Events, such as a caseworker forgetting to send in a diploma for validation or the absence of accurate information about university studies in Sweden, are read as an institutional neglect of this group of refugees' main aspiration, namely higher education. The withdrawal of cash distributions when refugees concentrate on things other than learning Swedish is taken as proof of the caseworkers' lack of understanding and even lack of appropriate professional knowledge. Dealing with their disappointments when they have not succeeded in taking up their studies, my interlocutors either re-negotiate their aspirations, by becoming employed and thereby securing a financially 'good life', or by dreaming of migrating onwards, in the search for education and jobs. Ironically, the introductory programme, which aims to include refugees in Sweden, makes some give up hope of a satisfactory life there. Instead, they are softly impelled to fill spots in a racialised labour market, rather than educate themselves.

Moreover, the experiences of my interlocutors show that the institutional difficulties in taking the refugees' more long-term educational goals seriously are not only due to budget limits or shortage of staff, but are intertwined with the labelling of refugees. A refugee cannot be highly educated or hold ambitions to be so; it is a contradiction in terms. Within the institutional frames of the Swedish introductory programme, my informants' ambitions to get a higher education and/or re-establish their former identities as professionals collide with their main reason for seeking refuge, which is to reach safety from political violence and persecution. Their experiences show that bureaucratic practices end up being a hindrance, rather than support.

## Notes

1 Although many Palestinians from the occupied territories are used to the hostile and extensive bureaucracy of the Israeli Civil Administration when, for instance, applying for travel permissions, family reunification or work permits, Israel does not intend to turn them into 'good citizens' or decide on their daily whereabouts. The Swedish introductory programme does. Israel, rather, uses its military forces to interfere in people's daily routines through arbitrary decisions to block a road, close off a specific geographical area or refuse to let a Palestinian through a checkpoint despite having a valid permit (Calis, 2017).
2 They thus have previous refugee statuses with UNRWA since they belong to families that fled the first Israeli-Arab war in 1948. UNRWA's ability and mandate to protect Palestinian refugees is, however, very limited. My interlocutors travelled independently to Sweden to seek asylum.
3 A recent study, however, has pointed out that with diminishing beliefs in Palestinian self-determination and in an end to Israeli occupation, many Palestinian youth understand education in a more instrumental manner and as a route to individual economic improvement (Pherali and Turner, 2018).
4 It can, however, also be argued that in practice, refugees have been more or less deliberately kept out of the labour market during various time periods, for instance by high demands on Swedish language proficiency and Swedish, rather than foreign, educational degrees (Schierup et al., 2006, p. 207).
5 http://arbeidslivinorden.org/artikler/insikt-og-analyse/nyheter-2015/article.2015-05-27.1719982153.
6 Arbetsförmedlingens återrapportering 2012. Etablering av vissa nyanlända -samverkan och samordning, Dnr: AF-2011/414101, p. 44. Available at: https://arbetsformedlingen.se/download/18.3e623d4f16735f3976e9be/%C3%85terrapport_8b_-_Etablering_av_vissa_nyanl%C3%A4nda_-_Samverkan_och_samordning.pdf (Accessed 15 March 2020).
7 This is also clear from a special law, the so-called *Gymnasielagen*, which gave a second chance to young asylum-seekers, most from war-torn Afghanistan, in July 2018. Those 'failed' asylum-seekers with a deportation decision can stay in Sweden as long as they attend upper secondary school. After finishing school, they will have to leave unless they can find a job. The uncertain security situation in Afghanistan and any wishes for higher education are thus insignificant. (Khosravi, 2014 https://lesvosmosaik.org/stolen-time-shahram-khosravi/).
8 There are government-subsidised forms of employment for job-seekers considered 'difficult to employ' in Sweden. Normally, the employer will pay a smaller amount of the salary and social fees, while the SPES pays up to 80 per cent of the salary (Ennerberg 2017, p. 115).

## References

Akesson, B. (2014). 'School as a Place of Violence and Hope: Tensions of Education for Children and Families in Post-Intifada Palestine', *International Journal of Educational Development* 41, pp. 192–199.

Appadurai, A. (1996). *Modernity at Large: Cultural Dimensions of Globalization*. Minneapolis: University of Minnesota Press.
Appadurai, A. (2013). *The Future as Cultural Fact: Essays on the Global Condition*. London and New York: Verso.
Arbetsförmedlingen (2013). *Arbetsförmedlingens återrapportering. Etablering av vissa nyanlända: Analys av genomförandet* (Response of the Public Employment Service. The Establishment of Certain Newly Arrived: An Analysis of the Implementation). Report AF-2011/414101.
Bauman, Z. (1989). *Modernity and the Holocaust*. Cambridge: Polity Press.
Belevander, P. and Pendakur, R. (2012). 'Citizenship, Co-Ethnic Populations, and Employment Probabilities of Immigrants in Sweden', *International Migration and Integration* 13, pp. 203–222.
Borevi, K. (2014). 'Multiculturalism and Welfare State Integration: Swedish Model Path Dependency', *Identities: Global Studies in Culture and Power* 21(6), pp. 708–723.
Bourdieu, P. (2000). *Pascalian Meditations*. Stanford: Stanford University Press.
Byström, M. (2015). 'When the State Stepped into the Arena: The Swedish Welfare State, Refugees and Immigrants 1930s–50s', *Journal of Contemporary History* 49(3), pp. 599–621.
Calis, I. (2017). 'Routine and Rupture: The Everyday Workings of Abyssal (Dis)order on the Palestinian Food Basket', *American Ethnologist* 44(1), pp. 1–12.
Christou, F. (2017). *La territorialisation de la mobilization politique de la diaspora palestinienne en Suède* (The Territorialisation of the Political Mobilisation of the Palestinian Diaspora in Sweden). PhD, Université de Poitiers.
Cochrane, G. (2018). *Max Weber's Vision for Bureaucracy: A Casualty of World War I*. London, New York, Shanghai: Palgrave Macmillan.
Diedrich, A. and Hellgren, H. (2018). *Organizing Labour Market Integration of Foreign Born Persons in the Gothenburg Metropolitan Area*, GRI-Report 2018: 3.
Eastmond, M. (2011). 'Egalitarian Ambitions, Constructions of Difference: The Paradoxes of Refugee Integration in Sweden', *Journal of Ethnic and Migration Studies* 37(2) pp. 277–295.
Eisenstadt, S. N. (1959). 'Bureaucracy, Bureaucratization, and Debureaucratization', *Administrative Science Quarterly* 4(3), pp. 302–320.
Engebrigtsen, A. I. (2007). 'Kinship, Gender and Adaptation Processes in Exile: The Case of Tamil and Somali Families in Norway', *Journal of Ethnic and Migration Studies* 33(5), pp. 727–746.
Ennerberg, E. (2017). *Destination Employment? Contradictions and Ambiguities in Swedish Labour Market Policy for Newly Arrived Migrants*. PhD, Lund University.
Gabiam, N. (2016). *Politics of Suffering: Syria's Palestinian Refugee Camps*. Bloomington: Indiana University Press.
Graham, M. (2003). 'Emotional Bureaucracies: Emotions, Civil Servants, and Immigrants in the Swedish Welfare State', *Ethos* 30(3) pp. 199–226.
Gren, N. (2015). 'Being at Home Through Learning Palestinian Sociality: Swedish-Palestinians' Houses in the West Bank', in Kläger, F. and Stierstorfer, K. (eds.) *Diasporic Constructions of Home and Belonging*. Berlin and Boston: De Gruyter, pp. 229–247.

Gren, N. (2017). 'Unruly Boys and Obedient Girls: Gender and Education in UNRWA Schools in the West Bank', *Nidaba: An Interdisciplinary Journal of Middle East Studies* 2(1), pp. 36–47.

Jackson, M. (2008). 'The Shock of the New: On Migrant Imaginaries and Critical Transitions', *Ethnos* 73(1), pp. 57–72.

Janmyr, M. and Mourad, L. (2018). 'Modes of Ordering: Labelling, Classification and Categorization in Lebanon's Refugee Response', *Journal of Refugee Studies* 31(4), pp. 544–565.

Khosravi, S. (2014). 'Waiting', in Anderson, B. and Keith, M. (eds.) *Migration a COMPAS Anthology*. Oxford: COMPAS.

Larsson, J. K. (2015). *Integration och arbetets marknad. Hur jämställdhet, arbete och annat 'svenskt' göras av arbetsförmedlare och privata aktörer* (Integration and the Labour Market. How Equality, Work and Other 'Swedish Things' Are Done by Caseworkers at SPES and Private Actors). Falun: Bokförlaget Atlas.

Lindholm Schulz, H. with Hammer, J. (2003). *The Palestinian Diaspora: Formation of Identities and Politics of Homeland*. London: Routledge.

Lister, R. (2007). *Gendering Citizenship in Western Europe: New Challenges for Citizenship Research in a Cross-National Context*. Bristol: Policy.

Ludwig, B. (2013). '"Wiping the Refugee Dust from My Feet": Advantages and Burdens of Refugee Status and the Refugee Label', *International Migration* 54(1), pp. 5–18.

Lundberg, A. and Strange, M. (2017). 'Struggles over Human Rights in Local Government – The Case of Access to Education for Undocumented Youth in Malmö, Sweden', *Critical Policy Studies*, 11(2), pp. 146–165.

Lundborg, P. (2013). 'Refugees' Employment Integration in Sweden: Cultural Distance and Labor Market Performance', *Review of International Economics* 21(2), pp. 219–232.

Malkki, L. (1996). 'Speechless Emissaries: Refugees, Humanitarianism and Dehistoricization', *Cultural Anthropology* 11(3), pp. 377–404.

Migrationsverket (n.d.). Available at: www.migrationsverket.se/download/18.39a9cd9514a346077211283/148555605662/Beviljade%20uppeh%C3%A5llstillst%C3%A5nd%201980-2014%20flyktingar%20m.fl.pdf (Accessed 4 December 2019).

OECD (2016). *Working Together: Skills and Labour Market Integration of Immigrants and their Children in Sweden*, OECD Publishing, Paris. http://dx.doi.org/10.1787/9789264257382-en. Accessed 10 March 2020).

Olwig, K. F. (2011). '"Integration": Migrants and Refugees between Scandinavian Welfare Societies and Family Relations', *Journal of Ethnic and Migration Studies* 37(2), pp. 179–196.

Pappe, I. (2004). *A History of Modern Palestine. One Land, Two Peoples*. Cambridge: Cambridge University Press.

Peteet, J. M. (2005). *Landscape of Hope and Despair: Palestinian Refugee Camps*. Philadelphia: University of Pennsylvania Press.

Pherali, T. and Turner, E. (2018). 'Meanings of Education Under Occupation: The Shifting Motivations for Education in Palestinian Refugee Camps in the West Bank', *British Journal of Sociology of Education* 39(4), pp. 567–589.

Regeringens proposition (Governemnt Bill) (2009/10:60). *Nyanlända invandrares arbtsmarknadsetablering. Egenansvar med professionellt stöd* (Newly Arrived

Immigrants' Establishment at the Labour Market: Self-Responsibility with Professional Support), Stockholm: Arbetsmarknadsdepartementet.
Rosenfeld, M. (2004). *Confronting the Occupation: Work, Education and Political Activism of Palestinian Families in a Refugee Camp*. Stanford, California: Stanford University Press.
Rytter, M. (2018). 'Made in Denmark. Refugees, Integration and the Self-Dependent Society', *Anthropology Today* 34(3), pp. 12–14.
Salazar, N. (2011). 'The Power of Imagination in Transnational Mobilities', *Identities: Global Studies in Culture and Power* 18, pp. 576–598.
Schierup, C., Hansen, P. and Castles, S. (2006). *Migration, Citizenship, and the European Welfare State A European Dilemma*. Oxford: Oxford University Press.
Valenta, M. and Bunar N. (2010). 'State Assisted Integration: Refugee Integration Policies in Scandinavian Welfare States: The Swedish and Norwegian Experience', *Journal of Refugee Studies* 23(4), pp. 463–483.
Weber, M. (2013) [1922]. *Economy and Society: An Outline of Interpretative Sociology*, Volume 2. Roth, G. and Claus Wittich, C. (eds.) Berkeley, Los Angeles, London: University of California Press.
Zetter, R. (1991). 'Labelling Refugees: Forming and Transforming a Bureaucratic Identity', *Journal of Refugee Studies* 4(1), pp. 39–62.
Zetter, R. (2007). 'More Labels, Fewer Refugees: Remaking the Refugee Label in an Era of Globalization', *Journal of Refugee Studies* 20(2), pp. 172–192.

## 10 Wendy Pearlman

# Aspiration, appreciation, and frustration: Syrian asylum seekers and bureaucracy in Germany

> The university system here is very complicated and bureaucratic. In the German system, universities demand a 2.5 GPA. That is 80–85 per cent in the Syrian system. The student who is ranked number one in all of Syria got 80 per cent. I graduated from university in Syria with a GPA of 70 per cent, which is very good for the system there. But here they do not understand the difference in the systems. They recognize my degree, but with bad grades. I am trying to resolve the issue. I finished taking German. Now I am looking for a university that accepts a GPA that is less than 2.5 in the German system. … We are not here for money. I am an educated person and I am trying to learn more. I have dignity here, but I am trying to increase it by finding my own job. I do not want assistance from the state. I am looking forward to such a day when I earn a living by myself. I now have to compete with people who are more qualified in terms of language and high degrees. I am seeking those things, too. I will get my Master's and then I will show them what I can do. (Bilal, Tübingen, Germany)

On 21 August 2015, German Chancellor Angela Merkel invited Syrian refugees to Germany when her government suspended the de-facto policy (the Dublin system, see the Introduction of this volume) of sending asylum seekers back to their European country of entry. Against this backdrop, asylum applications exceeded one million in 2015–2016. The plurality of those attaining refugee or subsidiary protection status was Syrian.

In granting asylum, the German state was not only extending legal protection to individuals fleeing violence and persecution, but also social welfare provisions to meet their essential needs and support their integration into society and the labour market. The subsequent sweeping government expenditures have fed debates preoccupied with distinguishing 'deserving' war refugees worthy of care from 'undeserving' migrants exploiting state largesse (Holzberg et al., 2018). German Interior Minister Thomas de Maizière spoke for many citizens in suspecting that generous benefits were a major 'pull-factor' attracting refugees in the first place (Bröcker and Kessler, 2017; Staudenmaier, 2017). Critics denounced his words, insisting that Germany's social transfers simply matched its high cost of living (Die Welt, 2017), and that welfare benefits still left many refugees below the poverty line (Bierbach, 2017).

These and other host society perspectives can be traced in press debates, public opinion surveys, and political party rhetoric. We know less, however, about the different ways that refugees and asylum seekers themselves are debating their encounters with the social welfare state. This chapter probes this spectrum of experiences and evaluations. Analysing my interviews and field research with Syrian asylum seekers in Germany since 2016, I find two powerful yet contradictory sentiments. On the one hand, many Syrians voice a keen appreciation for the social services and the ways that they aid their new lives in Europe. On the other hand, many articulate intense frustration with the bureaucratization of daily life.

At first glance, the identification of appreciation and frustration as prominent strands in asylum seekers' encounter with social welfare bureaucracies might seem to affirm the discourse of 'refugee gratitude'. That is, it can be read as insinuating that refugees' primary orientation toward states and societies should be one of thanks, and that a major problem in state–refugee relations lies in refugees' failure to be grateful. Scholarly and popular writing has rightly criticized such constructs, arguing that humanitarian protection is not a gift but an obligation (Nayeri, 2017). They suggest that viewing it otherwise reproduces demeaning hierarchies that subordinate refugees to dependency (Moulin, 2012), if not a tyrannical paternalism or eternal debt (D'Cruz, 2014).

Gratitude, however, is not the only lens with which to understand appreciation and frustration with the welfare state. Offering a different perspective, I argue that asylum seekers are primarily motivated by desires to rebuild their lives and pursue their dreams for a better future. Attention to the intensity of such personal, professional, and educational aspirations can help us see that asylum seekers do not seek social welfare for its own sake, and that their struggles with state bureaucracy relate to concerns much larger than the mere hassle of paperwork and red tape. As Bilal's testimony illustrates, many asylum seekers' appreciation for social welfare stems chiefly from its power to facilitate realization of their hopes and ambitions. Their frustration, on the flip side, flows from the violence that it does to those ambitions (see also chapter 9). Exploration of these ways that aspiration drives asylum seekers' experiences of appreciation and frustration allows us to detach these very real sentiments from discourses implying that refugees are powerless, voiceless, and passive receivers of help. Instead, it allows us to interpret those sentiments with respect for refugees' agency as political beings who critically evaluate state practices no less than do citizens, and who similarly appraise them in the context of their own drive to be productive members of society.

This chapter explores these arguments in five parts. The first establishes the context for this analysis by using published sources to provide an overview of Germany's social welfare system and bureaucratic landscape, as it pertains to asylum seekers. The second section briefly presents my research methodology. The third section uses testimonials from a cross-section of Syrian asylum seekers to illustrate how personal aspirations for a better future shape sentiments of appreciation for German social welfare. The fourth section shows how the same aspirations produce and shape asylum seekers' articulations of frustration with social welfare bureaucracies. The final section concludes with reflections on what analysis of the linkages between aspiration, appreciation, and frustration can teach us about both asylum seekers' lived experiences and European social welfare bureaucracy in general.

## Social welfare and bureaucracy: key domains for asylum seekers

Syrian asylum seekers' interactions with the social welfare state begin almost immediately upon arrival in Germany. Upon submitting an asylum application, asylum seekers receive a temporary residency identity card while the Federal Office of Migration and Refugees (BAMF) evaluates their applications. As few asylum seekers have income to cover their own expenses, federal states provide asylum seekers with 'basic benefits for food, housing, heating, clothing, healthcare and personal hygiene, and household durables and consumables; benefits to cover personal daily requirements (cash and "pocket money"); benefits in case of sickness, pregnancy and birth; as well as further benefits which depend on the individual case under special circumstances' (BAMF, 2018).

As they await a decision on their asylum applications, most asylum seekers' principal encounter with the German social welfare landscape is their assignment to live in a reception centre for their first three months (Laubenthal, 2016). As long as asylum seekers live in reception facilities, basic benefits are typically provided as benefits-in-kind, such as meals and donated second-hand clothing (BAMF, 2018). Some states provide shelter-dwellers with an additional cash allowance (Deutsche Welle, 2017; Trevelyan, 2018). The asylum application review process often takes longer than these three months. For example, Syrians waited an average of 7.1 months from arrival in Germany to receipt of their asylum decision in 2016, a wait-time that rose to 10.7 months in 2017 (Deutsche Welle, 2018).

Once asylum seekers' applications are reviewed, their relationships to the social welfare state evolve. Of 295,040 decisions on Syrian asylum applications in 2016, the state granted 56 per cent refugee status, which offered a three-year residence permit with rights to apply for family reunification. It granted 41 per cent of Syrian applicants subsidiary protection, which entailed a one-year residence permit that was extendable for two years and carried no eligibility for family reunification during a transitional period (BAMF, 2017).

Once granted asylum or subsidiary protection, individuals receive social welfare and unemployment benefits according to the same general rubrics as German citizens. Meanwhile, they begin a relationship with another key component of the social welfare state: education. The law requires children of those seeking asylum to attend school after three months in the country. Since 2016, the government has also offered integration classes to asylum seekers 'from countries with good prospects to remain', even when they have yet to be granted asylum. Syria was included in this category (while many countries well represented among asylum seekers were not). Integration courses consist of 600 hours of German language instruction and 30 hours of orientation focused on Germany's history, culture, and legal system. New legislation in 2016 went further in making integration courses not only more available, but also obligatory. Still, in some places language courses remained oversubscribed and undersupplied (Rietig, 2016).

Language learning is crucial for both everyday life and for integration into the German work force. In 2016, to expedite asylum seekers' engagement in 'meaningful work', the federal government announced its plan to create 100,000 'One Euro Jobs'. These invited asylum seekers to do tasks such as laundry, cleaning, or food distribution in reception centres for a one-euro-per-hour supplement to their default welfare benefits (Deutsche Welle, 2016). The scheme was met with as much criticism as praise (Agence France-Presse, 2018) and, as of November 2016, only 4,392 asylum seekers were employed in such jobs (Deutsche Welle, 2016).

Until September 2013, asylum applicants had to wait one year for applications to be processed before being allowed access to the labour market. That time limit was later reduced to nine months and, in 2014, to three months (Information Network on Asylum and Migration, n.d.). The state allowed asylum seekers to apply for training courses after three months of residence and for funding for job training programmes after fifteen months (The Federal Chancellor, 2016). In accessing such resources, individuals who have been granted asylum, like unemployed citizens, access help from the Federal Employment Agency. The Agency provides services such as career counselling and assistance with job and training placement. Nevertheless, many asylum seekers find it very difficult to find employment. As of January 2018, 143,000 refugees were officially employed in Germany, while 482,000 refugees were registered at state agencies as searching for jobs (Klaus and Kriegbaum, 2018).

Language proficiency is a significant hurdle to employment, as basic German is necessary even for low-level positions (Breitenbach, 2016, see also chapter 9). Recognizing this problem, the federal government funded an extra 100,000 seats in job-related language classes, which provide refugees with German training beyond standard integration courses (Trines, 2017). It also launched a four-year, EUR 100 million initiative to bolster refugees' access to university education (Federal Ministry for Education and Research, 2015). This campaign included measures to improve recognition of students' existing competencies, expand linguistic and technical preparedness, and support integration into universities. This effort included increased advising; expanding opportunities for testing in foreign languages; funding of up to 10,000 new seats in preparatory colleges and institutions serving as pathways to German universities; improved online information about educational opportunities in multiple languages; and increased access to government student loans.

These and other measures illustrate the German government's efforts to meet asylum seekers' needs in the wake of the 'refugee crisis'. How have Syrians experienced both the benefits that the social welfare state extends and the bureaucratic hang-ups that they often carry?

## Methodology

The chapter is based on approximately seven months of fieldwork in Germany in the summers of 2016, 2017, and 2018, during which I conducted ninety interviews with Syrian asylum seekers and refugees. This built upon a larger ongoing project in which I have interviewed more than 400 Syrians in eight countries in the Middle East, Europe, and North America since 2012 (Pearlman, 2017a; Pearlman, 2017b). I identified interviewees using snowball sampling (Goodman, 2011), employing multiple entry points into different social networks in different towns to obtain as diverse a sample as possible. To this end, I made use of the robust, cross-continental linkages that I have established with displaced Syrians over the years. I also met Syrians through consultation with German colleagues, volunteer work at refugee shelters, participation in a range of civil society activities targeting newcomers, and attendance at Syrian-organised events.

My interviews, all but a few in Arabic, ranged from twenty-minute one-on-one conversations, to group discussions involving several individuals over hours, to oral histories recorded over days. Interviews were open-ended; I usually began with a general prompt that invited interviewees to speak about their lives. While I did not set out to learn specifically about their experiences with German social welfare and bureaucracy, I was struck by the extent to which such issues emerged spontaneously in our conversations. The information that they relayed in this context is valuable because open-ended interviews create spaces for people to raise concerns, feelings, and experiences that researchers might not think to elicit in questionnaires (Patterson and Monroe, 1998).

# Aspiration, appreciation, and frustration

Still, individuals' post-hoc explanations of their actions can carry deliberate or inadvertent misrepresentations, harden into social scripts, or assert lofty motivations rather than admit to base ones. I thus analyse narratives with an ethnographic sensibility, in the sense of seeking to glean the meaning of behaviour to the actors involved (Schatz, 2009, p. 5). I have developed the knowledge with which to do so through my general immersion in Syrian refugee communities during fieldwork. Multi-site, cross-temporal participant-observation has given me a bedrock of context in which to make sense of individuals' self-reporting. Beyond this, I compare my interview data to a range of published sources, including journalistic reports and essays by Syrian writers. These published materials, cited in this chapter where appropriate, allow me to confirm that my interlocutors' reflections resonate with those of an exponentially larger number of Syrian asylum seekers.

## Aspiration and appreciation

Ahmed, an unmarried thirty-something from Homs with a vocational trade, recounted two years of life in a town in the former East Germany, where, on the one hand, he experienced the joy of new Syrian friendships made in exile and on the other, the indignities of racist slurs endured on public transport. These and other experiences, however, paled beside what he insisted was the dominant force guiding both his new life in Germany and that of his compatriot asylum seekers: the aspiration to rebuild, achieve, and live dignified lives:

> We are driven to improve ourselves. Some are studying in university, and some have already finished language courses. You can see them in every step in life. This one is trying to get a place in a school. That one is a dentist, but is working as a physician's assistant so he can learn medical vocabulary. Another one is trying to find an internship, and is working as a car mechanic. People are everywhere. They won't just stay at home. They started again from zero, but didn't give up. The first reason for all of this is that people love life. The second is people's desire to build and improve themselves. I will be nothing if I just live here as a refugee. But if I get an education or finish learning the language, I'll improve myself and be someone of value to society. I believe that's people's only motivation to keep going like this ... We're hoping for a better future. We're all living on hope.

This aspiration structures a bedrock of appreciation for German social welfare services that I heard expressed repeatedly in my conversations with Syrian asylum seekers from different walks of life. For many, goals for personal advancement or growth, and the sense that the welfare state could facilitate realization of those goals, was what drove them to undertake great costs to try to get to Germany in the first place. This was a particularly common sentiment among Syrians who spent months or years living in one of the countries on Syria's borders before embarking on dangerous journeys to Europe. Mohammed, a young engineer from Damascus, described his life in Istanbul, where he worked long hours, was laughed at and exploited by others in the office, and still barely earned enough to get by. A young newlywed in the prime of life, Mohammed found life in Turkey to be a deadening cycle of work-sleep-work with no possibility of improving his lot. Information that reached him about Germany convinced him that the social welfare allowed greater chances to achieve his ambitions:

> Salaries [in Turkey] are very low, but expenses are the same as in Germany. I earned 400 euros per month and paid 300 for rent. So my wife and I had 100 euros left to live on. It was very difficult. My goal was to continue my education, but there was no way in Turkey. I tried to study at university and found that they needed 20,000 Turkish liras over two or three years, which is the equivalent to 6,000 euros per year. My salary was one hundred euros, what was left after the rent. How could I study? I tried to apply to language schools but they asked about 200 euros per month. I couldn't do it. My work was from eight in the morning until six in the evening. There was no money, no time, no way to study … I heard that here [in Germany] education is almost free. They teach you the language, they put you in a house and so on … So I decided that either I live in humiliation in Turkey or I grab my future in Germany.

For Mohammed, the promise of social welfare was its delivery from a life of humiliation to one that offered a future. In his telling, free education is not an end in itself, but a means to the end of building a life that fulfilled his potential. The yearning for such opportunity was a main driver of his decision to risk his life on a dinghy across the Mediterranean in 2015.

I found similar expressions of appreciation for the social welfare state, and its role in facilitating life aspirations, among Syrian refugees after they had settled in Germany. Yusra, a mother from Aleppo, had stopped her formal education in primary school before gaining basic literacy. Having arrived in Germany after a perilous journey alone with three children, she was thankful for the range of provisions that the welfare state offered her family. What she appreciated most, however, was the educational opportunities made available to refugees and the future that she hoped it would enable her children to attain:

> The most wonderful thing here is the schools. They take really good care of kids. They teach them until they understand … Also, they help them with their homework. It's so different from schools in Syria. In Syria, if you didn't do your homework, you'd be beaten. And at the end of the year, the student passes, even if he was lazy and didn't understand anything. Just to get rid of him. Here, they'll teach the kid until he understands. They know that there's something that can come out of him … I hope that my daughter will be an engineer or a doctor one day. I'm also going to school, and I started to learn the letters.

Yusra was one of many who emphasized how the services they enjoyed in Germany surpassed those that they had known back home, regardless of rhetoric about socialism and a social safety net in Ba'ath party-ruled Syria (Perthes, 1995). Several of my interlocutors similarly compared German state practices to their experiences of the state in Syria, and grounded their appreciation for the former in their assessment of the shortcomings of the latter. 'It's very good to have a system and make sure that no one is above the law', Fadi, a student from Swayda, said about his encounters with the German state. Others made similar nods to the principles of fairness, rule-abiding, and equal treatment – the benefits of bureaucracy as described by Max Weber and values among those most prized by public administration in Germany (Zudeick, 2012). By contrast, many people with whom I spoke regarded corruption, nepotism, abuse of power, legalistic harassments, and general disrespect toward citizens as synonymous with Syrian government bureaucracy. Back home, in other words, many experienced negative dimensions of bureaucracy as a vehicle for illegitimate use of state power. In Germany, they experienced some positive aspects of bureaucracy as a system regulating legitimate uses of state power. This safeguarded persons' basic rights and security, but also removed arbitrariness and abuses that distorted meritocracy, and created a fairer playing field on which individuals could pursue their ambitions. As Mohammed the engineer put it, 'Here there is hard work. People don't cheat, they don't trick people. They don't say one thing and do another. I see that I can build something here.'

Others of my Syrian interlocutors assessed Germany's social welfare state favourably, not only in comparison to Syria, but also relative to other countries in the Global North. Kareem escaped Syria for Jordan, where he continued his work as a doctor until increasingly restrictive conditions convinced him that he needed to take his family elsewhere. He received a visa to the US and spent ten days there exploring options for asylum. He discovered that the relative lack of social assistance for those who receive asylum, as for residents and citizens in general, would make it extremely difficult for him to survive the transition period requisite for him to become certified again as a physician, no less a surgeon. Kareem thus travelled onward to Germany, where he immediately requested protection as a displaced Syrian. Assigned to a shelter, he studied general German and then medical German, worked as a guest auditor at a local hospital, and was eventually invited to work at a hospital on a one-month, unpaid trial. The social welfare benefits that he received as an asylum seeker enabled him and his family to get by during these many months with minimal or no wages. Pleased with his performance, the hospital offered him a full position. Now a licensed doctor, he reflected on the social welfare state:

> I am doing my duty in the best way I can in this country. Thank God I have been fortunate enough to do that. The taxes we pay are very high. I sometimes

pay 45 per cent of my paycheque in taxes. Plus, you have to pay an extra 20 per cent in taxes on everything you buy. On the other hand, the social security here is excellent. For example, if I get injured, I will stay at home and get my full paycheque, and the government will help … In the US you won't get that. Here, when receiving treatment, a janitor and a doctor lay down on cots next to each other. Life here is very comfortable and affordable … Those with high salaries pay more in taxes than from those with low salaries. There is a true sense of social equality, and an even stronger sense of social security. [This system] really deserves respect.

Kareem's appreciation for social welfare was grounded in the ways that it helped him rebuild the life upturned by war in Syria and continue to grow his personal, professional, and familial dreams. Many others I spoke with echoed his eagerness to 'give back' to Germany, not least by being a taxpayer. Fadi, the student, fled Syria before finishing his degree, and was enrolled in German classes in hopes of resuming higher education: 'The most important thing that Germany gave me is a chance to live', he explained. 'I want to work here and pay taxes.' Mustafa, a man from a working-class background who did not finish high school, expressed this sentiment dramatically: 'Germany has done more for me than anyone else ever did. It gave me more than even my own mother and father could give me.' He invoked an expression in Arabic along the lines of, 'If someone looks at you with one eye, look back at them with two eyes', meaning that, when someone helps, you should return the help several times over. That, he explained, was his attitude toward Germany.

I re-emphasize that these sentiments were not merely 'gratitude' as suggested by the discourses that refugees are powerless receivers who should thank host states for their generosity. Rather, they give voice to agency, ambition, and a yearning to build productive futures. These Syrians looked forward to paying taxes, not simply to reimburse a debt, but because it signified dignity, independence, and participation as full members of society. In other words, their appreciation for social welfare was grounded in their aspiration to construct futures in which they were not dependent on social welfare.

**Frustration and the bureaucratization of daily life**

The flipside of appreciation for social welfare is frustration with the bureaucratic burdens that often accompany its provision. Just as many asylum seekers value welfare assistance due to its ability to facilitate realization of their goals, so can they sometimes feel that red tape and interminable waiting thwart those very hopes and dreams.

For the more than 325,000 asylum seekers arriving in Germany during the second half of 2015, the shock of bureaucracy came when 'logistical nightmares' required people to wait outside for days before they could

# Aspiration, appreciation, and frustration

even submit their asylum applications. 'It took me forty days even to enter the building', Ghayth told me of his experience in Berlin. 'I got a number, and then it took another thirty days for my number to show up on the screen.'

Asylum seekers' frustrations with bureaucracy evolved with their interactions with the multiple organs managing social welfare provisions in various realms of everyday need. For example, the social welfare state covered rent for independent housing. Nevertheless, tight housing markets could make it difficult to find affordable rentals. In addition, refugees' apartment searches were encumbered by complex rental rules and the need to pull together a considerable amount of paperwork to submit a rental application (Anwalt.org, n.d.). If asylum seekers managed to obtain a rental agreement, they then had to obtain approval from the appropriate social services office, which might be any number of different agencies, depending on asylum seekers' stage in the process. All of this could be so time-consuming that asylum seekers frequently lost the desired apartment in the interim (Bakir, 2015). I met Sami when he was completing his first year living in an emergency shelter that is an inflated structure dubbed 'the balloon'. He put the experience of bureaucratic red tape in these terms:

> If a miracle happens and you're able to find a room in a shared apartment, then you go to the Immigration Office to submit the paperwork. They'll tell you to come back in two weeks. And then if a second miracle happens and the landlord agrees to wait for you, then you go back to the Immigration Office, and they study your application for another month. And then if God really loves you, you'll get approved. So the whole process takes one-and-a-half to two months. But the problem is that no apartment is going to wait that long for you. There is a long list of other people who also want that room.

For Sami, like the dozens of others who described their time in shelters as among their most demoralizing life experiences, the problem with bureaucracy was not that it required time and paperwork. Rather, frustration came from the intensity of his desire to re-establish a life of normalcy, stability, and dignity, and the sense that bureaucratic obstacles blocked the path towards the achievement of those goals. I heard similar reflections from Sarah, a trained librarian who was working as a volunteer at a library in Germany for nearly a year. The uncertain hope that her work might transform into a paid position was the source of a considerable amount of worry. Her greatest source of pressure, however, was keeping up with the everyday paperwork demanded by the social welfare state:

> We've been here for two years, and we've been running the whole time. The day starts and ends, and you're always stressed, always running. The paperwork, the courses ... All the [refugees] here are very active. We're not just sitting doing nothing. And still, you feel that the results don't amount to much.

Nour described similar frustration with the health care bureaucracy, while also mentioning linguistic issues that compounded the challenge. For years, her English fluency had enabled her to hold her own as a professional working with international agencies. In navigating the German welfare bureaucracy, however, the expectation of German proficiency added further difficulty to those of complicated authorizations and delays:

> If you want to go to a doctor, you have to wait and wait. And make appointments. And wait again ... And then there's the issue of language. You have to prepare what to say when you talk on the phone. You can't make mistakes. I freak out ... I always thought of English as my 'exit' language that can connect me with anyone else, but that has become useless in Germany. They know that you're not a tourist and they want you to learn German. Try to speak English in official governmental places. [They'll respond], *'Deutsch bitte'* [i.e. 'German, please'].

Here again, the expectation of German language was not frustrating for its own sake as much as for its role in adding a touch of indignity to a situation in which the difficulties of meeting basic needs already seemed to hamper aspirations for building a new life. In my conversations with asylum seekers, I heard the most intense frustrations of this sort with regard to the bureaucratic obstacles to labour market access. Yahya, a journalist whose writing featured keen observation of the challenges of newcomers in Germany, reflected on his compatriots' aspirations and aspirations stymied:

> There are two main things the refugee asks about once he enters Germany: 'Will I be able to find a job' and 'Will I be able to continue studying?' ... The refugees who come here don't come just to eat and drink. They want to work and to build a life. But the situation here is hopeless. There are many job opportunities in Germany. The problem is that the labour market is filled with so many complexities ... There are many people from Syria who have excellent experience, but can't find a job here because their certificates are not accepted, or they require something additional, or they need to attend training courses for years. So many people decide not to work in their careers any more ... Instead you'll find many of them working as security guards. You can't blame someone like that. He needs to live. In Syria, he was an engineer, or a manger, or had his own business, or had a clinic, or worked in a hospital. But he needs to work now to be able to live. He's fed up of living off the Job Centre [the official name of the German employment agency] ... There're so many people who have good experience, but no one will hire them without first going through more training. I know many people like these, and they are losing their ambition to work. They're just hoping that their kids will grow up and go to work. Technically those people have no life. They're just numbers. They're doing nothing, except going to the supermarket or walking the streets or getting into arguments with their families. In Syria, their lives were whole. Here, life is empty.

# Aspiration, appreciation, and frustration

As Yahya suggests, state requirement of official certification of degrees, trainings, and other qualifications erect significant bureaucratic obstacles to refugees' entry into the work force, and thus their ability to fulfil their aspirations for occupational fulfilment and economic independence. Particularly confounding in this regard is Germany's apprenticeship system, whereby complex rules and standards require workers in dozens of areas to complete three-year vocational courses and pass exams in order to work legally. This system creates a layer of obstacles for refugees, many of whom had worked for years back home without formal instruction, often learning their craft from a young age in a family business. Lacking paperwork to verify their past experience or training, some face the choice of starting over with an apprenticeship alongside much younger novices, working in the 'black market', or abandoning their trade completely. Fadi gave voice to a sense of bewilderment that he and other acquaintances had with these administrative constraints:

> Here, everyone needs papers. Even carpenters, painters, and so on … I know many people who are very talented in the work they did in Syria, but don't have any sort of certificate because they didn't need it there … The system here is so different … Most people don't even know where to start. Like if I have an idea … or you just want to try something, you're not sure who are the right authorities to contact.

Frustration was thus less to do with the sheer magnitude of the bureaucracy than with its discouraging impact on asylum seekers' ambitions. This frustration co-existed with appreciation for the considerable funds that the German government was dedicating toward refugees' education and job training. Feras, an aspiring IT specialist, described this duality of excitement for state-made opportunities and dismay with bureaucratic hang-ups:

> I got an internship at a telecommunications company. I was there three months and I learned so much. They really liked me and they offered me a job. But I can't work until I get my residency permit, and I'm still waiting for it. A sister company also offered me a job. They said I could do another internship from September until December. They're willing to pay me, but the law allows you to have only one paid internship, and I already had one.

The sum of this red tape leaves many asylum seekers feeling that they devote the bulk of their first years in Germany to dealing with bureaucracy. This causes frustration first and foremost when they feel that they put on hold their larger ambitions in order to recover what they have lost and achieve new things. Starting a new life and learning the ropes of a new system is not simply difficult because it is different and time-consuming. Resonating with other chapters in this volume, it is difficult because the encounter does violence to the refugees' dreams and ability to rebuild dignified lives.

## Conclusion

Syrian newcomers' experiences of appreciation and frustration with the social welfare bureaucracy form a critical part of their everyday lives, and no understanding of their settlement in Germany is complete without it. Using interviews to probe those experiences, I have traced them to asylum seekers' overarching ambitions to reconstitute their lives and accomplish new goals. In doing so, I have grounded asylum seekers' position vis-à-vis the welfare state in a framework not of gratitude, but of aspiration.

Scrutiny of the linkages between aspiration, appreciation, and frustration can help us investigate refugee integration as a lived process. European politicians and publics are engaged in intense debates regarding what integration should entail and who bears responsibility for its success or failure. Some of these debates are based on assumptions about cultural clashes rather than grounded listening. Prioritising the latter, I have turned the spotlight on refugee encounters with welfare bureaucracy because it emerged as a recurring topic in open-ended conversations with refugees about their lives. Work with such an orientation can shift the study of integration from the realm of the conceptual to the practical, and thereby allows us to trace the quotidian operations of public policy and state–society relations as they truly unfold in offices, classrooms, homes, and the lives of ordinary people.

Beyond this, study of asylum seekers' encounters with social welfare states can shed light on the social welfare state itself. In interacting with a conspicuously different system, newcomers might observe, experience, feel, and articulate aspects of that system which might be buried, subdued, taken for granted, or simply unnoticed by locals too accustomed to those aspects to regard them as noteworthy. What strikes newcomers as triggering appreciation or frustration, or countless other reactions, can thus bring to the fore norms, practices, and institutions that are otherwise obscured due to their sheer normality for native-born society. In this way, research on refugees' interactions with social welfare states not only yields understandings about newcomers to Northern Europe but can teach us about Europe, as well.

## References

Agence France-Presse (2018). 'Germany Puts Refugees to Work … For One Euro', *The Local*, 16 May, www.thelocal.de/20160516/germany-puts-refugees-to-work-for-one-euro (Accessed 16 March 2020).

Anwalt.org (n.d.). 'Wohnungen mieten: Für Flüchtlinge ist das nicht immer leicht' [Renting Apartments: It's Not Always Easy for Refugees], *Anwalt*, www.anwalt.org/asylrecht-migrationsrecht/wohnungen-fluechtlinge/ (Accessed 19 March 2020).

Bakir, D. (2015). 'Kann ich Flüchtlinge aufnehmen und was muss ich beachten?' [Can I Take in Refugees and What Do I Have to Consider?] *Stern*, 12 November, www.stern.de/wirtschaft/immobilien/fluechtlinge-aufnehmen-das-muessen-sie-bei-der-vermietung-beachten-6548070.html (Accessed 16 March 2020).

BAMF (2017). *Das Bundesamt in Zahlen 2016* [The Federal Bureau in Numbers 2016], *BAMF*, www.bamf.de/SharedDocs/Anlagen/DE/Statistik/Bundesamtin Zahlen/bundesamt-in-zahlen-2016.html?nn=284738 (Accessed 10 May 2020).

BAMF (2018). 'The responsible reception facility', *BAMF*, 28 November, www.bamf.de/EN/Themen/AsylFluechtlingsschutz/AblaufAsylverfahrens/Aufnahmeein richtung/aufnahmeeinrichtung-node.html (Accessed 10 May 2020).

Bierbach, M. (2017). 'How Much Money Do Refugees in Germany Get?' *Info-Migrants*, 12 September, www.infomigrants.net/en/post/5049/how-much-money-do-refugees-in-germany-get (Accessed 16 March 2020).

Breitenbach, D. (2016). 'The Challenge of Finding Jobs for Refugees in Germany', *Deutsche Welle*, 29 November, www.dw.com/en/the-challenge-of-finding-jobs-for-refugees-in-germany/a-36574268 (Accessed 16 March 2020).

Bröcker, M. and Kessler, M. (2017). 'Leistungen für Flüchtlinge sind ziemlich hoch in Deutschland' [Benefits for Refugees Are Quite High in Germany], *Rheinische Post Online*, 9 September, www.rp-online.de/politik/deutschland/bundestagswahl/interview-mit-thomas-de-maiziere-leistungen-fuer-fluechtlinge-sind-ziemlich-hoch-in-deutschland-aid-1.7070203 (Accessed 16 March 2020).

D'Cruz, J. R. (2014). 'Displacement and Gratitude: Accounting for the Political Obligation of Refugees', *Ethics & Global Politics* 7(1), pp. 1–17.

Deutsche Welle (2016). '"One-Euro Job" Program for Refugees Off to a Slow Start in Germany', *Deutsche Welle*, 2 December, www.dw.com/en/one-euro-job-program-for-refugees-off-to-a-slow-start-in-germany/a-36618371 (Accessed 16 March 2020).

Deutsche Welle (2017). 'European Parliament Head Calls for Harmonizing Asylum Policy', *Deutsche Welle*, 11 September, www.dw.com/en/european-parliament-head-calls-for-harmonizing-asylum-policy/a-40446615 (Accessed 16 March 2020).

Deutsche Welle (2018). 'Asylverfahren dauern fast elf Monate' [Asylum Procedures Take Nearly Eleven Months], *Deutsche Welle*, 11 January, http://p.dw.com/p/2qfNH (Accessed 16 March 2020).

The Federal Chancellor (2016). 'Integration Act to Support and Challenge', 8 July, www.bundeskanzlerin.de/Content/EN/Artikel/2016/07_en/2016-05-25-integrationsgesetz-beschlossen_en.html (Accessed 16 March 2020).

Federal Ministry for Education and Research (2015). 'Flüchtlingen den Zugang zum Studium ermöglichen' [Enabling Refugees to Study in Higher Education], *Federal Ministry for Education and Research*, 13 November, www.bmbf.de/de/fluechtlingen-den-zugang-zum-studium-ermoeglichen-1980.html (Accessed 16 March 2020).

Goodman, L. A. (2011). 'Comment: On Respondent-Driven Sampling and Snowball Sampling in Hard-to-Reach Populations and Snowball Sampling Not in Hard-to-Reach Populations', *Sociological Methodology* 41(1), pp. 347–353.

Holzberg, B., Kolbe, K., and Zaborowski, R. (2018). 'Figures of Crisis: The Delineation of (Un)deserving Refugees in the German Media', *Sociology* 52(3), pp. 534–550.

Information Network on Asylum and Migration (n.d.). 'Access to the Labour Market: Germany', *AIDA: Asylum Information Database*, www.asylumineurope.org/reports/country/germany/reception-conditions/employment-education/access-labour-market (Accessed 16 March 2020).

Klaus, A. and Kriegbaum, S. (2018). 'Fluchtmigration' [Forced Migration], *Bundesagentur für Arbeit Statistik/Arbeitsmarktberichterstattung*, January, https://statistik.

arbeitsagentur.de/Statischer-Content/Statistische-Analysen/Statistische-Sonderberichte/Generische-Publikationen/Fluchtmigration.pdf (Accessed 16 March 2020).

Laubenthal, B. (2016). 'Political Institutions and Asylum Policies: The Case of Germany', *Psychosociological Issues in Human Resource Management* 4(2), pp. 125–131.

Moulin, C. (2012). 'Ungrateful Subjects? Refugee Protests and the Logic of Gratitude', in Nyers, P. and Rygiel, K. (eds.), *Citizenship, Migrant Activism, and the Politics of Movement*. London, New York: Routledge, pp. 54–72.

Nayeri, D. (2017). 'The Ungrateful Refugee: "We Have No Debt to Repay"', *The Guardian*, 4 April, www.theguardian.com/world/2017/apr/04/dina-nayeri-ungrateful-refugee (Accessed 16 March 2020).

Patterson, M. and Monroe, K. R. (1998). 'Narrative in Political Science', *Annual Review of Political Science* 1, pp. 315–331.

Pearlman, W. (2017a). 'Culture or Bureaucracy? Challenges in Syrian Refugees' Initial Settlement in Germany', *Middle East Law and Governance* 9(3), pp. 313–327.

Pearlman, W. (2017b). *We Crossed a Bridge and It Trembled: Voices from Syria*. New York: Custom House.

Perthes, V. (1995). *The Political Economy of Syria under Asad*. London: I. B. Tauris.

Rietig, V. (2016). 'Moving Beyond Crisis: Germany's New Approaches to Integrating Refugees into the Labour Market', *Migration Policy Institute*, October 2016, www.migrationpolicy.org/research/moving-beyond-crisis-germany-new-approaches-integrating-refugees-labor-market (Accessed 16 March 2020).

Schatz, E. (2009). 'Introduction: Ethnographic Immersion and the Study of Politics', in Schatz, E. (ed.), *Political Ethnography: What Immersion Contributes to the Study of Power*, University of Chicago Press: Chicago, pp. 1–23.

Staudenmaier, R. (2017). 'Refugee Benefits in Germany Are "Quite High", Interior Minister de Maizière Says', *Deutsche Welle*, 9 September, www.dw.com/en/refugee-benefits-in-germany-are-quite-high-interior-minister-de-maiziere-says/a-40426704 (Accessed 16 March 2020).

Trevelyan, M. (2018). 'Factbox: Benefits Offered to Asylum Seekers in European Countries', *Reuters*, 15 September, www.reuters.com/article/us-europe-migrants-benefits-factbox/factbox-benefits-offered-to-asylum-seekers-in-european-countries-idUSKCN0RG1MJ20150916 (Accessed 16 March 2020).

Trines, S. (2017). 'Lessons From Germany's Refugee Crisis: Integration, Costs, and Benefits', *World Education News and Reviews*, 2 May, https://wenr.wes.org/2017/05/lessons-germanys-refugee-crisis-integration-costs-benefits (Accessed 16 March 2020).

Die Welt (2017). 'De Maizière für einheitliche Asylverfahren in Europa' [De Maizière in Favour of Uniform Asylum Procedure in Europe], *Die Welt*, 9 September, www.welt.de/newsticker/dpa_nt/afxline/topthemen/article168477893/De-Maiziere-fuer-einheitliche-Asylverfahren-in-Europa.html (Accessed 16 March 2020).

Zudeick, P. (2012). 'Germans and Bureaucracy', *Deutshe Welle*, 14 December, www.dw.com/en/germans-and-bureaucracy/a-16446787. (Accessed 16 March 2020).

# 11 Nerina Weiss

# The trauma of waiting: understanding the violence of the benevolent welfare state in Norway

Bisrat, a refugee from Eritrea, was granted asylum in Norway after a relatively short waiting period of ten months. However, it took another two years before he was settled in a municipality. Asked about how he experienced his time in the reception centre after he was granted asylum, Bisrat answered as follows:

> It completely changed my behaviour. It is difficult when you have to spend three years of your life waiting for something. It is a very expensive time. Nothing means anything. ... I like joking, playing, sharing experiences. I had a book club in my home country. I liked to read books and watch movies, share experiences with my friends. Those times are gone. It affects you emotionally, completely. You see people coming and going and you ask yourself 'What did I do to spend three years here?' I got a chance to go to school, a chance to communicate with people. I got many chances when I was in the first reception centre, but the biggest question for me was this: The system says that once a person gets his papers, he is supposed to leave the reception centre, to be settled in a municipality, to start his life. My life was stalled in the reception centre, waiting for the next chapter to begin. My next chapter was stalled in the asylum centre.

He continues:

> I did not expect things to be like this in Norway. Things were really difficult in my home country. I saw the worst things. I do not expect to be forgotten in a reception centre in a free country in Europe, especially not in Norway. I say that maybe they forgot me. I know the government declared that there was a lack of houses. Shelter and food are basic priorities in life. ... But life means more than that. I hurt myself two or three times. I did not talk to anyone. Sometimes you stop breathing, stop thinking, your dream is crushed. Everything stops, for three years.

Norway's welfare system has historically been conceived as inherently good and caring (Vike et al., 2016). An institutional apparatus is in place to host asylum seekers and integrate refugees as so-called, 'new citizens'. After a short transit, asylum seekers are placed in ordinary reception centres. These are characterised as 'simple accommodations' [*nøktern botilbud*], which should secure the inhabitants' basic needs and security (UDI Rundskriv RS 2008-031). Such centres are either centralised, that is refugees living in the same building as the camp administration – former hotels, schools or other institutions, or decentralised, in which case the refugees and asylum seekers are allocated ordinary flats or houses in vicinity to the camp administration. Such decentralised reception centres are usually preferred, as the refugees live an (almost) normal life integrated in the local community. Asylum seekers have the right to 250 hours of Norwegian classes and activities organised by the reception centre. After they are granted asylum, refugees are to be settled in a municipality within six months, and are enrolled in an intensive and comprehensive introductory programme, which lasts about two years. Settlement procedures within the Norwegian system are based on a collaboration between state institutions and municipalities (Djuve and Kavli, 2007), with municipalities having relative discretionary power to choose how many and what kind of refugees they want to resettle (Weiss et al., 2017). The governments' expressed aim is to have a speedy process and to resettle the refugees as quickly as possible. Due to organisational and bureaucratic shortcomings of the system, however, refugees have to wait up to several years until a suitable municipality is found and they may be settled. In fact, refugees spend on average more than 600 days in reception centres from the day of their first admission to Norway until their settlement in municipalities (Weiss et al., 2017). Much of this waiting time is spent *after* refugees have been granted asylum, and refugees with a residence permit make up a third of the population in Norwegian reception centres (UDI, 2017).

From the perspective of the Norwegian ethnic majority, the link between welfare and violence might seem at odds. However, we do know that modern secular states, committed to preventing pain and suffering, abandon specific groups of citizens (Biehl, 2004; Povinelli, 2011) and generate pervasive forms of exclusion and violence (Asad, 2003; Mahmood, 2015). In this chapter, I explore the experiences of refugees who have been waiting in reception centres for years, investigate how this waiting is experienced, and question whether and how their experience in the reception centres affects their relationship to the Norwegian state. As the initial quote by Bisrat already indicates, I argue that refugees waiting for resettlement often experience the welfare state as imponderable, negligent and, at times, as utterly violent.

In referring to violence, I explore the ordinary, chronic and cruddy quasi-events (Povinelli, 2011; Das, 2015), situations that are experienced as difficult or exhausting (Kublitz, 2015). I therefore tease out three factors which contribute to aggravating the experience of waiting as existential insecurity (Haas, 2017). I first explore the camp as a waiting zone in which time seems lost. I then explore how the absence of family members, the fear for their safety and the longing for their arrival not only increase insecurity but also prolong the refugees' sense of waiting. Finally, I link the two factors above to the refugees' experience of the state. Refugees and immigrants who are subjected to the integration bureaucracy in the Scandinavian welfare states feel trapped in a vicious circle created by bureaucratic rules that they can neither understand nor escape from (Khosravi, 2009; Whyte, 2011). Whereas refugees may acknowledge attempts at empathy and care from street-level bureaucrats, the bureaucratic system often resembles a Kafkaesque state bureaucracy rather than a benevolent welfare state.

The refugees I am writing about had received resident permits and, as such, had a secure future in Norway. However, this future was indefinitely far away, as the refugees were waiting to be settled, and their lives were put on hold. Many refugees describe this waiting period as extremely difficult and stressful, as we see in the quotes from Bisrat (see also chapter 10 above). In the following pages, I describe refugees' reports of severe stress, mental illness, depression and hopelessness. Such symptoms cannot only be traced back to their traumatic experiences in their country of origin or during flight. Waiting in the refugee camp, the inability to build a future and the frustration over wasted time are often experienced as equally traumatic as the trauma of war and refuge (Berg et al., 2005; Laban et al., 2008). Being made to wait has been analysed as a demonstration of power (Bourdieu, 2000), a technology of governance, as power is effectuated through its exercise over other people's time and in how they are made to wait (Auyero, 2012; Janeja and Bandak, 2018, p. 4). It is also a weapon to make existence intolerable for certain groups of people (Gaibazzi, 2012). Therefore, researchers have argued that the uncertainty inherent in waiting is not an accidental aspect of the immigration detention system, but intrinsic to its functioning (Whyte, 2011; Griffiths, 2013; Turnbull, 2016). Ironically, some would argue, the Norwegian government has acknowledged the long waiting period of refugees as very unfortunate and as a hindrance to integration (Stortingsmelding, 2015–2016). Reducing the time spent in reception centres after asylum has been granted is, therefore, one of its prioritised immigration practices. Until now, however, this priority has had very little success.

**Methodology**

This chapter is the result of a larger mixed-method project conducted in 2015–2016. The project was funded by the Norwegian Directorate of Immigration to explore the short- and long-term structural effects of long stays in reception centres after asylum had been granted (Weiss et al., 2017, Weiss and Gren, forthcoming). Even though the ethnographic research partly coincided with the construction of the refugee crisis in 2015, the latter had but little significance for this research. After all, the project focuses on refugees who had come to Norway prior to 2015 and who had already spent a considerable amount of time in Norwegian asylum centres.

This chapter is based on the qualitative part of the research, which was conducted by the author and Wendy Hamelink. We conducted ethnographic interviews with thirty-four refugees, half of whom had already been settled in municipalities whereas the other half were still waiting in reception centres. With the exception of six refugees who had managed to find a municipality on their own, the refugees had waited between two months and more than three years, with an average waiting period of sixteen months, after receiving their residence permit. We also interviewed thirty-five street-level bureaucrats working with refugees in Norwegian asylum centres, municipalities and the Directorate of Immigration. Their experiences and reflections have been explored elsewhere (Weiss and Gren, forthcoming) and only serve as background information in this chapter. In order to control for the way structural frames impact waiting, we selected refugees from six municipalities in three different regions in Norway. We also recruited refugees from different types of reception centres (centralised, decentralised, and those which offered housing to people with special needs). Interestingly, however, the type of reception centre had little impact on the waiting experiences, a fact which confirmed the importance of waiting in and of itself. Initial contact with the refugees was established through the reception centres and municipalities in which they had been settled. In addition, we used personal networks and snowball techniques to reach more interviewees. All of our interlocutors had already obtained their residence permit.

For contextualisation, I also draw on the quantitative dataset of the above-mentioned research project. We analysed the re-settlement histories of 19,000 refugees who had come to a Norwegian refugee centre between 2005 and 2010, and who were later resettled in a municipality (Weiss et al., 2017).

## Waiting and unbecoming

> People get ill from waiting. If they stay long at reception centres, they get more and more stressed. They sleep badly, think a lot and have little future. (Hassan, a Syrian living in a reception centre, who has waited for resettlement for almost a year)

Waiting is considered as an inherent ingredient of migratory practices (Elliot, 2016; Janeja and Bandak, 2018; Barber and Lem, 2018). As a process, migration often takes time – sometimes several years until the final destination is reached. Migrants wait for an opportunity to emigrate. They wait for transport, tickets and money. They wait at border crossings, in camps, and at immigration offices. They wait for their asylum application to be approved. In the meantime, they wait to hear back from their lawyers and to receive a date for their hearing. They wait for being given a municipality and being settled. After having waited that long, waiting continues if they have applied for family reunion. Not surprisingly, therefore, waiting and its detrimental effects have been explored in research on paperless migrants (Bendixsen and Eriksen, 2018), in detention centres (Turnbull, 2016), asylum seekers (Rotter, 2016) and among those who stayed behind (Kwon, 2015; Elliot, 2016). In these studies, waiting is often described as painful, exhausting and associated with a lack of respect and dignity (Schwartz, 1974). Haas (2017) argues that waiting in the asylum system may be described as an 'extreme situation', in which uncertainty and investment are simultaneously maximised. People are forced to live with a dual uncertainty of time, in which change is both absent and imminent (Griffith, 2014 in Haas, 2017, p. 82). This total uncertainty, described by Haas, points to Bourdieu (2000), who made the direct link between time and power: 'Waiting is one of the privileged ways of experiencing the effect of power, and the link between time and power' (Bourdieu, 2000, p. 228). Where the one who is made to wait is forced into submission, the powerful is the one 'who does not wait but who makes others wait'. Therefore, 'absolute power is the power to make oneself unpredictable and deny other people any reasonable anticipation, to place them in total uncertainty by offering no scope to their capacity to predict' (Bourdieu, 2000, p. 228).

Prolonged insecurity, as waiting in the asylum system entails, may severely impact mental health, and researchers and migrants alike refer to this prolonged insecurity as psychological torture (Turnbull, 2016, p. 69). We also know that long stays in reception centres after being granted asylum may have serious consequences for the refugees' psychosocial health (Laban et al., 2004; Berg, 2012; Weiss, 2013; Weiss et al., 2017). Asylum seekers and refugees are already more vulnerable to certain psycho-somatic and physical illnesses (Marshall et al., 2005; Jakobsen et al., 2007; Bughra and Gupta, 2011) due to traumatic experiences in their home country and refuge, the loss of resources and social networks, and so on. Research on asylum seekers has shown that such experiences intensify through insecurity, passivity and lack of meaningful future perspectives (Berg et al., 2005; Laban et al., 2008; Sveaas et al., 2012). Also, among the refugees who had been granted asylum but who were still waiting for resettlement in municipalities, feelings of insecurity, passivity and the lack of a meaningful future prevailed. The majority of our interlocutors reported experiences of depression, sleeplessness and other psychosomatic inflictions.

Being forced to wait affects experiences of temporality (Barber and Lem, 2018), as the abundance of time, and the indefinite time left to wait, does something to people. Time is expensive, as Bisrat expressed in the introduction, 'time is lost' (Simonsen, 2018), or negated (Rotter, 2016) as people live in the 'nothing' (Kublitz, 2015), while they watch those outside, in the 'normal' world, getting on with their lives. The notion of life in nothing is explored in Kublitz's (2015) article on the experiences of catastrophe by Palestinian refugees in Danish housing projects. Her interlocutors insist that the present catastrophe is worse than the past and recollect an abundance of life in spite of conflict, war and danger in Palestine and in Lebanese refugee camps. Their current life in Denmark, however, 'was marked by decline and disillusion'. Kublitz draws our attention to the ordinary, chronic and cruddy in her interlocutors' lives, and to the quasi-events, a concept coined by Povinelli (2011). 'If events are things that we can say happened such that they have certain objective being, then quasi-events never quite achieve the status of having occurred or taken place. They neither happen nor not happen' (Povinelli 2011, p. 13). Povinelli furthermore theorises the effect of these quasi-events. She speaks of the violence of enervation, 'the weakening of the will rather than the killing of life' and that 'hopes and despair are conjured through the endurance of the exhaustion of numerous small quasi-events' (Povinelli 2011, p. 13). As will become clear throughout this chapter, it is the violence of enervation, coupled with the imponderability of the bureaucracy, which constitutes much of the experienced violence and negligence described below.

### The reception centre as a waiting zone

> The reception centre becomes like an open prison. Sometimes a prison could even be better, since you can get a proper education and a proper everything. In the reception centre, I cannot express it in English, it is a bad life. (Nasih, refugee from Eritrea who waited for three years to be settled)

Norwegian reception centres are voluntary accommodation offers [*frivillig botilbud*] (Weiss et al., 2017). This indicates that – at least on paper – refugees and asylum seekers are not obliged to stay there during and after their asylum application has been processed. Asylum seekers and refugees are free to find their own accommodation, as long as that they inform the police and immigration authorities about their whereabouts and can provide for themselves. Asylum seekers and refugees have the right to allowances while in the immigration system. These allowances, however, are tightly linked to the stay in reception centres, and people lose the right to financial support upon leaving the reception centre. As Gordon, a refugee from Kenya who had chosen to leave the reception centre and to manage on his own, explains:

> When I left [the reception centre] and came to Oslo everything stopped. Because in Norway, unlike in Sweden, when you leave the camp you are on your own. ... Once you leave the camp, then that is the end of it. No allowances from immigration so you really have to either get a job, or get somebody to help you. It was that simple.

# The trauma of waiting

While Gordon had a social network in Norway that supported him and helped him to find accommodation and work, many refugees have neither resources nor networks. In spite of the voluntary nature of reception centres, most refugees therefore feel bound to stay there. They find themselves in a paradoxical situation well formulated by Turner (2015): 'First, they cannot settle where they are because they are supposedly "on the move"' and 'second, they cannot remain "on the move" as they possibly are not going anywhere, either now or in the near future'. Refugees thus end up in a 'time pocket, where time grinds to a halt inside the camp while normal time continues outside the camp'. Refugees often referred to their stay in reception centres as a period of powerlessness and constraint. Dependency on the reception centre for housing and financial support made it difficult for the refugees to take decisions over their own lives, to move or settle where they wished. Of course, refugees were allowed to move in and out of the centre – especially during daytime. However, there were strict rules as to when and how long a resident could leave the reception centre overnight (see also chapter 12).

> You can leave the camp. You may go, but you have to report that you are going. You could not go away for more than I think a week, and you could not go frequently. There was a limit, because we were attending orientation classes and these kinds of things, so you could not miss them. (Gordon, Kenyan refugee, now settled)

Refugees had to apply for permission to leave the reception centre for longer periods, even after their asylum application had been processed and they had been granted residency. Although such permission was granted in most cases, the fact that refugees had to apply before leaving the centre aggravated their feelings of isolation and incapacitation. Fethawi, a refugee from Syria in his twenties who had arrived in Norway after the outbreak of the Syrian Civil War, compared the reception centre and its control regime to life in prison:

> Reception centres are like a prison. People control me [even] when I go out. If I want to go away for some days, the staff get angry with me and inquire where I have been. They threaten to sign me out [thus also threatening him with a cut in allowance]. (Fethawi, Syrian artist, still living in a reception centre and who has been waiting for a municipality for one year)

References to prisons were made frequently. Fethawi referred to what he called a control regime. Others mentioned the remoteness of the centres and the lack of transportation or money to get around (see also chapter 12 below). However, associations to places of confinement came often simply from the fact that the reception centres were waiting zones, where time was lost. This temporal dimension, of course, refers to the fact that reception centres by definition are meant to be temporary, while in practice this temporariness may become – if not permanent – then still indefinite. This became quite clear in the quote from Nasih, mentioned above: 'The reception centre becomes like an open prison'. Nasih had received his residence permit after only a few months, but waited for three years to be settled in a municipality. Waiting in the reception centre was so difficult that he even would have preferred to stay in prison. At least in prison, time would not have been entirely lost. He could have found useful activities and maybe even continued his education. In the reception centre he only waited, waited for a municipality and for life to go on. For him, in experiencing his waiting time as indefinite, time was lost. As Bourdieu (2000) has reminded us, it is in the way time is spent that power relations become visible. While the powerful are able to fill time well, time is 'killed' for those who are made to wait. Of course, the confinement to a space, where time passes or maybe is killed, further accentuates the power imbalance. Several researchers have therefore pointed to the 'time work' (Rotter, 2016) that refugees engage in – an active but exhaustive attempt to find 'distractions' (Brux et al., 2018), which might make time pass.

Authorities and front-line bureaucrats knew of the importance of meaningful activities, and of the detrimental effect of long-time passivity. Therefore, refugees who lived in reception centres were encouraged to stay active and to partake in organised or unorganised activities outside. People went fishing, visited a church, or participated in the activities organised by the centre. Per decree, reception centres were required to provide their inhabitants with meaningful activities (UDI Rundskriv RS 2008-027). There were, however, no specific guidelines as to which activities and how many should be organised. The lack of specifications and the relative discretion of the centres' administrators as to the allocation of resources has led to a quite unequal offer in the different reception centres (Weiss, 2013; Lillevik et al., 2017; Weiss et al., 2017). Furthermore, what is considered meaningful for some makes no sense for others. As Hassan, a Syrian refugee points out: 'We have lectures about FGM [Female Genital Mutilation], but there is no FGM in Syria. So this is totally meaningless for me.' In general, therefore, it was mostly up to the refugees to fill their day with more or less meaningful activities.

> I do things to let the time pass by. I go fishing and do sports, do whatever I can find, so that the time passes by. The time passes by but it is of no benefit, because I do not do anything useful. I do not do anything to build up my life. Those who are already in municipalities, they are learning the language. They can start with university or do a job. But, whatever you do here is without any benefit. (Harun, Syrian refugee still living in reception centre)

In spite of the considerable energy refugees invested to make time pass and to be active, they still found themselves living in 'nothing'. Waiting for life to start in an indeterminate future, enduring life in the waiting zones and maintaining life under conditions of the 'nothing' required an enormous effort.

## The absence and the living in nothing

> It is not so easy to wait for a year – especially if you do not know whether it is a year or more. People who wait for a long time, they think of their family. I am tired of waiting – both physically and mentally. I am very afraid for my family. The longer my family reunion case takes, the longer my family will be exposed to war and violence. (Ali, a Syrian refugee, having waited 9 months in reception centre)

The notion of living in 'nothing' has, as I outlined earlier, been coined by Kublitz (2015). The author demonstrated how this 'nothing' was 'characterised by absences: of homeland, family members, close friends, jobs, and good health' (Kublitz, 2015, p. 230). The absence of security, of a future, and not least the absence of family members, was of course also very central in the lives of many refugees.

Adiba, a woman in her late twenties and mother of two children, had fled Sudan and arrived in Norway in 2011. 'The whole family left because of problems and misery in my country. We left, and from that day onwards it had only been problems.' The family came to Norway via Malta, and whereas Adiba and her two children were granted asylum in Norway, her husband was sent back to Malta under the Dublin agreement. (It seemed that her husband's fingerprints had been taken in Malta, whereas Adiba's and the children's had not.) The family was thus forcefully split. Her husband returned several times illegally to Norway in order to visit the family. Sometimes he stayed for weeks, sometimes for months. The last time he had visited, he had been forcefully deported from their home and sent back to Malta.

Adiba has now employed a lawyer who is looking into her case, and she is hopeful that once they are finally settled in a municipality she will be able to bring her husband on the basis of family reunion. However, there were a number of possible issues with that plan. Firstly, Adiba was unsure whether and how her husband's repeated illegal entry into Norway and his forceful deportation would influence an application for family reunion. Secondly, she did not know when she would be settled. At the time of our interview, Adiba had already waited two years for a municipality, and nothing pointed to a quick change in her situation. Abida did not consider a positive outcome for family reunion likely until she was settled in a municipality. When asked about her health, Adiba shrugged: 'I try to keep myself occupied, but there is not much to do'. She had wanted to start with her obligatory introduction programme and was looking forward to Norwegian courses and job training. The municipality in which her reception centre was based, however, had little resources and offered the programme only to refugees who had settled there. As Adiba was not one of those, she had to wait. In the meantime, she had to stay in good health, she said, because of her children. 'But I feel extremely sad and tired.' As much as waiting for a municipality, it was the waiting for her husband to come and her family to be complete again that exhausted Adiba.

Families who migrate together only make up 8 per cent of the refugee population in Norway; 27 per cent of the refugee population in our quantitative dataset had children who did not live with them, and 19 per cent had fled with children, but without their spouse (Weiss et al., 2017). Reuniting with their loved ones was therefore a major concern of many of the refugees we interviewed. While around 80 per cent of all applications for family unification had been approved in 2015 to 2017, getting their families safely to Norway was still highly challenging. The waiting time until their application was processed was between one-and-a-half to two years. In the meantime, the refugees had to cope with continued fear for their family members, who either still lived in the conflict zones or in refugee camps, and the need to provide for their loved ones without necessarily being able to do so. The insecurity over whether and when they would be united seemed to overshadow all other concerns. Thus, the struggle to obtain family reunion seemed to have a detrimental effect on refugees' social and mental wellbeing.

When I met Mounir, a Syrian refugee, I met a man who was nearly out of his mind. His entire demeanour showed signs of extreme stress and anxiety. Mounir had arrived in 2014 and had been granted asylum very quickly – two months after his arrival. However, the system did not work as efficiently when it came to his family. Mounir had applied for family reunion with his wife and four children, who were living in destitute conditions in Turkey. He had been informed that the procession of his application would take at least eighteen months – if there were no problems along the way. However, there was a problem in Mounir's family. His daughter had a chronic illness, which required intensive – and thus expensive – care. Mounir feared that the Norwegian state was interested only in healthy refugees, those who were easy to integrate. After all, quota refugees were, and still are, handpicked to fulfil the high standards set by the Norwegian government (Enes, 2017). Mounir reckoned that his daughter would fall outside of that category. Her condition was chronic, and she would need expensive care for the rest of her life. He therefore saw his chances for reunion with his family and resettlement in a municipality as meagre: 'I am sitting here and waiting. I am afraid that the municipalities do not want us, since my child is handicapped.' He had heard that municipalities refused to accept refugees who were considered an obvious financial burden, a rumour that was partially confirmed in our research (Weiss et al., 2017). Mounir was thus left in limbo, and in indeterminate anxiety and uncertainty, knowing that he had the right to family reunion but also knowing that this right would not be effectuated in any immediate future.

### Bureaucracy and unpredictable futures

> I have now been waiting for five months and again nothing. I went to Oslo, but they said, we have a long list. But many friends of mine, who came after me, they got the municipality before me. That is what I do not understand. I do not understand what the problem is. (Harun, Kurdish refugee who has been waiting five months for resettlement after being accepted by a municipality)

While I agree with Whyte (2011) and others that the uncertainty inherent in the waiting for asylum is intrinsic to the immigration system, it is beyond my ethnographic material to state the same for the insecurity linked to waiting for resettlement. As I have mentioned, the Norwegian government did see the long stay in reception centres as highly problematic and has effectuated several measures to improve the situation – without any success, however. My point here is that there is at least an expressed will to care for these refugees in limbo, and to improve their living conditions.

Indeed, most street-level bureaucrats we talked to – be it the employees in reception centres or people working in the municipalities – said that they cared about the refugees and that they were deeply concerned for their wellbeing.

> I try to spread confidence in a very insecure everyday life. I try to smile at everyone, to look the residents into their eyes every day. I want to give them the feeling that I care, and to see whether they are stressed or whether they have managed to sleep. I try to detect those whose feelings of stress and frustration have become unbearable. Life in reception centres exhausts people. A reception centre is meant for a maximum stay of three to six months only, not longer. (Nurse in reception centre, Northern Norway)

Street-level bureaucrats were especially concerned for those refugees who had mental or physical illnesses or who had developed psychosocial health problems:

> Those with mental health issues or psychosomatic problems, they are the disadvantaged, and are treated unfairly. They are suffering even worse [than other refugees] under the long waiting period, I would say. They have more difficulties in handling the situation ... How can they understand that someone has said yes – and granted them asylum – whereas they do not get this other yes from the municipality [which would enable them to settle]? This maybe sounds strange, but some of these refugees with special needs, they sit and wait for years after having received a residence permit. (Manager of a reception centre with a special unit for refugees and asylum seekers with special needs)

This street-level bureaucrat had gone to great lengths in order to find municipalities for his residents. At one point, he had put a notice in one of the main newspapers, advertising on behalf of a refugee with severe mental health issues. The notice had been picked up by the national press and been widely discussed. This effort produced results: after having spent more than five years waiting for a municipality, the refugee was finally able to resettle and to get proper treatment. 'But you cannot advertise for all of the residents, can you?' he added.

Many of the refugees I talked to acknowledged the attempts at empathy and care by the street-level bureaucrats. However, these bureaucrats could only alleviate their everyday struggles, not reduce their insecurity. Whether and when a refugee was given a municipality to resettle was often beyond the knowledge of the employees in reception centres. In spite of attempts of empathy and care, the benevolent welfare state was often experienced as utterly violent.

## Conclusion

In several of his works, Kafka explores the hopelessness, or rather the continuous crushed hopes, 'as the protagonists are led from one false hope to another' (Huber and Munro, 2014). Redemption is promised, but never tangible, never in sight. In the case of some of the refugees whose stories were told in this chapter, redemption was finally achieved. At some point, the refugees were assigned a municipality and allowed to start with the introduction programme, to learn Norwegian and to find a job. More than 80 per cent of all applications for family reunion are granted. This means that at some point in the future, the vast majority of refugees ought to be able to reunite with their loved ones and to start their lives outside the camp, to return to normalcy.

Indeed, some of the refugees we talked to had managed to find a job or continue their education. Fethawi found a job in the local supermarket, Gordon is today well established with a family and job, and also Harun has finally been settled in a municipality and resumed his studies. The last time we met, he had married and was full of optimism for the future. Unfortunately, not all of the refugees we interviewed had managed to go on with their lives as they had planned. Several are still waiting for family reunion. Among those settled, a third have not managed to find a full-time job; they are more or less dependent on social welfare and their hopes and plans for their future remain remote. They continue to live in the 'nothing' and to experience the Norwegian welfare system as a Kafkaesque bureaucracy, which remains imponderable (see chapter 9 above). Their hopes were projected on the next generation, for whom hopefully the Norwegian

# The trauma of waiting

welfare state will be experienced as inherently caring, instead of ignorant, negligent and even violent.

## References

Asad, T. (2003). *Formations of the Secular: Christianity, Islam, Modernity*. Stanford: Stanford University Press.
Auyero, J. (2012). *Patients of the State: The Politics of Waiting in Argentina*. Durham: Duke University Press.
Barber, P. G. and Lem, W. (2018). *Migration, Temporality, and Capitalism: Entangled Mobilities across Global Spaces*. New York: Palgrave Macmillan.
Bendixsen, S. and Eriksen, T. H. (2018). 'Timeless Time Among Irregular Migrants: The Slowness of Waiting in an Accelerated World', in Janeja, M. K. and Bandak, A. (eds.) *Ethnographies of Waiting: Doubt, Hope and Uncertainty*. London: Bloomsbury Academic, pp. 87–112.
Berg, B. (2012). 'Mottakssystemet: Historikk og utviklingstrender' (The Reception System: History and Development Trends), in Valenta, M. and Berg, B. (eds.) *Asylsøker: I velferdstatens venterom* (Asylum Seeker: In the Waiting Room of the Welfare State). Oslo: Universitetsforlaget, pp. 17–34.
Berg, B., Lauritsen, K., Meyer, M. A., Neumayer, S. M., Tingvold L., and N. Sveaass (2005). "Det hainnle om å leve…". Tiltak for å bedre psykisk helse for beboere i asylmottak (It's all about the living: Measures to improve mental health for residents in asylum centers. Trondheim: SINTEF IFIM.
Biehl, J. (2004). 'Life of the Mind: The Interface of Psychopharmaceuticals, Domestic Economies, and Social Abandonment', *American Ethnologist* 31(4), pp. 475–496.
Bourdieu, P. (2000). *Pascalian Meditations*. Stanford: Stanford University Press.
Brux, C., Hilden, P. K. and Middelthon, A.-L. O. (2018). '"Klokka tikker, tiden går": Time and Irregular Migration', *Time & Society* 28(4), pp. 1429–1463.
Bughra, D. and Gupta, S. (eds.) (2011). *Migration and Mental Health*, Cambridge: Cambridge University Press.
Das, V. (2015). 'Lecture Two: What Does Ordinary Ethics Look Like?' in Lambek, M., Das, V., Fassin, D. and Webb, K. (eds.) *Four Lectures on Ethics: Anthropological Perspectives*. Chicago: HAU Books, pp. 53–125.
Djuve, A. B. and Kavli, H. C. (2007). *Integrering i Danmark, Sverige og Norge* (Integration in Denmark, Sweden and Norway). Oslo: Fafo Research Foundation.
Elliot, A. (2016). 'Paused Subjects: Waiting for Migration in North Africa', *Time & Society* 25(1), pp. 102–116.
Enes, A. W. (2017). Overføringsflyktninger i Norge: Rekordmange har kommet fra Syria siste par år. (Migration Refugees in Norway: Record Numbers have Come from Syria in the Last Couple of Years). Oslo: Statistisk sentralbyrå.
Gaibazzi, P. (2012). '"God's Time is the Best": Religious Imagination and the Wait for Emigration in The Gambia', in Graw, K. and Schielke, J. S. (eds.) *The Global Horizon: Expectations of Migration in Africa and the Middle East*. Leuven: Leuven University Press.

Griffiths, M. (2013). 'Living with Uncertainty: Indefinite Immigration Detention', *Journal of Legal Anthropology* 1(3), pp. 263–286.

Haas, B. M. (2017). 'Citizens-in-Waiting, Deportees-in-Waiting: Power, Temporality, and Suffering in the U.S. Asylum System', *Ethos* 45(1), pp. 75–97.

Huber, C. and Munro, I. (2014). '"Moral Distance" in Organizations: An Inquiry into Ethical Violence in the Works of Kafka', *Journal of Business Ethics* 124(2), pp. 259–269.

Jakobsen, M., Sveaas, N., Johansen, L. E. E. and Skogøy, E. (2007). Psykisk helse i mottak: Utprøving av instrumenter for kartlegging av psykisk helse hos nyankomne asylsøkere (Mental Health in Reception: Testing of Instruments for Mapping Mental Health in Newly Arrived Asylum Seekers). Oslo: Nasjonalt kunnskapssenter om vold og traumatisk stress.

Janeja, M. K. and Bandak, A. (2018). *Ethnographies of Waiting: Doubt, Hope and Uncertainty*. London: Bloomsbury Publishing.

Khosravi, S. (2009). 'Displaced Masculinity: Gender and Ethnicity among Iranian Men in Sweden', *Iranian Stidies* 42(4), pp. 591–609.

Kublitz, A. (2015). 'The Ongoing Catastrophe: Erosion of Life in the Danish Camps', *Journal of Refugee Studies* 29(2), pp. 229–249.

Kwon, J. H. (2015). 'The Work of Waiting: Love and Money in Korean Chinese Transnational Migration', *Cultural Anthropology* 30(3), pp. 477–500.

Laban, C. J., Gernaat, H. B. P. E., Komproe, I. H., Schreuders B. A., and de Jong, J. T. V. M. (2004). 'Impact of a Long Asylum Procedure on the Prevalence of Psychiatric Disorders in Iraqi Asylum Seekers in the Netherlands'. *The Journal of Nervous and Mental Disease* 192(12), pp. 843–851.

Laban, C. H., Komproe, I. H., Gernaat, H. B. and de Jong, J. T. (2008). 'The Impact of a Long Asylum Procedure on Quality of Life, Disability and Physical Health in Iraqi Asylum Seekers in the Netherlands', *Social Psychiatry* 43, pp. 507–515.

Lillevik, R., Sønsterudbråten, S. and Tyldum, G. (2017). Evaluering av tilrettelagt avdeling i asylmottak: Et tilbud til asylsøkere med helseproblemer (Evaluation of an Asylum Reception Facility: An Offer to Asylum Seekers with Health Problems). Oslo: Fafo Research Foundation.

Mahmood, S. (2015). *Religious Difference in a Secular Age: A Minority Report*. Princeton: Princeton University Press.

Marshall, G. N., Schell, T. L., Elliott, M. N., Berthold, S. M. and Chuun, C.-A. (2005). 'Mental Health of Cambodian Refugees Two Decades after Resettlement in the United States', *Journal of Marican Medical Association* 294, pp. 571–579.

Povinelli, E. A. (2011). *Economies of Abandonment: Social Belonging and Endurance in Late Liberalism*, Durham: Duke University Press.

Rotter, R. (2016). 'Waiting in the Asylum Determination Process: Just an Empty Interlude?' *Time & Society* 25(1), pp. 80–101.

Schwartz, B. (1974). 'Waiting, Exchange, and Power: The Distribution of Time in Social Systems', *The American Journal of Sociology* 79(4), pp. 841–870.

Simonsen, A. (2018). 'Migrating for a Better Future: "Lost Time" and Its Social Consequences Among Young Somali Migrants', in Barber, P. G. and Lem, W. (eds.) *Migration, Temporality, and Capitalism: Entangled Mobilities across Global Spaces*. London: Palgrave Macmillan.

Stortingsmelding (2015–2016). *Fra mottak til arbeidslivet. En effektiv integrering-spolitikk* (From Reception to Working Life: An Effective Inetgration Policy). Oslo: Justis- og beredskapsdepartementet.

Sveaas, N., Vevstad, V. and Brekke, J.-P. (2012). 'Sårbare asylsøkere i mottak: Identifisering og oppfølging' (Vulnerable Asylum Seekers in Reception: Identification and Follow-up), in Valenta, M. and Berg, B. (eds.) *Asylsøker: I velferdsstatens venterom* (Asylum Seeker: In the Waiting Room of the Welfare State). Oslo: Universitetsforlaget.

Turnbull, S. (2016). "Stuck in the Middle': Waiting and Uncertainty in Immigration Detention', *Time & Society* 25(1), pp. 61–79.

Turner, S. (2015). 'What is a Refugee Camp? Explorations of the Limits and Effects of the Camp', *Journal of Refugee Studies* 29(2), pp. 139–148.

UDI 2017. *Beboere i asylmottak etter statsborgerskap og status i søknad (2017)* (Residents in Asylum Reception by Citizenship and Status in Application (2017)). Oslo: Utlendingsdirektoratet.

UDI Rundskriv RS 2008-027 *Krav til fritidsaktiviteter under opphold på statlig mottak* (Circular RS 2008-027 Requirements for Leisure Activities During Stays at State Reception). Oslo: Utlendingsdirektoratet.

UDI Rundskriv RS 2008-031 *Krav til innkvarteringstilbud i ordinære statlige mottak* (Circular RS 2008-031 Requirements for Accommodation in Ordinary State Reception). Oslo: Utlendingsdirektoratet.

Vike, H., Debesay, J. and Haukelien, H. (2016). *Tilbakeblikk på velferdsstaten: Politikk, styring og tjenester* (Looking Back on the Welfare State: Politics, Governance and Services). Oslo: Gyldendal akademisk.

Weiss, N. (2013). *Normalitet i limbo: Asylbarn med endelig avslag* (Normality in Limbo: Asylum Children with Final Refusal). Oslo: Fafo Research Foundation.

Weiss, N. and Gren, N. (forthcoming). 'Mission Impossible? The Moral Discomfort in Swedish and Norwegian Welfare for Refugees', *PoLAR: Political and Legal Anthropology Review*.

Weiss, N., Djuve, A. B., Hamelink, W. and Zhang, H. (2017). *Opphold i asylmottak: Konsekvenser for levekår og integrering* (Staying in Asylum Reception: Consequences for Living Conditions and Integration). Oslo: Fafo Research Foundation.

Whyte, Z. (2011). 'Enter the Myopticon: Uncertain Surveillance in the Danish Asylum System', *Anthropology Today* 27(3), pp. 18–21.

## 12 Victoria Canning[1]

# Bureaucratised banality: asylum and immobility in Britain, Denmark and Sweden

Bordering is not new to Northern and Western Europe. Although the erosion of physical and invisible boundaries is often celebrated – from the fall of the Berlin Wall and the Iron Curtain, to the implementation of the Schengen Agreement in 1985 – a resurgence of bureaucratic bordering is manifest (see also the Introduction in this volume). Gaining entry to European countries has become ever more restrictive, particularly since the 1980s. Meanwhile, as Ana Aliverti (2012; 2013; 2015) has shown in depth, there has been a long term shift to administrative bordering through social policy, whilst Juliet Stumpf (2006; 2015) has concretely conceptualised the conflations between criminal law and immigration (or 'crimmigration') in ways which entangle border transgressors in criminal justice systems in the Global North.

This chapter briefly explores the impacts of increased external borders before developing an empirical analysis of the increase in internalised bordering. Focusing on Britain,[2] Denmark and Sweden as Northern cases, I outline ways in which people are kept out of these countries, and how this increased in the aftermath the European refugee crisis, which I term a refugee reception crisis.[3] I will then turn my attention to the micro-level, everyday forms of bordering which impact on the wellbeing of people seeking asylum. These specifically relate to the deliberate erosion of autonomy through spatial isolation, destitution, detention, informal confinement, and social control. Those are experiences of bureaucratic violence (see the Introduction in this book).

The arguments drawn out here stem from multiple projects over a ten-year period. Primary empirical data included in this chapter are based on interviews across three periods: reflections from a decade of activist participation and ethnography with women seeking asylum in the North West of England; interviews with psychologists and psychotraumatologists from a research project focusing on state and organisational responses to survivors of sexual torture in Denmark;[4] and a two-year project on women's experiences of seeking asylum in Britain, Sweden and Denmark, funded by the

Economic and Social Research Council.[5] The last mentioned project incorporated seventy-four in-depth semi-structured interviews with psychologists, detention custody officers, support workers, border agents, refugee rights activists and other such social actors working with people seeking asylum. The material has been further enriched with six oral histories with women seeking asylum. The project also included visits to two immigration detention centres in Sweden, one in Denmark, a Danish deportation centre (*udrejsecenter* or *udvisningscentre*[6]) and ethnographic reflections from one month of visits to a Danish Red Cross asylum centre.

## After the borders

'There has been a narrowing of all the gaps through which people can obtain permission to stay legally in the state or permission to enter the state legally.' This statement, made by an immigration lawyer I interviewed in the UK, is certainly reflective of the responses taken by Northern European countries in the aftermath of the European refugee reception crisis of 2015. In 2015, Sweden received considerably more people seeking asylum than the UK and Denmark did (Clante Bendixen, 2018). Whilst Sweden's neighbouring countries worked to ferment hostile environments for the increasing numbers of people arriving to seek asylum, the Swedish government had a more welcoming attitude (Barker, 2018, pp. 1).

As the year progressed, however, so too did a politicised anti-immigrant sentiment in Sweden. The most obvious physical manifestation of border-anxiety came with the closure of the Öresund Bridge which, from 24 November 2015, was policed with travellers required to produce valid IDs and/or relevant visas. Although aspects of immigration control – such as detention, dispersal and deportation – were long embedded in all three countries, Denmark and Sweden, in particular, have seen substantive legislative shifts since 2015, aspects of which are discussed as this chapter progresses. On the whole, however, Sweden's reputation as being open for migration shifted almost overnight (see chapters 2 and 7).

At the time of writing, Sweden has maintained its use of the Temporary Law of 2016, which limits stay to thirteen months before a requirement to reapply for asylum; and residence permits in Denmark have been reduced since 2015 from five-to-seven years, to one-to-two years. As such, although external border controls were not new, as the title of this section indicates, people I spoke with often referred to a point 'after the borders' or 'since the borders', in particular in Denmark and Sweden.

At the same time as Denmark and Sweden were hardening their internal and external borders, Britain, entrenched with a neoliberal island mentality, had long worked to build an externalising scaffold, which facilitated a buffering zone far from its own borders, lest such a crisis might unfold

(Carr, 2012; Andersson, 2014). Whilst the UK has maintained a five-year stay for those granted refugee status, the number of refusals has gradually increased, and the number of grounds on which to appeal a refusal have been reduced from seventeen to four (Immigration Act, 2014). Unlike Denmark and Sweden, Britain has always refused participation in the Schengen Agreement and has long outsourced visa restrictions, even to its own former colonies (Webber, 2012). Considering that Sweden, for example, is geographically further North than the UK, it should go without saying that the disproportionately low number of applications is not due simply to physical distance. It is instead the result of a long-term strategy to reduce the mobility capacity for people outside of the EU[7] to reach British shores (Webber, 2016).

It was thus through these strategies that the UK was able to retain a kind of exclusivity in its response to the movements of migrants north. Two outcomes of these strategies are as follows: Britain received comparatively low numbers of asylum applications in 2015 and 2016, and facilitated instead a bottle neck build-up of people stranded at camps in Calais in France who were not able to make the final border crossing toward Britain. Controversially, this has included unaccompanied minors who otherwise had the right to be with their families already in the UK. In the aftermath of the European refugee reception crisis, the exacerbation of physical and bureaucratic boundaries to prevent and deter the mobilisation of people into (predominantly richer, Northern) countries became more concrete than ever.

### The increasing internalisation of immigration controls

Compounding the problems that people experience in gaining entry to Britain, Denmark and Sweden is the increased use of internalised borders (Crawley and Sigona, 2016; Barker, 2018). For some time, clear and deliberate decisions have been made to make living in each country a lot more difficult for migrants generally and people seeking asylum specifically. In the UK, this has become widely known as the 'Hostile Environment', a term used by then Home Secretary (2010–2016), and later Prime Minister (2016–2019), Theresa May, to characterise an environment being developed for those living in Britain who, it was considered, should not be there (Kirkup and Winnett, 2012).

'Enhanced motivation techniques' have been employed in Denmark since 1997 – a way of encouraging coercive self-deportations by encouraging reductions in autonomy and welfare allowances (Suárez-Krabbe et al., 2018). However, a much harsher policy – more similar to the UK's – was later promoted by the former Danish Minister for Immigration, Integration and Housing, Inger Støjberg, who promised to make life 'intolerable' for people on 'tolerated stay' (see chapter 4). As the coordinator of a national support service for refugees in Denmark bluntly summarised it in the context of deportation centres: 'They are designed to make life as intolerable as possible, to persuade people to go back.' Also, people who have been accepted as refugees are affected, as a director at a Danish support facility for survivors of torture told me: 'The new policies that have come into place for refugees that have achieved asylum are really tough, they've never been tougher than they are right now and we're seeing levels of poverty that we have never experienced before. I mean this is really devastating.'

The policies to which he refers were known as Halvtreds Stramninger, or The Fifty Restrictions (as of April 2019, increased to 114 restrictions). The most internationally controversial of these was the introduction of The Jewellery Law (see chapters 2 and 4 above), which reminded many Europeans of the Anti-Semitic politics of Nazi Germany. However, as this chapter goes on to evidence, it is the infliction of banality and isolation, including but not limited to deportation centres, which is most grinding in the everyday.

In Sweden, the general feeling amongst practitioners was that the state had created two borders. As one support worker for unaccompanied minors argued: 'There are two border controls, and they took one away now and instead they said they would focus on controls inside the borders. So instead of checking IDs at the border, they said there are no safe zones right now'. The idea that there are 'no safe zones' is a direct reference to the increased efforts which have been gradually placed by states and state affiliated actors to infiltrate areas that are otherwise seen as safe from securitised controls. From interviews and conversations in the field, this has included the targeting of religious buildings, organisations working with unaccompanied minors and undocumented migrants, and attempts by police to enter a popular informal language class.

The exacerbation of these controls was sharply experienced by Nour,[8] a woman seeking asylum who had lived in Sweden for thirteen years and with whom I undertook the beginnings of an oral history within one of the two Swedish detention centres I visited. Nour is a survivor of multiple forms of male violence, and had originally sought asylum to avoid being returned to her husband, who she stated is a significant figure in Hezbollah. Having had her asylum application refused twice, she had been able to live in relative obscurity as a refused asylum applicant, living with Swedish friends who were able to provide her with legitimate and legal work. As internalised borders tightened, however, Nour was refused asylum once more – this time within two weeks of her application in 2017. She recalled:

> The third time was really awful, because I have heard that it would take around two to three years before you got a response, either positive or negative, but this time they dropped all the other cases and were just focussing on me and they handed me over to the police immediately and I got a negative result in only two weeks.

The period within which she was refused fell at the same time that Sweden was responding to unprecedented numbers of asylum applicants and – as a staff member at the Migration Agency (*Migrationsverket*) informed me – had hired new staff to organise the backlog. Having not known immigration detention centres even existed, Nour was subsequently arrested and moved to the centre where we met. She was confused and disorientated,[9] remembering, 'the first four days I didn't eat at all [Crying]. But now I'm starting to adapt to the environment'. Nour also argued that her refusal for asylum was in a way bureaucratic, in that the Migration Agency did not believe Lebanon to be unsafe for women due to inaccurate in-country information, and that 'they listened but they didn't believe me and I don't understand who gave them the information that I was safe in my home country because I really wasn't'. She was subsequently deported to Lebanon before the latter sections of her oral history could be developed.

**Eradicating autonomy, eroding dignity**

Whilst events such as deportation or detention are of serious significance and incredibly traumatic experiences in the lives of individuals affected, it is in the everyday that the impacts of grinding bureaucracies are often felt in the longer term. This is enacted through the deliberate reduction or removal of autonomy, and is a key facet of micro-level controls (see Canning, 2019b). Across all three countries, asylum-seeking people's access to everyday activities are reduced – access to further and higher education is limited; nutritious food is often unaffordable, culturally specific foods often unobtainable; and travel unfeasibly expensive. These create what I have discussed elsewhere as autonomy harms and relational harms (Canning, 2017, pp. 75–85), whereby people are (deliberately) infantilised and degraded through processes of forced dependence, social isolation and waiting (see also chapters 9 and 11).

These bureaucratic borders are no less barbed in the everyday, but are differentially enforced. In all three countries, they are compounded by spatial isolation. In Britain, this can be seen in the practice of dispersal, whereby people are placed in towns and cities without any say on where, but which are often far from amenities and networks which could have promoted inclusion. Furthermore, many of these are situated in some of the poorest areas of the UK, since, 'All of the top 10 areas for highest concentration of asylum seekers are in the north of England, Scotland and Wales and just one of the top 31 is in the south of England' (Wheatstone, 2016).

Asma's case is an example of bureaucratic temporality. She has been 'stuck' in the British asylum system for more than a decade with no right to work and – given that she has a young child with learning disabilities – is unlikely to be deported. Instead, she feels she is made to 'waste the best years of [her] life'. For Asma, a survivor of domestic violence living in the North West of England and whom I regularly visited, the distance from the city centre was compounded by two further impacts on autonomy. The first was her fear of the Home Office, the government body responsible for handling asylum claims and with which she had to report every week. As well as this appointment impacting on other duties and childcare, she reflected that: 'I feel very scared when I go to the Home Office because they can detain with children as well. Oh yeah, I feel very, very scared'. The second related to the long-term experience of racist abuse and threats to report her from her housing officer, employed by a private company which was contracted by the Home Office. She stated that, 'Even my manager is very bad, racist, all the time the comment that he gives me, he said, "Why have you people come to this country? You have to go back! Home Office will come and soon this house will be empty".' This was one example in a long line of many. At the time of writing, the housing officer in question has been suspended from his duties pending multiple investigations from various complainants.

In Denmark and Sweden, spatial isolation is a central facet of housing, since many people seeking asylum live in (often remote) asylum centres (see Asylum Information Database, 2017). Although technically open, and so not the same as the detention centres which will be discussed later, these centres are typically located on the periphery of towns or cities, if not altogether isolated in Sweden's rural north, or as Zachary Whyte documents, on small Danish islands (Whyte, 2011).

Denmark is a unique example in that, on application, people first live in Centre Sandholm, a reception (or processing) centre in former military barracks approximately one-and-a-half hours from Copenhagen by bus and train – which are largely unaffordable for migrants.[10] As Mahira, a survivor of domestic abuse and false imprisonment, reflected, 'you don't have money and you cannot go out if you don't have money so how do you pay for the bus, for the train? So you cannot go out, you can walk ... but you cannot go out. You can get a ticket, a bus ticket, a bus pass, only if you have an appointment with your doctor'. Alongside the spatial isolation, Mahira felt that the process itself was degrading, reflecting on hours of standing in lines for food and post (see Boochani, 2018 for discussions on 'queuing as torture'), due to which she preferred to eat only twice a day. Moreover, her reflections on Sandholm embedded experiences of public 'embarrassment' and indeed an Othering of the non-Danish migrant body:

> You have to wait there for the post and if you want to know something or you want to say something you have to wait in the gate. It took such a long time for me. And if they gave you the post and you collect the post it is in Danish. You are an asylum seeker from another country, you cannot read Danish, but you get the letter in Danish. So you need to ask, 'Can you read this letter for me?' And they read the letter in English and other people hear you. I was really embarrassed.

Controversially, and as with the Ellebæk 'Alien's Centre' – a closed detention centre – and Sjælsmark deportation centre, Sandholm is situated next to an active military camp. As a psychologist working nearby in Sandholm told me in 2014: 'Sometimes you have military rehearsals around Sandholm. So they stand practising how to throw a grenade like 100 metres away, and all the people in Sandholm are just like, back in the war. People with PTSD ... it's completely absurd.'

People generally spend at least three to four weeks at Sandholm[11] before they are transferred to an *asylcenter*. At the height of the so-called refugee crisis in 2015, Denmark opened multiple new centres. Many of these closed as the number of applications for asylum dropped, with only around nine centres in operation (not including departure or deportation centres) most of which are situated in rural, isolated areas in Jutland (*Jylland*).

Prior to its closure, I spent one month undertaking visits with women in an asylum centre in the rural southwest of Zealand (*Sydvestsjælland*). The centre was two hours away from Copenhagen by train, with limited resources in the town where it was situated. In any case, the lack of funds people had meant that few residents were able to exercise autonomy over meals, although collaborative cooking was a key way to maintain friendships, healthy eating and collegiality. Whilst some organisations in Copenhagen were able to offer travel reimbursements to people attending meetings, any women who had children were not able to benefit from this since they were expected to ensure their children were collected from nursery or school during the days – it was not possible to get to or from Copenhagen in the short time available. As Antonia, a survivor of sexual trafficking, reflected, 'I go to church when I have money for a ticket. Last week, I didn't have money. It's only when I go to church, when they pay us, every two, three weeks, so I will get money'. The political and bureaucratic decision to house people in spatial peripheries thus impacts on religious and cultural practices and social lives.

In essence, isolation at centres is both spatial and, for some, an exercise in self-confinement. During visits I spent many hours in women's rooms watching Danish or Nigerian television, kneading chapatti dough or talking. Any suggestions of other activities or exercise were met with exasperation, with the exception of one walk and some hours of cycling with one woman. There were numerous reasons for this. For Jazmine, a transwoman who had been persecuted in her country of origin, her experience of transphobia had, at the time, left her feeling vulnerable and thus choosing to stay alone in the asylum centre:

> I was a lone trans in my room. They gave me a room alone and every day I sit in my room, there was no TV, no internet, nothing. I only see the trees and houses. A very difficult life I see... I have also right to work, eat, to live as I want, as a woman, but the Red Cross did not help me that time, that's why due to the Red Cross, I [attempted] suicide [shows me scars on wrists].

For Antonia, there was a strong feeling of living in a prison, and that the people she was surrounded with were unsettling. Antonia had travelled by foot and car from Nigeria to Morocco, survived thirst by drinking her own urine in the desert, and endured significant levels of fear on a boat crossing to Spain at night. She was a survivor of sexual trafficking, first in Italy, then Denmark and Sweden, and had been living in camps for more than two years when we first met. She felt that, 'asylum makes people crazy, when you're sick in asylum, it's not what you expect when you are in asylum, sister. [In] asylum [centres] you will not know your whereabouts, where you are going to. But they just got you like prisoners in the camp'.

As we can see here, Antonia's life was reduced to feelings of confinement and isolation on the peripheries of Danish society. It was banal. 'You eat, you sleep, did you come to Europe to eat and sleep?' she had asked. The centre claimed to support vulnerable women – survivors of sexual violence, trafficking and domestic abuse – and yet there was no sustained psychological support for people living there. Antonia spent much of her time in her small room, with only one bed between herself and her son, curtains closed and a Nigerian Christian television channel on repeating church services throughout the day. Her son, who was almost two, was unable to speak, much like many of the other children I met there. At the time she was thankful for not being in one of the (even more) isolated centres, since, 'right now they are taking some people to Jutland. They are moving them from here to Jutland. But anyway, it's not my business. It's too far away'. Sadly, when I last visited Avstrup departure centre in 2018 I unexpectedly met a friend of Antonia's who informed me that she and her son had been moved to a centre in Jutland.

**Internal detention as a tool for externalisation**

Thus far I have focused on the informal aspects of spatial isolation that facilitate banality: poverty, asylum housing and dispersal, and self-confinement in asylum centres. To reiterate earlier points, many aspects of internalised bordering were already being developed or implemented *prior* to 2015, but these were exacerbated and – as we will see in this section – exponentially increased *since* 2015. One aspect of this has been penal expansionism in the form of the immigration detention estate in all three countries, and the implementation of departure centres in Denmark.

Immigration detention is one further tactic of control which has been used differentially across Denmark, Sweden and the UK. Denmark has only two formal detention centres – literally referred to as Aliens Centres. In Sweden there are currently five centres, with (as informants working in two centres told me) views to expand over the next three years. The UK is an anomaly here. At present, there are seven immigration detention centres – termed Immigration Removal Centres, also linguistically sanitised as IRCs.

Two key disparities sit between them: the capacity for detention, and the length of time people can be confined. At present, approximately 3,500 people can be detained at any given time in the UK (Silverman, 2017), whilst in Denmark this is around 358 (Global Detention Project, 2016) and in Sweden around 700.[12] Both Denmark and Sweden have a time limit for detention, respectively six months (with an option for an extension of twelve months) and twelve months (possibly longer in exceptional circumstances). There is no time limit for detaining people in British IRCs.

Although inherently harmful and violent, the objectives of immigration detention are clearer in Denmark and Sweden than in the UK. In Denmark, this is to contain people who are either deemed at risk of absconding or 'going underground' (interview with centre governor) before they are deported, whilst in Sweden it is specifically meant as a final holding area prior to deportation, with exceptional circumstances where detainees are successful in appealing their refusal to stay in Sweden. One detention custody officer in a Swedish centre I visited synopsised: 'we're here to make sure that they're available for deportation' (see also Khosravi, 2009). As Mary Bosworth (2014) has shown in depth, the objectives of detention are much less clear in the UK, and this is hard felt as punishment by people who are confined. Apart from the prison-like regime and architecture, which itself is often under scrutiny (Bosworth and Turnbull, 2015; Shaw, 2016; Women for Refugee Women, 2016), some people are left languishing even whilst appeals are ongoing or when their rights to refugee status are under review (Hasselberg, 2016).

The risk and threat of detention is a central driver of control in the UK. In 2017 alone, the UK detained 27,300 people in IRCs (Silverman and Griffiths, 2018). As argued elsewhere (Canning et al., 2017), the potential for detention becomes a key factor of anxiety for people seeking asylum, since they can be arbitrarily detained, often when attending weekly or monthly signings at the Home Office (a strategy to bureaucratically control the whereabouts and temporal autonomy of people seeking asylum). Moreover, the reasons for detaining people are incredibly broad, and work to further control the actions of people who are thus coerced into acting as docile bodies, compliant and apolitical since 'women and men awaiting decisions to stay in Britain can be detained indefinitely when the "decision has been reached" on the basis of one or more of 13 reasons, with the thirteenth being "your unacceptable character, conduct or associations"' (Canning, 2014, p. 11).

Similar to Cohen's (1985) visions of social controls, law breaking is extended to state interpretations of non-criminalised actions or associations. It is, in effect, easy to be detained in the UK without necessarily being able to avoid it.

## Denmark's departure centres: the extraordinary case of false freedom

> The more powerful and concerted political will is directed at keeping asylum seekers at a distance, socially disconnected, so as to facilitate their possible deportation. (Whyte, 2011, pp. 21)

At surface level then, one might be drawn to conclude that – compared to the UK – Denmark and Sweden are relatively 'soft' on detention (Barker, 2013; Pratt and Eriksson, 2013; Ugelvik, 2013). I have contested this and addressed the harms of detention in Sweden elsewhere (Canning, 2019c). However, for the purposes of emphasising the pains of bureaucratic violence, it is worth focusing on the harms of deportation centres in Denmark.

In response to the rising number of asylum applications, and perhaps as a pre-emptive measure against applications yet to come, the Danish state established Udrejsecenter Sjælsmark in 2015, the country's first deportation centre. Near to the centre for arrivals (Sandholm) and Ellebæk Aliens Centre, it is built in former military barracks approximately 25 kilometres north of Copenhagen, and takes around one hour and forty-five minutes to reach by public transport from the city centre.

Unlike Ellebæk detention centre, Sjælsmark is an open camp and although there is a curfew, residents are technically 'free' to come and go as they wish. With around 140 people living there at the time of writing, it is sprawling but not overcrowded. People have the option of eating three times a day at stipulated hours, and can travel to other cities. However, many are fundamentally limited by the lack of money to do so, and the potential reliance on food from the canteen if they cannot afford to eat elsewhere.

As figures 3 and 4 show, the militaristic architecture of the centre is quite clearly prisonlike – although people can leave, they must first pass through a guarded gate. Likewise, fences surround the communal areas, which was a point of discussion with a member of staff I interviewed:

> D12: I think it's hard for families to live there, when it looks like that, and there's so many lawns there that you could sit on when it's sunny but you can't because there's fences everywhere …
> VC: Why do you think the fences are there?
> D12: I dunno. I think it's to make it … I dunno. To make it look like a prison?

This was reiterated by five other members of staff whom I interviewed. Indeed, there is no purpose for these wire fences other than to create a sense of confinement. They do not actually physically confine, but instead reduce autonomy and enforce banality: where children could play on the grass or meet in communal areas, the sense of imprisonment will stay pervasive, restricting where and how one moves through the centre. Banality is thus inflicted through the removal of options to live how one might wish to, or take part in activities ranging from basic rights, such as eating, to having

3 Accommodation at *Udrejsecenter Sjælsmark*

4 Image of walkway at *Udrejsecenter Sjælsmark*

options for leisure. The aim of such a bureaucratised violence is therefore to induce a sense of nothingness, so that returning to any other circumstances in ones' country of origin (or indeed a third party country) becomes preferable to banally watching time slip away.

Faiza was moved to the asylum centre in the southwest of Zealand in early 2017. She had endured a marriage with a man who controlled her until a point when, after having been brought to Denmark to marry and after the birth of two children, she could not endure the relationship any further. On the occasions I visited her at Sjælsmark, frustrations were clear, not only with the failures of her legal representative to open her case and thus move her from Sjælsmark (which did eventually happen), but the restrictions on food times and school times meant she was not able to leave the camp when she otherwise would go to get food she was culturally accustomed to. This was compounded by the withdrawal of funds: the 'pocket money' which is given to people seeking asylum is removed once they enter the departure centre unless they agree to 'comply' with orders for removal and deportation. As Faiza argued: 'I'm ... fighting with life because they stopped my money. They don't continue my pocket money, even though I cooperate with the police, because there's immigration law, if we cooperate with the police then they give you money.'

The impacts of this extension of bureaucratic controls were personal and, for Faiza, highly gendered. She reflected that it was, 'so bad because I have no more social life, I have nothing to do, I have nothing ... anything [that's] my own choice, I can't do. So it's the worst. I get tired a lot from my life, mainly physically I'm tired a lot, but just as a woman sometimes I feel I've died'. Moreover, as a survivor of domestic violence, Faiza felt that, 'my husband and Danish immigration are the same for me. They are playing the same role, they're both playing the same role for me. So I'm very tired'.

What has been made integral to Danish deportation centres is the deliberate strategy to induce banality. Although Red Cross staff I spoke with were working hard to implement activities for people living there, the politically driven objective was the opposite, as one staff member pointed out, since 'our [then] minister has stated that they should be as unpleasant as possible for people to actually want to leave the country'. Thus Sjælsmark has become the embodiment of motivation enhancement measures set out in the Aliens Act 1997 (see Suárez-Krabbe et al., 2018), which aim to encourage people to leave 'voluntarily'.

The message is clear: residents are technically free, but all means to survive independently are reduced and ultimately eradicated as a way to speed up removal. As a staff member working there told me, 'It's deliberately not trying to make people stay, so there weren't concerts every Friday night so you have something to look forward to', whilst another synopsised, 'We're discussing whether you should be allowed to do anything because it's supposed to be motivating, for motivating people to depart'. Like closed detention centres, the intended outcome is the same: the removal of unwanted migrant bodies, spatially isolated so that out of sight becomes out of mind for the majority society. Existential confinement, banality and the reduction of autonomy replace formal confinement as a means to externalisation. It is thus only the strategies of the three countries I discuss which inherently differ.

## Conclusion

There have been clear efforts to reduce and deter people from seeking asylum in Northern Europe. Whilst calls have indeed been made for states such as Britain, Denmark and Sweden to 'do their fair share', in accommodating refugees (Morgan Johansson, cited in Orange, 2015), they have arguably not done so. Instead, fewer people are able to reach safety in Northern shores, and the lives of people seeking asylum in Northern Europe have been progressively made worse through bureaucratic controls and the infliction of harmful practices.

It is this point that has been the central focus of this chapter: the means by which people are deterred, degraded, detained, and, for some, deported. In the case of the UK, long-term bureaucratic efforts to offshore and outsource border control responsibilities were ultimately successful in their bid: the UK was broadly unaffected by the increase in people seeking asylum as 2015 and 2016 progressed. As I have argued, externalisation works to refuse entrance before people even leave their country of origin through visa regulation. For those who have made it further North, the final reach to Britain has been blockaded by the increased financing of physical border expansionism.

As 2015 progressed, so too did Danish and Swedish efforts to reduce entry by securitising the borders between Denmark and Sweden as well as between Denmark and Germany through border controls and increased deportations. These have been supplemented by strategies to deter – some tactics are new, some are bolstered versions of policies already in existence. From the empirical data reflected on throughout this chapter, it is clear that the realities of poverty, uncertainty and lack of autonomy render people dependent on state agendas even to the micro-level – where they go, how they travel, who they spend time with, how long they spend it, where it is spent. Asylum centres in Denmark and Sweden may differ from dispersal in the UK, but spatial isolation remains a central facet of internalised controls – further embodied in the use of formal immigration detention.

To that end, it is worth drawing a conclusion from a national coordinator for a refugee women's support organisation in the UK. Although focusing on Britain, it is clear that the points she raises are increasingly applicable to Danish and Swedish state counterparts:

> the Home Office doesn't want to grant asylum to very many people and whether it has explicit ... numerical targets on that or not, the ethos of the asylum system, if you think about, all of the things that happen in it – from dispersing people, or giving them tiny amounts of money, to not letting them work, to detaining people – it just seems really clear that in all of these kinds of stages of the asylum process you've got a system that doesn't want those people to be here.

The outcome is uncertainty, threat of detention and ultimately deportation. It is the deliberate infliction of bureaucratic violence on and within Northern borders.

## Notes

1. Grant information: This research is funded by the Economic and Social Research Council, grant number ES/NO16718/1.
2. The term 'Britain' is used when referring to empirical research, which did not include Northern Ireland. Where relevant statistics or legislation are referred to, it is the UK.
3. This accounts for the fact that the increase in refugees arriving in Europe was predictable and predicted. It is instead more appropriate linguistically to address the crisis in responding adequately to refugees, which has exacerbated border harms and indeed border related deaths. Many thanks to Karam Yahya and Alaa Kassab for insightful conversations on framing this.
4. Undertaken in 2014. See Canning, 2016 for fuller context.
5. Entitled Gendered Experiences of Social Harm in Asylum: Exploring State Responses to Persecuted Women in Britain, Denmark and Sweden, grant number ES/NO16718/1.
6. The first translates as 'departure centre', but this is contested by Lindberg et al. who – along with people living there – refer to it as the second, translating as a 'deportation centre'. See Suárez-Krabbe et al (2018).
7. This case has now expanded in the aftermath of Brexit to further include EU migrants, including economic migrants and European students.
8. This is a pseudonym, as are all the other names in this chapter.
9. Considering Nour's upset state of mind, I repeatedly asked if she was sure she wanted to take part in any of the oral history, to which she vehemently asked to participate as she felt women's rights were not represented in the Swedish asylum system.
10. When I last visited Sandholm in 2018 a bicycle system had been introduced to facilitate free travel to the train station. Whilst a positive initiative, this does not solve the problem of inaccessible travel for a) people who cannot afford train travel and b) people with dependent children – a disproportionately gendered issue (see Canning, 2019a; 2019b).
11. Interviews I undertook with staff members working there raised concerns that some were staying for periods of months.
12. These numbers are based on interview information with governors working in Sweden. Statistics from the Global Detention Project suggest much fewer, with 255 spaces, but this is inconsistent with a) the numbers in the centres I visited, which across two already reach this, and b) the information given by staff.

## References

Aliverti, A. (2012). 'Making People Criminal: The Role of the Criminal Law in Immigration Enforcement', *Theoretical Criminology* 16(4), pp. 417–434.

Aliverti, A. (2013). 'Sentencing in Immigration-Related Cases: The Impact of Deportability and Immigration Status', *Prison Service Journal* 205, pp. 39–44.

Aliverti, A. (2015), 'Criminal Immigration Law and Human Rights in Europe', in Pickering, S. and Ham, J. (eds.) *The Routledge Handbook on Crime and International Migration*, Oxon: Routledge.

Andersson, R. (2014), *Illegality Inc.: Clandestine Migration and the Business of Bordering Europe*. California: University of California Press.

Asylum Information Database (2017), *Type of Accommodation: Sweden*. Available at: www.asylumineurope.org/reports/country/sweden/reception-conditions/housing/types-accommodation, (Accessed 5 February 2018).

Barker, V. (2013), 'Nordic Exceptionalism Revisited: Explaining the Paradox of a Janus Faced Penal Regime', *Theoretical Criminology* 17(1), pp. 5–25.

Barker, V. (2018), *Nordic Nationalism and Penal Order: Walling the Welfare State*. Oxon: Routledge.

Boochani, Behrouz (2018), *No Friend but the Mountains*. Sydney: Picador.

Bosworth, M. (2014). *Inside Immigration Detention*. Oxford: Oxford University Press.

Bosworth, M. and Turnbull, S. (2015), 'Immigration Detention and Criminalization', in Pickering, S. and Ham, J. (eds.) *The Routledge Handbook on Crime and International Migration*. Oxon: Routledge.

Canning, V. (2014). 'Violence in Britain: Behind the Wire at Immigration Removal Centres', *The Conversation*. Available at: http://theconversation.com/violence-in-britain-behind-the-wire-at-immigration-removal-centres-25519 (Accessed 16 March 2020).

Canning, V. (2016). 'Unsilencing Sexual Torture: Responses to Refugees and Asylum Seekers in Denmark', *British Journal of Criminology* 56(3), pp. 438–456.

Canning, V. (2017). *Gendered Harm and Structural Violence in the British Asylum System*. Oxon: Routledge.

Canning, V. (2019a). Reimagining Refugee Rights: Addressing Asylum Harms in Britain, Denmark and Sweden. Migration Mobilities Bristol, University of Bristol. Available at: www.statewatch.org/news/2019/mar/uk-dk-se-reimagining-refugee-rights-asylum-harms-3-19.pdf (Accessed 7 August 2019).

Canning, V. (2019b). 'Degradation by Design: Women Seeking Asylum in Northern Europe', *Race & Class* 61, p. 46–64.

Canning, V. (2019c), 'Keeping up with the Kladdkaka: Kindness and Coercion in Swedish Immigration Detention', *European Journal of Criminology* Available at: https://journals.sagepub.com/doi/abs/10.1177/1477370818820627 (Accessed 7 August 2019).

Canning, V., Caur, J., Gilley, A., Kebemba, E., Rafique, A. and Verson, J. (2017). *Migrant Artists Mutual Aid: Strategies for Survival, Recipes for Resistance*. London: Calverts Co-operative.

Carr, M. (2012). *Fortress Europe: Inside the War Against Immigration*. London: Hurst and Co.

Clante Bendixen, M. (2018). *How Many are Coming, and From Where?* Refugees Welcome Denmark. Available at: http://refugees.dk/en/facts/numbers-and-statistics/how-many-are-coming-and-from-where (Accessed 18 October 2018).

Cohen, S. (1985). *Visions of Social Control*. Cambridge: Polity Press.
Crawley, H. and Sigona, N. (2016). *European Policy is Driving Refugees to More Dangerous Routes Across the Med, The Conversation*. Available at: https://theconversation.com/european-policy-is-driving-refugees-to-more-dangerous-routes-across-the-med-56625 (Accessed 16 May 2016).
Global Detention Project (2016). *Sweden Immigration Detention Profile*. Available at: www.globaldetentionproject.org/immigration-detention-in-sweden (Accessed 5 February 2018).
Hasselberg, I. (2016). *Enduring Uncertainty: Deportation, Punishment and Everyday Life*. New York: Berghahn Books.
Khosravi, S. (2009). 'Sweden: Detention and Deportation of Asylum Seekers', *Race & Class* 50(4), pp. 38–56.
Kirkup, J. and Winnett, R. (2012). 'Theresa May Interview: We're Going to Give Illegal Immigrants a Really Hostile Reception', *The Telegraph*, 25 May 2012.
Orange, R. (2015). 'Britain will be Forced to Take "Fair Share" of Refugees, Swedish Minister Warns', *The Telegraph*, 27 August 2015.
Pratt, J. and Eriksson, A. (2013). *Contrasts in Punishment: And Explanation of Anglophone Excess and Nordic Exceptionalism*. New York: Routledge.
Shaw, S. (2016). *Review into the Welfare in Detention of Vulnerable Persons*. Available at: https://assets.publishing.service.gov.uk/government/uploads/system/uploads/attachment_data/file/490782/52532_Shaw_Review_Accessible.pdf (Accessed 17 March 2020).
Silverman, S. (2017). *Immigration Detention in the UK, The Migration Observatory*. Available at: www.migrationobservatory.ox.ac.uk/resources/briefings/immigration-detention-in-the-uk/ (Accessed 16 January 2018).
Silverman, S. and Griffith, M. (2018). *Immigration Detention in the UK*, Oxford Migration Observatory. Available at: https://migrationobservatory.ox.ac.uk/resources/briefings/immigration-detention-in-the-uk/ (Accessed 6 May 2019).
Stumpf, J. (2006). 'The Crimmigration Crisis: Immigrants, Crime and Sovereign Power', *American University Law Review* 52(2), pp. 367–419.
Stumpf, J. (2015). 'Crimmigration: Encountering the Leviathan', in Pickering, S. and Ham, J. (eds.) *The Routledge Handbook on Crime and International Migration*. Oxon: Routledge.
Suárez-Krabbe, J., Lindberg, A. and Arce, J. (2018). *Stop Killing Us Slowly: A Research Report on the Motivation Enhancement Measures and Criminalisation of Rejected Asylum Seekers in Denmark*. Roskilde University.
Ugelvik, T. (2013). 'Seeing like a Welfare State: Immigration Control, Statecraft and a Prison with Double Vision', in Aas, K. and Bosworth, M. (eds.) *Borders of Punishment: Citizenship, Crime Control and Social Exclusion*. Oxford: Oxford University Press.
Webber, F. (2012). *Borderline Justice: The Fight for Refugee and Migrant Rights*. London: Pluto Press.
Webber, F. (2016). *The UK Government's Inversion of Accountability*, Open Democracy. Available at: www.opendemocracy.net/uk/shinealight/frances-webber/uk-government-s-inversion-of-accountability (Accessed 1 June 2016).

Wheatstone, R. (2016). Poorest Areas Used as "Dumping Ground" for Asylum Seekers as Map Shows North-South Divide, *The Mirror*. Available at: www.mirror.co.uk/news/uk-news/poorest-areas-britain-used-dumping-7253485 (Accessed 15 February 2018).

Whyte, Z. (2011). 'Enter the Myopticon: Uncertain Surveillance in the Danish Asylum System', *Anthropology Today* 27(3), pp. 18–21.

Women for Refugee Women (2016). *The Way Ahead: An Asylum System without Detention*. London: W4RW.

# Index

Act (1994: 137) on the reception of asylum seekers and others 94
  see also LMA
anti-immigrant
  attitudes 124
  party 61–62
  sentiment 211
  see also discourse(s)
asylum
  appeal 8, 39, 44, 155, 212, 218
  application(s) 39–41
    number of 2, 70, 109, 180, 182, 212, 219
  asylum law 6, 53, 59
    see also law
  centre 79, 91, 132, 195, 198, 215–217, 220
    see also reception facility
  claim 41–42, 44, 90
  processes 95, 182, 200–201
  rejection/refusal 92, 94, 97, 213
asylum seeker 32–35, 37–45
  as a threat 150, 155
  bogus 10, 45, 150, 154
    see also migrants, undeserving
  genuine 106, 150, 154
  see also refugee
asylum systems 2, 5, 31, 44–46
  in Denmark 41, 89, 92
  in Germany 39–40
  in Sweden 35, 37, 39, 58, 89, 92, 128–130, 223
  in the UK 214, 222
  see also refugee, refugee regime

border
  border bureaucracy 86, 214
    border bureaucrats 89, 91, 97, 113
    see also bureaucracy, street-level bureaucrats
  Border Spectacle 42–43, 114
    see also De Genova, Nicholas
  controls 6, 20–21, 50, 55, 58–59, 61, 70, 72, 80, 89–90, 129, 131, 135, 154, 211, 213, 222
    see also re-bordering
  police 85, 89–90, 113–115
Bourdieu, Pierre 14, 31, 40, 108, 170, 197, 199, 202
bureaucracy
  'audit culture' 17
  bureaucratisation 3–5, 15, 17, 71, 76, 149, 161, 164
  of daily life 20, 161, 164, 175, 181, 188
  street-level bureaucrats 2, 9, 15, 17, 20, 87, 89, 94, 161, 197–198, 205–206
  Weber's 'iron cage' 3, 5, 13, 163

class 18, 31–34, 40, 42–43, 45–46, 88, 106, 133, 188
crisis
  construction of 2–3, 19–20, 106, 118, 123–125, 127, 129–136
  declaration of 1, 11, 86, 89
  framing of 18–19, 67–69, 71–72, 80, 110, 115

management of 53
theory of 52
*see also* Koselleck, Reinhart
Common European Asylum System (CEAS) 44, 46
*see also* Dublin Regulation

De Genova, Nicholas 42–43, 75, 114–116
*see also* border, Border Spectacle
deportation 74–76, 80–81, 85–87, 92, 94–95, 124, 144, 203, 211, 214, 218, 222
  anti-deportation 68
  centres 75, 79, 92–93, 97, 211, 213, 216, 219
  deportable populations 18, 68, 75–76, 80–81
  self-deportation 212
destitution 20, 95–97, 210
deterrence 43, 89–92, 94–96, 117
  logic 94, 96
  policies 18, 67–68, 71, 73–74, 77, 78, 80–81, 86, 89, 90–92, 95
  (symbolic) politics of 86, 89
discourse(s)
  anti-immigrant 61
  civil society 145, 155
  criminalisation 114
  crisis 106
  dominant 31, 33, 118, 124
  exclusionary 153–154
  hostile 9, 61–62
  humanising 116
  inclusionary 153–154
  institutionalised 145
  legal 151–152
  (mass) media 2, 12, 14, 69, 106, 123, 145
    *see also* media
  political 11, 18, 44, 51, 69, 118, 123, 145
  post-shame 132–133, 136
  public 2, 12, 62, 144–146, 150, 153
  securitisation 114

welfare state 6
*see also* the Other, othering
Dublin Regulation 5, 21, 41, 46, 90, 180, 203
Dublin transfers 95
*see also* Common European Asylum System (CEAS)

economic capital 31, 38, 40, 44–45
exclusion 5, 11–12, 14, 19, 42, 88, 94–97, 109, 145, 147–148, 153, 196
  exclusionary mechanism 77, 87
  exclusionary practices 16, 86, 154
  political 51
  social 34, 45, 51
  *see also* discourse(s); inclusion

Facebook 144, 154
family 38, 40, 69, 91, 116–117, 166, 172, 186–187, 203–206
  reunification 8, 41, 50, 59, 71, 73, 75–76, 78, 85, 176, 182–183, 199, 203–206

gender 33, 88, 106, 111, 113, 153, 172, 221
governance 2–3, 17, 50–51, 53, 97, 129–130, 197

Habermas, Jürgen 144–146, 151, 155
  'deliberative legitimation process' 145, 155
  legitimacy 144–146, 150, 155
  moral norms 151
  public sphere 146
  *see also* discourse(s), public
humanisation 109–110, 114, 116–118, 155
  dehumanisation 15, 19, 145, 155
  human attributes 107

inclusion 5, 19, 34, 51, 78, 145, 147–148, 153–154, 214
  subordinate inclusion 42, 88, 96
  *see also* exclusion
institutional uncertainty 18, 68, 76

# Index

integration 9, 19, 34, 68, 75, 77, 81, 86, 127, 129–130, 132, 134–135, 149, 162, 167–168, 172, 180, 192, 197
  benefit 74
  criteria 73
  debates on 130, 192
  programmes 4, 9, 20, 183–184
Islamophobia 34

Kærshovedgaard 75, 79
Khosravi, Shahram 14, 34
  *see also* waiting
Koselleck, Reinhart 52–53

labelling 4, 162, 164, 170, 175
language
  learning 77, 164, 167–171, 183–186, 202, 213
  proficiency 38, 40, 147, 167, 172, 176, 183, 190
  teachers 9, 118, 174
law 18, 21, 50, 54, 57, 147–148, 171, 183
  Geneva Convention 33, 45, 54, 75, 133
  international human rights 54–55, 90, 137, 144
  (im)migration law 37, 78, 95, 146, 152, 154–155, 210, 221
  Jewellery Law 11, 22, 42–43, 73, 91, 213
  rule of 6, 54, 62, 114, 146, 171, 187
  temporary law 8, 59, 85, 90, 94, 97, 211
  *see also* asylum, asylum law
lawyer 34–35, 37–41, 45, 51, 199, 203
lay judge 35, 39, 44–45
Lea, Susan 148, 150–152, 154
legal instance 35, 37, 39, 42, 46
LMA 56, 94–95, 97
Lynn, Nick 148, 150–152, 154

Mbembe, A. 86, 88, 93, 97
  *see also* necropolitics

media 17–18, 70, 79, 105, 110, 114, 116, 145, 150
  frame(s) 19, 51, 67, 71–72, 107, 109–118, 123, 125–127, 136–137, 152
    ambivalence 12, 93, 118
    diffused representation 118
    visual frames 19, 109–110, 118
  mainstream 45, 50, 61, 123–125, 136
  representations 123–125
  social 144–147, 151, 153–155
  *see also* discourse(s)
migrants
  economic 31–33, 41, 43
  illegal immigrant 59, 76, 79, 114
  rights 10, 73
  scapegoating 11, 132
  transit 127, 130, 136
  undeserving 33, 94, 181
    *see also* refugee, undeserving refugee
  unwanted 6, 9, 20, 43, 72, 86, 221
  wanted 21, 43
migration court 31, 36, 39, 41, 44–45, 62, 144
  Sweden's Migration Court of Appeal 32, 35–36, 46, 144, 152
minimum rights approaches 18, 86–88, 95, 97
minimum welfare 87–88
social rights 6, 50, 87, 92, 94–96
moral evaluation 147–152
mythopoesis 147–148

necropolitics 34, 86–88, 93, 97
  *see also* Mbembe, A.
neoliberalism 211
  neoliberal governmentality 10
  neoliberal policies 20, 61
  neoliberal turn 5

Other, the 12, 15, 88, 117–118, 122, 149, 155
  othering 106, 124, 149, 155, 215
  *see also* discourse(s)
  'us' and 'them' 107–108, 151, 154

paradigmatic shift 68, 72, 80–81
power
  disciplinary power 10
  discretionary power 76
  dynamics 3, 17, 52
  exclusionary power 87–88, 97
  imbalance 16, 35, 37, 53
  sovereign power 52, 55, 62
  structures 3, 51, 62, 105, 108
powerless(ness) 4, 13–14, 79, 181, 188, 201

racialisation 106
  racial crisis 115–116
  racialised 15, 33, 88, 107, 113, 115, 175
  racism 35, 46, 150
rationalisation 125, 147, 149, 151–153, 163
reception 3, 8–9, 16, 19, 56, 59–60, 87, 89, 91, 94, 96, 109–110, 112, 115, 118, 129, 135
  reception facility 41, 182–183, 195–203, 205–206, 215
  *see also* asylum, centre
  reception policies 122, 128, 134, 137
    *see also* asylum; asylum systems; refugee policies
  reception programmes 40
  refugee reception crisis 210–212
  welcome 110, 115–117
re-bordering 6, 9, 11, 16, 71–73, 154–155
refugee
  refugee body 17, 19, 106–110, 112–114, 116–118, 130
  refugeeness 4, 19, 106–107, 110
  refugee regime 4, 19, 21, 33, 44, 165
  *see also* asylum systems
  undeserving refugee 43
  *see also* asylum seeker
regimes of mobility 16–18
residence permit 8, 21, 32, 37–39, 41, 59, 71, 80, 85, 135, 148, 151, 153–155, 182–183, 196, 198, 202, 205, 211

risk
  governance through risk 2, 9
  perception of risk 3, 9–11, 136, 149
  risk management 11–13, 18, 136
  risk mitigation 2, 9–10, 12, 136
  risk society 9–11, 135
  security risks 10, 76, 92
    *see also* security; threat(s), threat to national security

security 6, 22, 54, 62, 72, 88, 126, 187, 203
  insecurity 80, 196–197, 204–206
    prolonged insecurity 199
  securitisation 10–11, 19, 22, 109–110, 112–115, 117–118, 213, 222
  barbed wire 113–114
  fences 92, 113–114, 219
  police 1, 5, 9, 13, 41–42, 51, 58, 69–70, 85–86, 89–90, 94, 105, 110, 112–115, 130, 200, 213, 221
  *see also* risk, security risks; threat(s), threat to (national) security
Sjælsmark 75, 79
smuggler 33, 37, 77
  smuggling 113
social security 6, 117, 188
solidarity 77–79, 115, 149–150, 154
state of emergency 11, 54–55, 69, 72–73, 80
Swedish Migration Agency 1, 35, 51, 53, 56, 58–60, 63, 85, 90, 94–95, 112, 127–129, 131–132, 134, 144, 146, 148–149, 152, 155, 165, 167, 173, 214
surveillance 10, 16, 91

threat(s) 3, 126, 150
  (discursive) construction of threat 20, 22, 152
  threat to (national) security 6, 46, 53–55, 58, 75, 106–107, 110, 113–114, 118
  threat to sovereignty 18, 19, 50, 52–53, 55, 109, 113, 116
  threat of terrorism 59

# Index

threat to welfare state 10, 58, 88–90, 96, 106, 151–152, 154

Van Leeuwen, Theo 144, 147–148, 151
  analytical tool 144, 147
victimisation 19, 43, 106–107, 109–114, 118, 153
  child 107, 110–115, 117
  feminised 107, 111–112
  Madonna and Child 107, 111
  Male Madonna 111–112
violence 2, 10–11, 109, 116–117, 162, 172, 175, 180–181, 191, 196, 200, 213, 215, 217, 221
  bureaucratic violence 9, 13–15, 18, 20, 68, 96, 122–123, 210, 219–220, 223

discursive violence 19, 145, 147, 153–154
epistemic violence 15
indirect violence 87, 91, 96
police violence 114
slow violence 89, 91, 95
state violence 19–20, 86, 97
structural violence 13, 34, 45, 88
subjective violence 108
symbolic violence 108
volunteer 1, 115, 130, 184, 189
Venligboerne 77–81
*visAvis* 78–79

waiting 14, 20, 73, 112, 170, 188, 195–207, 214
  *see also* Khosravi, Shahram
welfare chauvinist ideology 90
whiteness 115–116, 118
Wodak, Ruth 132, 147–148

Lightning Source UK Ltd.
Milton Keynes UK
UKHW021030121220
374916UK00003B/58

9 781526 146830